e-tales
three

**more of
the best
& worst
of internet
humour**

e-tales
three

CASSELL

Cassell
Wellington House
125 Strand
London
WC2R 0BB

© Cassell 2002

British Library Cataloguing-in-Publication Data

A catalogue entry for this book is available from the British Library.

ISBN 0-304-36118-6

Distributed in the United States
by Sterling Publishing Co. Inc.
387 Park Avenue South
New York, NY 10016–8810

Designed by Richard Carr
Printed in Great Britain by Mackays of Chatham PLC, Chatham, Kent

Contents

Introduction

Like its two predecessors (*e-tales* and *e-tales two*), *e-tales three* offers a generous helping some of the best, the worst, the direst, the dirtiest and most tasteless jokes you are ever likely to hear, all of them derived from those non-work-related items of electronic mail that we all love to read when we should be working. The jokes in *e-tales three* are grouped under more or less the same chapters as before, but with two special chapters, *Bin-Liners – The War Against Terrorism* and *God Bless America*, covering the events of a tumultuous year in which a humble pretzel came desperately close to changing for ever the course of American and world history.

Here, in keeping with the *e-tales* formula, are hundreds of jokes that can safely be described by at least one – and almost certainly more – of the following adjectives: gratuitous, scatalogical, sexist, shocking, sick, silly, superficial – and absolutely uncensored. *E-tales three* will not only introduce you to such denizens of cyberspace as Birkenstock barbie, Bubba the redneck, Justin the prawn, Sandra Claus the feminist santa and Bernard the brown-nosed reindeer, it will also tell how you to satisfy a woman every time, how to upset a scouser, why fishing is better than sex, the truth about George Dubya's IQ, what happened to Osama bin Laden when he reached the Pearly Gates, and why David Beckham thinks that 'tactics' keep your breath fresh all day. And as if all this was not enough, 'Come Again' provides a helpful glossary of 25 different types of orgasm.

And yes, there are lots more really bad puns and really contrived punch lines, and plenty more blonde jokes, lawyer jokes and Jewish jokes.

And for nostalgia's sake, one, just one … last … Monica joke …

May your forwarding fingers remain ever primed and your inboxes full of laughs.

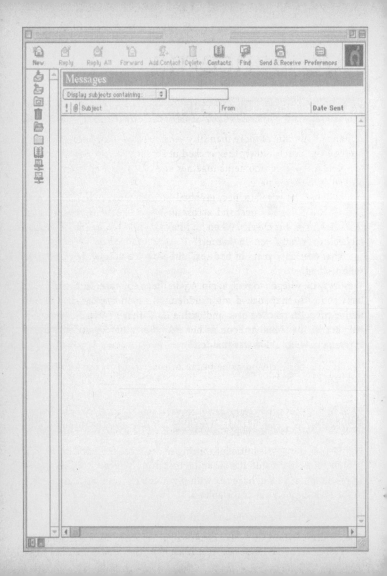

Age Concerns

After All These Years

A man and his wife of more than fifty years were rocking back and forth on the front porch. Slowly they rocked in rhythm, as this was their time to spend a few quiet moments together and after years of practice they rocked at the same pace.

Suddenly the wife stopped, grabbed her cane, and with a loud and hard WHACK hit her husband across the shins. His eyes watered and tears ran down his cheeks. When he finally caught his breath he gasped and asked, "What'd you do that fer?"

"That's fer fifty years of bad sex," she said. He nodded his head, but said nothing.

Slowly they began to rock again. Again they kept pace. Back and forth, back and forth they rocked, until suddenly the man stopped, and picked up his cane. He reached over and with a loud, sharp WHACK, he hit his wife across the shins. As soon as her eyes quit watering and she could speak she asked, "What was that fer?"

"That," said her husband as he began to rock again, "is for knowin' the difference."

Close Enough

Eighty-year-old Bessie burst into sitting room of the old folks' home. She held her clenched fist in the air and announced, "Anyone who can guess what's in my hand can have sex with me tonight!" An elderly gentleman in the rear shouted out, "An elephant?"

Bessie thought for a minute and said, "Close enough."

Wishing for Longevity

A man asked his doctor if he thought he'd live to be a hundred. The doctor asked the man, "Do you smoke or drink?"

"No," he replied, "I've never done either."

"Do you gamble, drive fast cars, and fool around with women?" inquired the doctor.

"No, I've never done any of those things either."

"Well then," said the doctor, "what do you want to live to be a hundred for?"

Wonderful for His Age

An 85-year-old man married a lovely 25-year-old woman. Because her new husband was so old the woman decided that on their wedding night they should have separate suites. She was worried that the old fellow might overexert himself.

After the festivities she prepared herself for bed and for the knock on the door she was expecting. Sure enough the knock came and there was her groom ready for action. They came together in conjugal union and all went well, whereupon he took his leave of her and she prepared to go to sleep for the night.

After a few minutes there was another knock on the door and there the old guy was again ready for more action. Somewhat surprised she consented to a further coupling, which was again successful after which the octogenarian bade her a fond goodnight and left.

She was certainly ready for slumber at this point and was close to sleep for the second time when there was another knock at the door and there he was again fresh as a 25-year-old and ready for more. Once again they did the horizontal boogie.

As they were lying in afterglow the young bride said to him, "I am really impressed that a guy your age has enough juice to go for it three times. I've been with guys less than half your age who were only good for one."

The old guy looked puzzled, turned to her and said, "Was I already here?"

Elderly Drivers: Part One

Two elderly women were out driving in a large car. Both could barely see over the dashboard. As they were cruising along they came to an intersection. The stoplight was red but they just went on through. The woman in the passenger seat thought to herself, "I must be losing it, I could have sworn we just went through a red light."

After a few more minutes they came to another intersection and the light was red again, and again they went right through. This time the woman in the passenger seat was almost sure that the light had been red but was really concerned that she was losing it. She was getting nervous and decided to pay very close attention to the road and the next intersection to see what was going on.

At the next intersection, sure enough, the light was definitely red and they went right through and she turned to the other woman and said, "Mildred! Don't you know we just ran through three red lights in a row! You could have killed us!" Mildred turned to her and said,

"Oh, silly me, I thought you were driving."

Elderly Drivers: Part Two

As a senior citizen was driving down the freeway, his car phone rang. Answering, he heard his wife's voice urgently warning him, "Herman, I just heard on the news that there's a car going the wrong way on 280. Please be careful!"

"Hell," said Herman, "It's not just one car. It's hundreds of them!"

Church Bells

On hearing that her elderly grandfather had died, Jenny went straight to visit her grandmother. When she asked how grandpa had died, her grandma explained, not holding back anything of course, "He had a heart attack during sex, Sunday morning!" Horrified, Jenny suggested that f**king at the age of 94 was surely asking for trouble!

"Oh no," Her grandma replied. "We had sex every Sunday morning in time with the church bells! In with the dings, out with the dongs ..." She paused to wipe away a tear.

"If it wasn't for that damn ice cream van passing by, he'd still be alive!"

You'll Be Next

I used to hate going to family weddings ... it seemed that all of my aunts and the grandmotherly types used to come up to me, poking me in the ribs and cackling, saying, "You'll be next."

They stopped that shit after I started doing the same thing to them at funerals.

The Senility Prayer

God, grant me the Senility
To forget the people
I never liked anyway,
The good fortune
To run into the ones I do,
And the eyesight
To tell the difference.

Thirteen ...

A young man was strolling down a street in south London. As he passed a large building with a fence around it, he heard a group of people chanting "Thirteen, thirteen, thirteen" over and over again.

Curious, he tried to see over the fence, but couldn't. Then he spotted a knot in the wood, and put his eye to the hole. He just managed to spy some old people sitting in deckchairs chanting, before a finger came out of nowhere and poked him in the eye.

As he staggered back, the old people started chanting,

"Fourteen, fourteen, fourteen ..."

Talkies

For the first time in many years, an old man travelled from his rural town to the city to see a movie. After buying his ticket, he stopped at the concession stand to purchase some popcorn. Handing the attendant

$1.50, he couldn't help but comment, "The last time I came to the movies, popcorn was only 15 cents."

"Well, sir," the attendant replied with a grin, "you're really going to enjoy yourself.

"We have sound now."

The Veteran Golfer

A young man who was also an avid golfer found himself with a few hours to spare one afternoon. He figured if he hurried and played very fast, he could get in nine holes before he had to head home. Just as he was about to tee off an old gentleman shuffled onto the tee and asked if he could accompany the young man as he was golfing alone. Not being able to say no, he allowed the old gent to join him.

To his surprise the old man played fairly quickly. He didn't hit the ball far, but plodded along consistently and didn't waste much time. Finally, they reached the ninth fairway and the young man found himself with a tough shot. There was a large pine tree directly between his ball and the green.

After several minutes of debating how to hit the shot the old man finally said, "You know, when I was your age I'd hit the ball right over that tree." With that challenge placed before him, the youngster swung hard, hit the ball up, right smack into the top of the tree trunk and it thudded back on the ground not a foot from where it had originally lain. The old man said,

"Of course, when I was your age that pine tree was only three feet tall."

🔖 🖳 The Smoking Aid

Two old ladies were outside their nursing home having a smoke when it started to rain. One of the ladies pulled out a condom, cut off the end, put it over her cigarette and continued smoking.

Lady 1: What's that?
Lady 2: A condom.
Lady 1: Where'd you get it?
Lady 2: You can get them at any drugstore.

The next day, Lady 1 hobbled into the local drugstore and announced to the pharmacist that she wanted to buy a package of condoms. The guy looked at her kind of strangely (she was, after all, in her 80s), but politely asked what brand she preferred.

"Doesn't matter," she replied, "as long as it fits a Camel."

🔖 🖳 In Miami

A little old lady was sitting on a bench in Miami Beach. A man walked over and sat down at the other end of the bench.

After a few moments, the woman asked, "Are you a stranger here?" He replied, "I used to live here years ago."

"So, where were you all these years?"

"In prison," he said.

"For what did they put you in prison?" He looked at her and very quietly said, "I killed my wife."

"Oh," says the woman. "So you're single …"

The Curve of Life

At age 4, success is … not peeing in your pants.

At age 12, success is … having friends.

At age 16, success is … having a driver's licence.

At age 20, success is … having sex.

At age 35, success is … having money.

At age 50, success is … having money.

At age 60, success is … having sex.

At age 70, success is … having a driver's licence.

At age 75, success is … having friends.

At age 80, success is … not peeing in your pants.

Granny's assets

The teenage granddaughter came downstairs for her date with a see-through blouse on and no bra. Her grandmother had a fit, telling her not to dare go out like that. The teenager said to her, "Loosen up Granny. These are modern times. You got to let your rosebuds show!" and out she went.

The next day the teenager came downstairs, to find her grandmother sitting with no top on, with her old wrinkled pair on show. The teenager wanted to die. She explained to her grandmother that she had friends coming over and that it just wasn't appropriate. The grandmother said, "Loosen up Sweetie. If you can show off your rosebuds,

"then I can display my hanging baskets."

Stroke

Two old ladies were sitting on a bench having a quiet chat, when a flasher approached from across the park. He stood right in front of them and opened his trench coat, exposing himself. One of the ladies immediately had a stroke.

The other lady, being older and more feeble, couldn't reach that far.

Then and Now

1970: Long hair
2002: Longing for hair

1970: The perfect high
2002: The perfect high-yield mutual fund

1970: Acid Rock
2002: Acid Reflux

1970: Moving to California because it's cool
2002: Moving to California because it's warm

1970: Growing pot
2002: Growing pot belly

1970: Trying to look like Marlon Brando or Liz Taylor
2002: Trying NOT to look like Marlon Brando or Liz Taylor

1970: Popping pills, smoking joints
2002: Popping joints

1970: Killer weed
2002: Weed killer

1970: Getting out to a new, hip joint
2002: Getting a new hip joint

1970: Rolling Stones
2002: Kidney stones

1970: Parents begging you to get your hair cut
2002: Children begging you to get their heads shaved

1970: Whatever
2002: Depends

Amazing but True(ish)

The Gold Coin Puzzle

You have ten stacks of identical-looking gold coins. Nine of the stacks contain real gold coins, and one of the stacks is made up entirely of fake gold coins. Each real gold coin weighs exactly 1 gram, while each fake gold coin weighs exactly 1.1 grams. Using a scale, how can you determine the stack of fake coins?

RULES: You can use the scale to take only one measurement. For example, stack what you want on the scale, press a button, and get a readout of the weight. You can do this only once, and once the readout is displayed it does not change if you remove any coins. You can mix the coins up in their stacks, separate them, mark them, whatever. How do you find out for sure which stack contains the fake gold coins?

Answer at the end of this chapter ...

Darwin Awards: 2002

It's that time again.

The Darwin Awards are an annual honour given to the person who did the gene pool the biggest service by killing themselves in the most extraordinarily stupid way. Last year's winner was the fellow who was killed by a Coke machine which toppled over on top of him as he was attempting to tip a free soda out of it. And the nominees are:

9. A young Canadian man, searching for a way of getting drunk cheaply, because he had no money with which to buy alcohol, mixed gasoline with milk. Not surprisingly, this concoction made him ill, and he vomited into the fireplace in his house. This resulting explosion and fire burned his house down, killing both him and his sister.

8. A 34-year-old white male found dead in the basement of his home died of suffocation, according to police. He was approximately 6' 2" tall and weighed 225 pounds. He was wearing a pleated skirt, white bra, black and white saddle shoes, and a woman's wig. It appeared that he was trying to create a schoolgirl's uniform look. He was also wearing a military gas mask that had the filter canister removed and a rubber hose attached in its place. The other end of the hose was connected to one end of a hollow wooden tube approximately 12" long and 3" in diameter. The tube's other end was inserted into his rectum for reasons unknown and was the cause of his suffocation. Police found the task of explaining the circumstances of his death to his family very awkward.

7. Three Brazilian men were flying in a light aircraft at low altitude when another plane approached. It appears that they decided to moon the occupants of the other plane, but lost control of their own aircraft and crashed. They were all found dead in the wreckage with their pants around their ankles.

6. A police officer in Ohio responded to a 911 call. She had no details before arriving, except that someone had reported that his father was not breathing. Upon arrival, the officer found the man face down on the couch naked. When she rolled him over to check for a pulse and to start CPR, she noticed burn marks around his genitals. After the ambulance arrived and removed the man, who was declared dead on arrival at the hospital, the police made a closer inspection of the couch, and noticed that the man had made a hole between the cushions. Upon flipping the couch over, they uncovered what had caused his death. Apparently, the

man had a habit of putting his penis between the cushions, down into the hole and between two electrical sanders (with the sandpaper removed, for obvious reasons). According to the report, after his orgasm the discharge shorted out one of the sanders, electrocuting him.

5. A 27-year-old French woman lost control of her car on a highway near Marseilles and crashed into a tree, seriously injuring her passenger and killing herself. As a commonplace road accident, this would not have qualified for a Darwin nomination, were it not for the fact that the driver's attention had been distracted by her Tamagotchi keyring, which had started urgently beeping for food as she drove along. In an attempt to press the correct buttons to save the Tamagotchi's life, the woman lost her own.

4. A 22-year-old man from Reston, Virginia, was found dead after he tried to use octopus straps to bungee jump off a 70-foot railroad trestle. Fairfax County police said Eric Barcia, a fast-food worker, taped a bunch of these straps together, wrapped an end around one foot, anchored the other end to the trestle at Lake Accotink Park, jumped and hit the pavement. Warren Carmichael, a police spokesman, said investigators thought Barcia was alone because his car was found nearby. "The length of the cord that he had assembled was greater than the distance between the trestle and the ground," Carmichael said. Police say the apparent cause of death was "Major trauma".

3. A man in Alabama died from rattlesnake bites. It seems that he and a friend were playing a game of catch, using the rattlesnake as a ball. The friend – no doubt a future Darwin Awards candidate – was hospitalized.

2. Employees in a medium-sized warehouse in west Texas noticed the smell of a gas leak. Sensibly, management evacuated the building extinguishing all potential sources of ignition; lights, power, etc. After the building had been evacuated, two technicians from the gas company were dispatched. Upon entering the building, they found they had difficulty navigating in the dark. To their frustration, none of the lights

worked. Witnesses later described the sight of one of the technicians reaching into his pocket and retrieving an object that resembled a cigarette lighter. Upon operation of the lighter-like object, the gas in the warehouse exploded, depositing pieces of it up to 3 miles away. Nothing was found of the technicians, but the lighter was virtually untouched by the explosion. The technician suspected of causing the blast had never been thought of as "bright" by his peers.

1. The Arizona Highway Patrol came upon a pile of smouldering metal embedded into the side of a cliff rising above the road at the apex of a curve. The wreckage resembled the site of an airplane crash, but it was a car. The type of car was unidentifiable at the scene. The lab finally figured out what it was and what had happened. It seems that a guy had somehow gotten hold of a JATO unit (Jet Assisted Take Off – actually a solid-fuel rocket) that is used to give heavy military transport planes an extra "push" when taking off from short airfields. He had driven his Chevy Impala out into the desert and found a long and straight stretch of road. Then he attached the JATO unit to his car, jumped in, got up some speed and fired off the JATO! The facts as best could be determined are that the operator of the 1967 Impala hit the JATO ignition at a distance of approximately 3 miles from the crash site. This was established by the prominent scorched and melted asphalt at that location. The JATO, if operating properly, would have reached maximum thrust within 5 seconds, causing the Chevy to reach speeds well in excess of 350 mph and continuing at full power for an additional 20–25 seconds. The driver, and soon-to-be pilot, most likely would have experienced G-forces usually reserved for dog-fighting F-14 jocks under full afterburners, causing him to become insignificant for the remainder of the event. However, the automobile remained on the straight highway for about 2.5 miles (15–20 seconds) before the driver applied and completely melted the brakes, blowing the tires and leaving thick rubber marks on the road surface, then becoming airborne for an additional 1.4 miles and impacting the cliff face at a height of 125 feet leaving a blackened

crater 3 feet deep in the rock. Most of the driver's remains were not recoverable; however, small fragments of bone, teeth and hair were extracted from the crater, and fingernail and bone shards were removed from a piece of debris believed to be a portion of the steering wheel.

Epilogue:

It has been calculated that this moron nearly reached Mach I, attaining a ground speed of approximately 420 mph.

A Late Nominee for This Year's Darwin Awards

Rising to a bet by the other members of his threesome, Everitt Sanchez tried to wash his own "balls" in a ball washer at the local golf course. Proving once again that beer and testosterone are a bad mix, Sanchez managed to straddle the ball washer and dangle his scrotum in the machine. Much to his dismay, one of his buddies upped the ante by spinning the crank on the machine with Sanchez's scrotum in place, thus wedging them solidly in the mechanism. Sanchez, who immediately passed his threshold of pain, collapsed and tumbled from his perch. Unfortunately for Sanchez, the height of the ball washer was more than a foot higher off the ground than his testicles were in a normal stance, and the scrotum was the weakest link. Sanchez's scrotum was ripped open during the fall, and one testicle was plucked from him forever and remained in the ball washer, while the other testicle was compressed and flattened as it was pulled between the housing of the washer and the rotating machinery inside. To add insult to injury, Sanchez broke a new $300 driver that he had just purchased from the pro shop and was using to balance himself. Sanchez was rushed to hospital for surgery, and the remaining threesome were asked to leave the course.

Bread: The Truth

1. More than 98% of convicted felons are bread users.

2. Fully HALF of all children who grow up in bread-consuming households score below average on standardized tests.

3. In the 18th century, when virtually all bread was baked in the home, the average life expectancy was less than 50 years; infant mortality rates were unacceptably high; many women died in childbirth; and diseases such as typhoid, yellow fever, and influenza ravaged whole nations.

4. More than 90% of violent crimes are committed within 24 hours of eating bread.

5. Bread has been proven to be addictive. Subjects deprived of bread and given only water to eat begged for bread after as little as two days.

6. Bread is often a "gateway" food item, leading the user to "harder" items such as butter, jam, peanut butter, and even cold meat.

7. Bread has been proven to absorb water. Since the human body is more than 90% water, it follows that eating bread could lead to your body being taken over by this absorbative food product, turning you into a soggy, gooey bread-pudding person.

8. Newborn babies can choke on bread.

9. Bread is baked at temperatures as high as 400° Fahrenheit. That kind of heat can kill an adult in less than one minute.

10. Most bread eaters are utterly unable to distinguish between significant scientific fact and meaningless statistical babbling.

Tube Announcements

Listed below are genuine announcements made by tube drivers on the London Underground:

"To the gentleman wearing the long grey coat trying to get on the second carriage, what part of 'stand clear of the doors' don't you understand?"

At Camden Town station (on a crowded Saturday afternoon): "Please let the passengers off the train first. Please let the passengers off the train first. Please let the passengers off the train first. Let the passengers off the train FIRST! Oh go on then, stuff yourselves in like sardines, see if I care, I'm going home."

"Ladies and Gentleman, upon departing the train may I remind you to take your rubbish with you. Despite the fact that you are in something that is metal, fairly round, filthy and smells, this is a tube train for public transport and not a bin on wheels."

"I apologize for the delay leaving the station ladies and gentlemen; this is due to a passenger masturbating on the train at Edgware Road. Someone has activated the alarm and he is being removed from the train."

"Ladies and Gentlemen do you want the good news first or the bad news? … The good news is that last Friday was my birthday and I hit the town and had a great time. I felt sadly let down by the fact that none of you sent me a card! I drive you to work and back home each day and not even a card. The bad news is that there is a points failure somewhere between Stratford and East Ham, which means that we probably won't reach our destination. We may have to stop and return. I won't reverse back up the line – simply get out, walk up the platform and go back to where we started. In the meantime if you get bored you can simply talk to the man in front or beside you or opposite you. Let me start you off: 'Hi, my name's Gary how do you do?'"

"Your delay this evening is caused by the line controller suffering from elbow and backside syndrome: not knowing his elbow from his backside. I'll let you know any further information as soon as I'm given any."

"Please mind the closing doors." The doors close ... the doors reopen. "Passengers are reminded that the big red slidey things on the side of the train are called the doors. Let's try it again. Please stand clear of the doors." The doors close. "Thank you."

"I am sorry about the delay, apparently some nutter has just wandered into the tunnel at Euston. We don't know when we'll be moving again, but these people tend to come out pretty quickly – usually in bits."

Bush IQ

Report: President Bush Has Lowest IQ of All Presidents of Past 50 Years

If late night TV comedy is an indicator, then there has never been as widespread a perception that a president is not intellectually qualified for the position he holds as there is with President G. W. Bush.

In a report published Monday, the Lovenstein Institute of Scranton, Pennsylvania, detailed the findings of a four-month study of the intelligence quotient of President George W. Bush. Since 1973, the Lovenstein Institute has published its research to the education community on each new president, which includes the famous "IQ" report among others.

According to statements in the report, twelve presidents over the past 50 years, from F. D. Roosevelt to G. W. Bush, have been rated based on scholarly achievements, writings that they alone produced without the aid of staff, their ability to speak with clarity, and several other psychological factors which were then scored in the Swanson/Crain system of intelligence ranking.

The study determined the following IQs of each president as accurate to within five percentage points:

147 Franklin D. Roosevelt (D)
132 Harry Truman (D)
122 Dwight D. Eisenhower (R)
174 John F. Kennedy (D)
126 Lyndon B. Johnson (D)
155 Richard M. Nixon (R)
121 Gerald Ford (R)
175 James E. Carter (D)
105 Ronald Reagan (R)
098 George H. W. Bush (R)
182 William J. Clinton (D)
091 George W. Bush (R)

The six Republican presidents of the past 50 years had an average IQ of 115.5, with President Nixon having the highest IQ, at 155. President G. W. Bush was rated the lowest of all the Republicans with an IQ of 91. The six Democrat presidents had IQs with an average of 156, with President Clinton having the highest IQ at 182. President Lyndon B. Johnson was rated the lowest of all the Democrats with an IQ of 126. No president other than Carter (Democrat) has released his actual IQ – 176.

Among comments made concerning the specific testing of President G. W. Bush, his low rating was due to his apparent inability to command the English language in public statements, his limited use of vocabulary (6500 words for Bush versus an average of 11,000 words for other presidents), his lack of scholarly achievements other than a basic MBA, and an absence of any body of work which could be studied on an intellectual basis. The complete report documents the methods and procedures used to arrive at these ratings, including depth of sentence structure and voice stress confidence analysis.

"All the Presidents prior to George W. Bush had a least one book under their belt, and most had written several white papers during their education or early careers. Not so with President Bush," Dr Lovenstein said. "He has no published works or writings, so in many ways that made it more difficult to arrive at an assessment. We had to rely more heavily on transcripts of his unscripted public speaking."

The Lovenstein Institute of Scranton, Pennsylvania, think-tank includes high-calibre historians, psychiatrists, sociologists, scientists in human behaviour, and psychologists. Among their ranks are Dr Werner R. Lovenstein, world-renowned sociologist, and Professor Patricia F. Dilliams, a world-respected psychiatrist.

National Park Feedback

Actual comments made by visitors to America's Great Wildernesses ...

"A small deer came into my camp and stole my bag of pickles. Is there a way I can get reimbursed? Please call."

"Escalators would help on steep uphill sections."

"Trails need to be wider so people can walk while holding hands."

"Ban walking sticks in wilderness. Hikers that use walking sticks are more likely to chase animals."

"Trails need to be reconstructed. Please avoid building trails that go uphill."

"Too many bugs and leeches and spiders and spider webs. Please spray the wilderness to rid the area of these pests."

"Please pave the trails so they can be ploughed of snow in the winter."

"Chairlifts need to be in some places so that we can get to wonderful views without having to hike to them."

"The coyotes made too much noise last night and kept me awake. Please eradicate these annoying animals."

"Reflectors need to be placed on trees every 50 feet so people can hike at night with flashlights."

"Need more signs to keep area pristine."

"A McDonalds would be nice at the trailhead."

"The places where trails do not exist are not well marked."

"Too many rocks in the mountains."

Thinking of You

Greetings cards that didn't quite make it:

My tire was thumping,
I thought it was flat,
when I looked at the tire,
I noticed your cat – Sorry.

You had your bladder removed
and you're on the mends
here's a bouquet of flowers
and a box of Depends.

You've announced that you're gay,
won't that be a laugh,
when they find out you're one
of the Joint Chiefs of Staff.

Heard your wife left you,
how upset you must be,
but don't fret about it –
she's moved in with me.

Job Applications

Here are some things people actually wrote on their application forms:

"Personal: I'm married with nine children. I don't require prescription drugs."

"I am extremely loyal to my present firm, so please don't let them know of my immediate availability."

"Qualifications: I am a man filled with passion and integrity, and I can act on short notice. I'm a class act and do not come cheap."

"Note: Please don't misconstrue my 14 jobs as 'job-hopping'. I have never quit a job."

"Number of dependants: 40."

"Marital Status: Often. Children: Various."

"Here are my qualifications for you to overlook."

REASONS FOR LEAVING LAST JOB:

"Responsibility makes me nervous."

"They insisted that all employees get to work by 8:45 every morning. Couldn't work under those conditions."

JOB RESPONSIBILITIES:

"While I am open to the initial nature of an assignment, I am decidedly disposed that it be so oriented as to at least partially incorporate the experience enjoyed heretofore and that it be configured so as to ultimately lead to the application of more rarefied facets of financial management as the major sphere of responsibility."

"I was proud to win the Gregg Typting Award."

"My goal is to be a meteorologist. Since I have no training in meteorology, I suppose I should try stock brokerage."

"I procrastinate – especially when the task is unpleasant."

PHYSICAL DISABILITIES:

"Minor allergies to house cats and Mongolian sheep."

Irrefutable Observations

1) Moles are always smaller than you imagine.

2) At the end of every party there is always a fat girl crying.

3) One of the most awkward things that can happen in a pub is when your pint-to-toilet cycle gets synchronized with a complete stranger's.

4) Everyone who grew up in the 80s has entered the digits 55378008 into a calculator.

5) Reading when you're drunk is horrible.

6) Sharpening a pencil with a knife makes you feel really manly.

7) You're never quite sure whether it's against the law or not to have a fire in your back garden.

8) Whatever your age the desire to make plastic dolls shag is almost impossible to resist.

9) Nobody has ever made cup-a-soup in a bowl.

10) You never know where to look when eating an apple.

11) It's impossible to describe the smell of a wet cat.

12) Prodding a fire with a stick makes you feel manly.

13) Rummaging in an overgrown garden will always turn up a bouncy ball.

14) You always feel a bit scared when stroking horses.

15) The most embarrassing thing you can do as schoolchild is to call your teacher mum or dad.

16) The smaller the monkey the more it looks like it would kill you at the first given opportunity.

17) Some days you see lots of people on crutches.

18) Every bloke has at some stage while taking a p*ss flushed halfway through and then raced against the flush.

19) Old women with mobile phones look wrong!

20) It's impossible to look cool while picking up a frisbee.

21) Driving through a tunnel makes you feel excited.

21) You never ever run out of salt.

22) Old ladies can eat more than you think.

23) You can't respect a man who carries a dog.

24) There's no panic like the panic you momentarily feel when you've got your hand or head stuck in something.

25) No one knows the origins of their metal coat hangers.

26) The most painful household incident is stepping on an upturned plug.

27) People who don't drive slam car doors too hard.

28) You've turned into your dad the day you put aside a thin piece of wood specifically to stir paint with.

29) Everyone had an uncle who tried to steal their nose.

30) Bricks are horrible to carry.

31) In every plate of chips there is a bad chip.

32) Triangle sandwiches taste better than square ones.

Classifieds

Real ads from newspapers:

FREE YORKSHIRE TERRIER.
8 YEARS OLD. HATEFUL LITTLE DOG.

FREE PUPPIES:
1/2 COCKER SPANIEL
1/2 SNEAKY NEIGHBOUR'S DOG

FOUND: DIRTY WHITE DOG.
LOOKS LIKE A RAT
BEEN OUT A WHILE
BETTER BE REWARD

1 MAN, 7 WOMAN HOT TUB – $850/offer

SNOW BLOWER FOR SALE
ONLY USED ON SNOWY DAYS

2 WIRE MESH BUTCHERING GLOVES:
1 5-finger, 1 3-finger, PAIR: $15

TICKLE ME ELMO, STILL IN BOX,
COMES WITH ITS OWN 1988 MUSTANG, 5L, AUTO,
EXCELLENT CONDITION $6800

COWS, CALVES NEVER BRED
ALSO 1 GAY BULL FOR SALE

FULL-SIZED MATTRESS
20-YR WARRANTY
LIKE NEW
SLIGHT URINE SMELL

FOR SALE:
LEE MAJORS (6-MILLION DOLLAR MAN) – $50

NORDIC TRACK $300
HARDLY USED, CALL CHUBBIE

BILL'S SEPTIC CLEANING
"WE HAUL AMERICAN-MADE PRODUCTS"

NICE PARACHUTE
NEVER OPENED – USED ONCE

JOINING NUDIST COLONY!
MUST SELL WASHER & DRYER – $300

Caddy's Revenge

Allegedly genuine caddies' comments:

Golfer: "I've played so poorly all day; I think I'm going to go drown myself in that lake."
Caddy: "I doubt you could keep your head down that long."

Golfer: "I'd move heaven and earth to be able to break 100 on this course."
Caddy: "Try heaven. You've already moved most of the earth."

Golfer: "Well, I have never played this badly before!"
Caddy: "I didn't realize you had played before, sir."

Golfer: "Caddy, do you think my game is improving?"
Caddy: "Oh yes, sir! You miss the ball much closer than you used to."

Golfer: "Please stop checking your watch all the time, caddy. It's distracting!"
Caddy: "This isn't a watch, sir, it's a compass!"

Golfer: "Caddy, do you think it's a sin to play golf on Sunday?"
Caddy: "The way you play, sir, it's a sin any day of the week!"

Golfer: "This golf is a funny game."
Caddy: "It's not supposed to be."

Golfer: "That can't be my ball, caddy. It looks far too old."
Caddy: "It's a long time since we started, sir."

Golfer: "Do you think I can get there with a 5-iron?"
Caddy: "Eventually."

Golfer (screaming): "You've got to be the worst caddy in the world!"
Caddy: "I doubt it. That would be too much of a coincidence!"

Year's Best Headlines – Of Course They're Real

1. Stud Tires Out

2. Married Priests In Catholic Church A Long Time Coming

3. Squad Helps Dog Bite Victim

4. Two Soviet Ships Collide, One Dies

5. Drunken Drivers Paid $1000 In 1984

6. British Union Finds Dwarves In Short Supply

7. Deaf College Opens Door To Hearing

8. Air Head Fired

9. Prosecutor Releases Probe Into Undersheriff

10. Old School Pillars Are Replaced By Alumni

11. Bank Drive-In Window Blocked By Board

12. Some Pieces Of Rock Hudson Sold At Auction

13. Sex Education Delayed, Teachers Request Training

14. Police Discovered Pot Plants Were Really Cannabis

15. Headless Body Found In Topless Bar

16. Mondale Gets Warm Response From French Head

The Gold Coin Puzzle - Answer

Very simple.

Take one coin from stack 1, two from stack 2 … nine from stack 9, ten from stack 10. Weigh all of them together.

Had they all been real they would weigh 55 grams.

If the dud is in stack 1 then the weight will be 55.1g, if in stack 2, 55.2g … and so on up to stack 10 (56g).

Bin-Liners

- THE WAR AGAINST TERRORISM

Presidential Hotline

Osama bin Laden phoned President Bush and said, "Mr President, I called you because I had this incredible dream last night. I could see all of America, and it was beautiful, and on top of every building there was a beautiful banner." Bush asked angrily, "And what was on the banner?" Osama responded, "It said 'Allah is God, and God is Allah.'"

Bush said, "You know, Binny, I'm really glad you called, because last night I had a dream too. I could see all of Kabul, and it was even more beautiful than before the Russian occupation. It had been completely rebuilt, and on every building there was also a beautiful banner." Bin Laden said, "What was on the banner?" Bush replied, "I really don't know.

"I don't read Hebrew."

UFO

An American fighter pilot was flying his F-16 aircraft over Afghanistan, when he noticed a flying carpet on his left-hand side, manned by a man with a machine gun. He looked to his right and saw another carpet alongside, also manned by a man with a machine gun.

"I've got to get out of this," he thought, so he accelerated flat out and put his plane into a high-speed loop and came up behind both carpets, which he shot down.

On arriving back at his Aircraft Carrier, he was told to report to the captain immediately.

"You idiot!" said the captain. "We saw what you did on radar and now we're in a load of trouble."

"What do you mean?" said the pilot. "I shot both carpets down!"

"I know that," said the captain,

"but they were Allied Carpets!"

I Say, I Say …

Q: What do bin Laden and General Custer have in common?
A: They both want to know where the hell those Tomahawks are coming from!

Q: What is the best Afghan job?
A: Foreign Ambassador.

Q: Why is it twice as easy to train Afghan fighter pilots?
A: You only have to teach them to take off.

Q: How do you play Afghan bingo?
A: B-52 … F-16 … B-2 …

Q: What is Afghanistan's national bird?
A: Duck.

Q: How is bin Laden like Fred Flintstone?
A: Both look out of their windows and see Rubble.

📥 🖭 Osama's Inter-Cave Memo

Hi guys.

We've all been putting in long hours and most of us are now deaf, but we've really come together as a group and I love that. Big thanks to Omar for putting up the poster that says "There is no I in team" as well as the one that says "Hang In There, Baby." That cat is hilarious.

However, while we are fighting a jihad, we can't forget to take care of the cave. While it's good to be concerned about bombers, cruise missiles, and those scary-ass little remote-controlled drones, we should also be concerned about the scorpions in our cave. Hey, you don't want to be stung and neither do I, so we need to sweep the cave daily. I've posted a sign-up sheet near the main cave opening.

Second, it's not often I make a video address but when I do, I'm trying to scare the most powerful country on earth, okay? That means that while we're taping, please do not run through the camera shot screaming bloody murder every time you hear a plane. It totally undermines the message I'm trying to send. Thanks.

Third point, and this is a touchy one. As you know, by edict, we're not supposed to shave our beards. But I need everyone to just think hygiene, especially after mealtime and PLEASE change your trousers after bombing raids. We're all in this together.

Fourth: food. I bought a box of Cheez-Its recently, clearly wrote "Osama" on the front, and put it on the top shelf by my bug repellent. Today, my Cheez-Its were gone. Consideration. That's all I'm saying.

Finally, we've heard that there may be American soldiers in disguise trying to infiltrate our ranks. I want to set up patrols to look for them. First patrol will be Omar, Muhammad, Abdul, and Bob.

Love you lots.
Osama

New Secret Weapon

French Intellectuals to be Deployed in Afghanistan to Convince Taliban of Non-Existence of God

The ground war in Afghanistan heated up yesterday when the Allies revealed plans to airdrop a platoon of crack French existentialist philosophers into the country to destroy the morale of Taliban zealots by proving the non-existence of God.

Elements from the feared Jean-Paul Sartre Brigade, or "Black Berets", will be parachuted into the combat zones to spread doubt, despondency and existential anomie among the enemy. Hardened by numerous intellectual battles fought during their long occupation of Paris's Left Bank, their first action will be to establish a number of pavement cafés at strategic points near the front lines.

There they will drink coffee and talk animatedly about the absurd nature of life and man's lonely isolation in the universe. They will be accompanied by a number of heartbreakingly beautiful girlfriends who will further spread dismay by sticking their tongues in the philosophers' ears every five minutes and looking remote and unattainable to everyone else.

Their leader, Colonel Marc-Ange Belmondo, spoke yesterday of his confidence in the success of their mission. Sorbonne graduate Belmondo, a very intense and unshaven young man in a black pullover, gesticulated wildly and said, "The Taliban are caught in a logical fallacy of the most ridiculous sort. There is no God and I can prove it. Take your tongue out of my ear, Juliet, I am talking."

Speculation was mounting last night that Britain may also contribute to the effort by dropping Professor Stephen Hawking into Afghanistan to propagate his non-deistic theory of the creation of the universe.

📥 📧 Are You Osama Bin Laden?

The FBI are having trouble locating Osama and would like you to complete this questionnaire to rule you out of the investigation.

AM I OSAMA BIN LADEN?

You win a two-week vacation in Florida, do you:
A) spend two weeks lying on a beach, visiting theme parks and relaxing.
B) try to sell your tickets, go anyway and spend all your time trying to become as fat as everyone else there.
C) take control of the aircraft en route to Disneyland, divert to New York and crash into the Brooklyn Bridge?

You inherit a plot of land, do you:
A) set up a fat camp to help jelly belly kids of the USA?
B) set up a holiday camp and try to make a fat wad of cash?
C) set up a terrorist training camp to create the suicide bombers of tomorrow?

You inherit your father's billion-dollar fortune, do you:
A) live moderately and donate to charity?
B) get very fat, visit poor, underdeveloped countries and exploit sex-trade workers?
C) live in a cave in Afghanistan?

A few friends offer to help you out if you need a favour, do you:
A) ask them to help you organize a community event?
B) ask them over to your house for a game of poker and then rig the game to rip them off?
C) ask them to strap bombs to their backs and go sightseeing in Manhattan?

A building collapses after a terrorist attack in downtown NY, do you:
A) feel sorry for the loss of innocent life?
B) run into the street waving the Stars and Stripes and shouting "USA, USA, USA"?
C) jump up and down, beat your head and fire your AK-47 in the air?

Answers:
All *A*s – you're not an American
All *B*s – you are an American
All *C*s – you're Osama bin Laden; please go to your nearest police station.

The World According to America

COLD Santa Claus lives here

See how America **valiantly** defends itself by bombing → Some this way too
small countries

COMMIES

COMMIES
Go away commies

Scotchland and Irland

CANADA
Our friendly but backwards neighbours

ENGLAND

Disney

Theme parks
go see the Queen

YUROP

Stay out commies

USA
Land of the free and of the brave etc.

McDonalds
Everybody loves them

Vietnam over here somewhere

Commies are our enemies they must be destroyed

Smelly people with big hats

MEXICO

No TV or escalators

COMMIES
They want to destroy our great democracy with their... err... cigars.

HERE BE DRAGONS

HERE BE... SOMETHING ELSE

HERE BE DRAGONS

No civilisation
People eat each other here

43

The War Against Dentistry

George W. Bush and Tony Blair are at a White House dinner. One of the important guests walks over to them and asks what they are talking about.

"We are making up the plans for WWIII," says Bush.

"Wow," says the guest. "And what are the plans?"

"We are gonna kill 14 million Muslims and one dentist," answers Bush. The guest looks to be a bit confused.

"One … dentist?" he says. "Why? Why will you kill one dentist?" Bush pats Blair on the shoulder and says:

"What did I tell you? Nobody is gonna ask about the Muslims."

Liberation

A journalist had done a story on gender roles in Afghanistan under the Taliban, and she noted then that women customarily walked about ten feet behind their husbands.

She returned there recently and observed that the men now walked several yards behind their wives. She approached one of the women for an explanation.

"This is marvellous," said the journalist. "What enabled women here to achieve this reversal of roles?"

Replied the Afghan woman, "Landmines."

📥 💻 Q & A

Q: What's the difference between Elvis and Osama bin Laden?
A: There have been at least three sightings of Elvis over the past two months.

📥 💻 Osama at the Pearly Gates

After getting nailed by a Daisy Cutter, Osama makes his way to the pearly gates. There he is greeted by George Washington.

"How dare you attack the nation I helped conceive!" yells Mr Washington, slapping Osama in the face. Patrick Henry comes up from behind.

"You wanted to end the Americans' liberty, so they gave you death!" Henry punches Osama on the nose.

James Madison arrives next, and says, "This is why I allowed the Federal government to provide for the common defence!" He drops a large weight on Osama's knee.

Osama is subject to similar beatings from John Randolph of Roanoke, James Monroe, and 65 other people who have the same love for liberty and America.

As Osama writhes on the ground, Thomas Jefferson picks him up to hurl him back toward the gate where he is to be judged. As Osama awaits his journey to his final very hot destination, he screams, "This is not what I was promised!"

An angel replies, "I told you there would be 72 Virginians waiting for you. What did you think I said?"

Boom-Boom

📥 🗄 Q and A

Q: What's a mixed feeling?
A: When you see your mother-in-law backing off a cliff in your new car.

Q: What's the height of conceit?
A: Having an orgasm and calling out your own name.

Q: What's the definition of macho?
A: Jogging home from your own vasectomy.

Q: What is the difference between a drug dealer and a hooker?
A: A hooker can wash her crack and sell it again.

Q: What's the difference between a G-Spot and a golf ball?
A: A guy will actually search for a golf ball.

Q: How can you tell the porno star at the gas station?
A: Just as the gas starts up the hose, he pulls out the nozzle and sprays the gas all over the car.

Q: Do you know how New Zealanders practise safe sex?
A: They spray-paint Xs on the back of the animals that kick.

Q: Why is divorce so expensive?
A: Because it's worth it.

Q: What is a Yankee?
A: The same as a quickie, but a guy can do it alone.

Q: What do a tupperware manufacturer and a walrus have in common?
A: They both like a tight seal.

Q: What do a Christmas tree and a priest have in common?
A: Their balls are just for decoration.

Q: What is the difference between "ooooooh" and "aaaaaaah"?
A: About three inches.

Q: What's the difference between purple and pink?
A: The grip.

Q: How do you find a blind man in a nudist colony?
A: It's not hard.

Q: How do you find Ronald McDonald on a nudist beach?
A: He's the one with the sesame seed buns.

Q: How do you circumcise a hillbilly?
A: Kick his sister in the jaw.

Q: What's the difference between a girlfriend and a wife?
A: 45 lbs.

Q: What's the difference between a boyfriend and a husband?
A: 45 minutes.

Q: Why do men find it difficult to make eye contact?
A: Breasts don't have eyes.

Q: What is the difference between medium and rare?
A: Six inches is medium, eight inches is rare.

Q: Why don't men fake orgasm?
A: Because no man would pull those faces on purpose.

Q: Why do most women pay more attention to their appearance than improving their minds?
A: Because most men are stupid but few are blind.

Q: Why do women rub their eyes when they get up in the morning?
A: They don't have balls to scratch.

Q: Why do women call it PMS?
A: Mad Cow Disease was already taken.

Q: If the dove is the bird of peace, what is the bird of true love?
A: The swallow.

Bumper Stickers: Part One

BUMPER STICKERS WE PROBABLY MISSED BECAUSE WE WERE
DRIVING SO FAST ...

Constipated People Don't Give A Crap.
~~~~~~~~~~~~~~~~~~~~~~~~~~~~~~~~~~
Practice Safe Sex, Go Screw Yourself.
~~~~~~~~~~~~~~~~~~~~~~~~~~~~~~~~~~
If You Drink Don't Park, Accidents Cause People.
~~~~~~~~~~~~~~~~~~~~~~~~~~~~~~~~~~
Please Tell Your Pants It's Not Polite To Point.
~~~~~~~~~~~~~~~~~~~~~~~~~~~~~~~~~~
If That Phone Was Up Your Butt, Maybe You Could Drive A Little Better.
~~~~~~~~~~~~~~~~~~~~~~~~~~~~~~~~~~
My Kid Got Your Honor Roll Student Pregnant.
~~~~~~~~~~~~~~~~~~~~~~~~~~~~~~~~~~
Thank You For Pot Smoking.
~~~~~~~~~~~~~~~~~~~~~~~~~~~~~~~~~~
To All You Virgins: Thanks For Nothing.
~~~~~~~~~~~~~~~~~~~~~~~~~~~~~~~~~~
Impotence: Nature's Way Of Saying "No Hard Feelings".

~~~~~~~~~~~~~~~~~~~~~~~~~~~~~~~~~~~~

If You Can Read This, I've Lost My Trailer.

~~~~~~~~~~~~~~~~~~~~~~~~~~~~~~~~~~~~

Horn Broken ... Watch For Finger.

~~~~~~~~~~~~~~~~~~~~~~~~~~~~~~~~~~~~

It's Not How You Pick Your Nose, But Where You Put The Booger.

~~~~~~~~~~~~~~~~~~~~~~~~~~~~~~~~~~~~

If You're Not A Hemorrhoid, Get Off My Tuchas.

~~~~~~~~~~~~~~~~~~~~~~~~~~~~~~~~~~~~

You're Just Jealous Because The Voices Are Talking To Me.

~~~~~~~~~~~~~~~~~~~~~~~~~~~~~~~~~~~~

The Earth Is Full – Go Home.

~~~~~~~~~~~~~~~~~~~~~~~~~~~~~~~~~~~~

So Many Pedestrians – So Little Time.

~~~~~~~~~~~~~~~~~~~~~~~~~~~~~~~~~~~~

Cleverly Disguised As A Responsible Adult.

~~~~~~~~~~~~~~~~~~~~~~~~~~~~~~~~~~~~

If We Quit Voting Will They All Go Away?

20 Deep (But Really Quite Stupid) Thoughts

1. Don't sweat the petty things and don't pet the sweaty things.

2. One tequila, two tequila, three tequila, floor.

3. Atheism is a non-prophet organization.

4. If man evolved from monkeys and apes, why do we still have monkeys and apes?

5. The main reason Santa is so jolly is because he knows where all the bad girls live.

6. I went to a bookstore and asked the saleswoman, "Where's the self-help section?" She said if she told me, it would defeat the purpose.

7. Could it be that all those trick-or-treaters wearing sheets aren't going as ghosts but as mattresses?

8. If a mute swears, does his mother wash his hands with soap?

9. If a man is standing in the middle of the forest speaking and there is no woman around to hear him … is he still wrong?

10. If someone with multiple personalities threatens to kill himself, is it considered a hostage situation?

11. Is there another word for synonym?

12. Isn't it a bit unnerving that doctors call what they do "practise"?

13. Where do forest rangers go to "get away from it all"?

14. What do you do when you see an endangered animal eating an endangered plant?

15. If a parsley farmer is sued, can they garnish his wages?

16. Would a fly without wings be called a walk?

17. Why do they lock gas station bathrooms? Are they afraid someone will clean them?

18. If a turtle doesn't have a shell, is he homeless or naked?

19. Why don't sheep shrink when it rains?

20. Can vegetarians eat animal crackers?

Bumper Stickers: Part Two

The Face Is Familiar, But I Can't Quite Remember My Name.
~~~~~~~~~~~~~~~~~~~~~~~~~~~~~~~~~~~~~
Eat Right, Exercise, Die Anyway.
~~~~~~~~~~~~~~~~~~~~~~~~~~~~~~~~~~~~~
Iliterate? Write For Help.
~~~~~~~~~~~~~~~~~~~~~~~~~~~~~~~~~~~~~
Honk If Anything Falls Off.
~~~~~~~~~~~~~~~~~~~~~~~~~~~~~~~~~~~~~
Cover Me, I'm Changing Lanes.
~~~~~~~~~~~~~~~~~~~~~~~~~~~~~~~~~~~~~
He Who Hesitates Is Not Only Lost But Miles From The Next Exit.
~~~~~~~~~~~~~~~~~~~~~~~~~~~~~~~~~~~~~
I Refuse To Have A Battle Of Wits With An Unarmed Person.
~~~~~~~~~~~~~~~~~~~~~~~~~~~~~~~~~~~~~
You! Out Of The Gene Pool!
~~~~~~~~~~~~~~~~~~~~~~~~~~~~~~~~~~~~~
I Do Whatever My Rice Krispies Tell Me To.
~~~~~~~~~~~~~~~~~~~~~~~~~~~~~~~~~~~~~
Where Are We Going And Why Am I In This Handbasket?
~~~~~~~~~~~~~~~~~~~~~~~~~~~~~~~~~~~~~
If Sex Is A Pain In The Posterior, Then You're Doing It Wrong.
~~~~~~~~~~~~~~~~~~~~~~~~~~~~~~~~~~~~~
Fight Crime: Shoot Back!
~~~~~~~~~~~~~~~~~~~~~~~~~~~~~~~~~~~~~
If You Can Read This, Please Flip Me Back Over
[seen upside down on a jeep]
~~~~~~~~~~~~~~~~~~~~~~~~~~~~~~~~~~~~~
Remember Folks: Stop Lights Timed For 35 mph Are Also Timed For 70 mph.
~~~~~~~~~~~~~~~~~~~~~~~~~~~~~~~~~~~~~

Guys: No Shirt, No Service.
Gals: No Shirt, No Charge.

~~~~~~~~~~~~~~~~~~~~~~~~~~~~~~~~~~~~~

If Walking Is So Good For You, Then Why Does My Mailman Look Like Jabba The Hut?

~~~~~~~~~~~~~~~~~~~~~~~~~~~~~~~~~~~~~

Ax Me About Ebonics.

Handy Hints for Campers

>Lint from your navel makes a handy fire starter. Warning: Remove lint from navel before applying the match.

>Get even with a bear who raided your food bag by kicking his favourite stump apart and eating all the ants.

>A hot rock placed in your sleeping bag will keep your feet warm. A hot enchilada works almost as well, but the cheese sticks between your toes.

>The best backpacks are named for national parks or mountain ranges. Steer clear of those named for landfills.

>While the Swiss Army Knife has been popular for years, the Swiss Navy Knife has remained largely unheralded. Its single blade functions as a tiny canoe paddle.

>Modern rain suits made of fabrics that "breathe" enable campers to stay dry in a downpour. Rain suits that sneeze, cough, and belch, however, have been proven to add absolutely nothing to the wilderness experience.

>You'll never be lost if you remember that moss always grows on the north side of your compass.

>You can duplicate the warmth of a down-filled bedroll by climbing into a plastic garbage bag with several geese.

>The canoe paddle, a simple device used to propel a boat, should never be confused with a gnu paddle, a similar device used by Tibetan veterinarians.

>When camping, always wear a long-sleeved shirt. It gives you something to wipe your nose on.

>Take this simple test to see if you qualify for solo camping. Shine a flashlight into one ear. If the beam shines out the other ear, do not go into the woods alone.

>A two-man pup tent does not include two men or a pup.

>A potato baked in the coals for one hour makes an excellent side dish. A potato baked in the coals for three hours makes an excellent hockey puck.

>In emergency situations, you can survive in the wilderness by shooting small game with a slingshot made from the elastic waistband of your underwear.

>The guitar of the noisy teenager at the next campsite makes excellent kindling.

>The sight of a bald eagle has thrilled campers for generations. The sight of a bald man, however, does absolutely nothing for the eagle.

>It's entirely possible to spend your whole vacation on a winding mountain road behind a large motorhome.

>Bear bells provide an element of safety for hikers in grizzly country. The tricky part is getting them on the bears.

>When using a public campground, a tuba placed on your picnic table will keep the campsites on either side vacant.

>In an emergency, a drawstring from a parka hood can be used to strangle a snoring tent mate.

Another Light Bulb Joke

Q: How many internet mail list/newsgroup subscribers does it take to change a light bulb?

A: 1343:
1 to change the light bulb and to post to the mail list that the light bulb has been changed;

14 to share similar experiences of changing light bulbs and how the light bulb could have been changed differently;

7 to caution about the dangers of changing light bulbs;

27 to point out spelling/grammar errors in posts about changing light bulbs;

53 to flame the spell checkers;

41 to correct spelling/grammar flames;

6 to argue over whether it's "lightbulb" or "light bulb";

6 more to condemn those 6 as anal-retentive;

156 to write to the list administrator about the light bulb discussion and its inappropriateness to this mail list;

109 to post that this list is not about light bulbs and to please take this email exchange to litebulb-l;

203 to demand that cross posting to grammar-l, spelling-l and illuminati-l about changing light bulbs be stopped;

111 to defend the posting to this list saying that we all use light bulbs and therefore the posts *are* relevant to this mail list;

306 to debate which method of changing light bulbs is superior, where to buy the best light bulbs, what brand of light bulbs work best for this technique and what brands are faulty;

27 to post URLs where one can see examples of different light bulbs;

14 to post that the URLs were posted incorrectly and post the corrected URLs;

3 to post about links they found from the URLs that are relevant to this list which makes light bulbs relevant to this list;

33 to link all posts to date, then quote them including all headers and footers and then add "Me too";

12 to post to the list that they are unsubscribing because they cannot handle the light bulb controversy;

19 to quote the "Me too"s to say "Me three";

4 to suggest that posters request the light bulb FAQ;

44 to ask what is "FAQ";

4 to say "Didn't we go through this already a short time ago on Usenet?"

143 to ask "What's Usenet?"

Bumper Stickers: Part Three

Body By Nautilus; Brain By Mattel.
~~~~~~~~~~~~~~~~~~~~~~~~~~~~~~~~~~~~~

Boldly Going Nowhere.
~~~~~~~~~~~~~~~~~~~~~~~~~~~~~~~~~~~~~

Caution – Driver Legally Blonde.
~~~~~~~~~~~~~~~~~~~~~~~~~~~~~~~~~~~~~

Don't Be Sexist – Bitches Hate That.
~~~~~~~~~~~~~~~~~~~~~~~~~~~~~~~~~~~~~

Heart Attacks ... God's Revenge For Eating His Animal Friends.
~~~~~~~~~~~~~~~~~~~~~~~~~~~~~~~~~~~~~

How Many Roads Must A Man Travel Down Before He Admits He Is Lost?
~~~~~~~~~~~~~~~~~~~~~~~~~~~~~~~~~~~~~

If You Can't Dazzle Them With Brilliance, Riddle Them With Bullets.
~~~~~~~~~~~~~~~~~~~~~~~~~~~~~~~~~~~~~

Money Isn't Everything, But It Sure Keeps The Kids In Touch.
~~~~~~~~~~~~~~~~~~~~~~~~~~~~~~~~~~~~~

Saw It ... Wanted It ... Had A Fit ... Got It!
~~~~~~~~~~~~~~~~~~~~~~~~~~~~~~~~~~~~~

My Hockey Mom Can Beat Up Your Soccer Mom.
~~~~~~~~~~~~~~~~~~~~~~~~~~~~~~~~~~~~~

Grow Your Own Dope – Plant A Man.
~~~~~~~~~~~~~~~~~~~~~~~~~~~~~~~~~~~~~

All Men Are Animals, Some Just Make Better Pets.
~~~~~~~~~~~~~~~~~~~~~~~~~~~~~~~~~~~~~

Some People Are Only Alive Because It Is Illegal To Shoot Them.
~~~~~~~~~~~~~~~~~~~~~~~~~~~~~~~~~~~~~

I Used To Have A Handle On Life, But It Broke.
~~~~~~~~~~~~~~~~~~~~~~~~~~~~~~~~~~~~~

WANTED: Meaningful Overnight Relationship.

~~~~~~~~~~~~~~~~~~~~~~~~~~~~~~~~~~

BEER: It's Not Just For Breakfast Anymore.

~~~~~~~~~~~~~~~~~~~~~~~~~~~~~~~~~~

So You're A Feminist ... Isn't That Precious.

~~~~~~~~~~~~~~~~~~~~~~~~~~~~~~~~~~

I Need Someone Really Bad ... Are You Really Bad?

~~~~~~~~~~~~~~~~~~~~~~~~~~~~~~~~~~

Beauty Is In The Eye Of The Beer Holder.

So I Said ...

I saw this bloke chatting up a cheetah and thought, "He's trying to pull a fast one."

So I said to the booking clerk, "I want to go to Paris." He said, "Eurostar?" I said, "Thanks, but I've not even been on telly."

So I said to my gym instructor, "Can you teach me to do the splits?" He said, "How flexible are you?" I said, "I can't make Tuesdays."

When I go away, what I love doing more than anything is trying to pack a small suitcase. I can hardly contain myself.

So I said, "Do you want a game of darts?" He said, "OK then." I said, "Nearest to bull starts." He said, "Baa." I said, "Moo." He said, "You're closest."

The other day I sent my girlfriend a huge pile of snow. I rang her and said, "Do you get my drift?"

So I went down the local supermarket and said, "I want to make a complaint; this jar of vinegar's got lumps in it." They said, "Those are pickled onions."

So I went to the Chinese restaurant and this duck came up to me with a red rose and said, "Your eyes sparkle like diamonds." I said, "Waiter, I asked for a-ROMATIC duck."

Did you know that if a stick insect lays its eggs in a jar of Bovril it will give birth to a litter of Twiglets.

So this bloke says to me, "Can I come in your house and talk about cleaning your carpets?" I thought, "That's all I need, a Je-Hoover's witness."

So I rang British Telecom and said, "I want to report a nuisance caller." They said, "Not you again."

So I was having dinner with Garry Kasparov and there was a check table-cloth. It took him two hours to pass me the salt. He said, "You remind me of a pepper-pot." I said, "I'll take that as a condiment."

Did you know all male tennis players are witches, for example Goran, even he's a witch.

And I've got a friend who's fallen in love with two school bags; he's bi-satchel.

The news reported that a lorry-load of tortoises had crashed into a train-load of terrapins. I thought, "That's a turtle disaster."

In the same bulletin, they said that a tanker of molasses had lost its load on the M1 and that drivers were advised to stick to the inside lane.

⬇🖳 Another 20 Deep Thoughts

21. If the police arrest a mime, do they tell him he has the right to remain silent?

22. Why do they put Braille on the drive-through bank machines?

23. How do blind people know when they are done wiping?

24. How do they get the deer to cross at that yellow road sign?

25. Is it true that cannibals don't eat clowns because they taste funny?

26. What was the best thing before sliced bread?

27. One nice thing about egotists: they don't talk about other people.

28. Does the Little Mermaid wear an algebra?

29. Do infants enjoy infancy as much as adults enjoy adultery?

30. How is it possible to have a civil war?

31. If God dropped acid, would he see people?

32. If one synchronized swimmer drowns, do the rest drown too?

33. If you ate pasta and antipasto, would you still be hungry?

34. If you try to fail, and succeed, which have you done?

35. Whose cruel idea was it for the word "lisp" to have a "s" in it?

36. Why are haemorrhoids called "haemorrhoids" instead of "asteroids"?

37. Why is it called tourist season if we can't shoot at them?

38. Why is the alphabet in that order? Is it because of that song?

39. Why does sour cream have an expiry date?

40. If the "black box" flight recorder is never damaged during a plane crash, why isn't the whole damn airplane made out of that stuff?

Booze and Boozers

Drunk

A guy stumbled in through the front door of a bar completely drunk. He walked up to the bartender and asked for a drink. The bartender kindly told the guy he couldn't give him a drink because he was already drunk. Angry, the guy stumbled back out the front door.

About five minutes later the guy stumbled in through the side door of the bar. He asked the bartender for a drink and once again the bartender told the guy no because he was already drunk. The guy stumbled back out through the side door.

A few minutes later the guy stumbled in through the back door of the bar. He walked up to the bar, looked at the bartender for a moment then said,

"Damn man, how many bars do you work at?"

Barspeak

"No, really, I'm OK to drive."
means
"I'm wasted, and I am too embarrassed to have anybody see who I am going home with."

"I'm not used to these darts."
means
"I'm not used to throwing anything smaller than a pool cue when I am this bombed."

"Let's go out to my car and get some cigarettes." (male to female)
means
"You would look great face down in my lap."

"You get this one, next round is on me."
means
"We won't be here long enough to get another round."

"I'll get this one, next one is on you."
means
"Happy hour is about to end: pints are currently £1.50, but by the next round they'll be £4.00 a pop."

"I haven't seen you around here for a long time."
means
"You stuck up little bitch, too good for your old friends??"

"Hey, where is that friend of yours?"
means
"I have no interest in talking to you except as a way to get your attractive friend into a compromising position."

"Can I have a glass of white Zinfandel?" (female)
means
"I'm easy."

"Can I have a glass of white Zinfandel?" (male)
means
"I'm gay."

"Ever try a body shot?" (male to female)
means
"I am even willing to drink tequila if it means that I get to lick you."

"Ever try a body shot?" (female to male)
means
"If this is how wild I am in the bar, imagine what I'll do to you on the ride home?"

"I don't feel well, let's go home." (female)
means
"You are paying more attention to your friends than me."

"I don't feel well, let's go home." (male)
means
"I'm horny."

"Excuse me." (male to male)
means
"Get the f*** out of the way."

"Excuse me." (male to female)
means
"I am going to grope you now."

"Excuse me." (female to male)
means
"Don't even think about groping me, just get the f*** out of the way."

"Excuse me." (female to female)
means
"Move your fat ass. Who do you think you are anyway? You are not all that, missy, and don't think for one minute that you are. Coming in here dressing like a ho … Get your eyes off of my man, or I'll slap you like the slut you are."

"Can I have a white Russian?" (female)
means
"I'm really easy."

"Can I have a white Russian?" (male)
means
"I'm really gay."

"That person looks really familiar."
means
"Did I sleep with him?"

"Can I just get a glass of water?" (female)
means
"I'm annoying, but just cute enough to get away with this."

"Can I just get a glass of water?" (male)
means
"It's 6:00 a.m. and I just stopped drinking half an hour ago. Hell, I probably dropped half of my paycheque in here last night, it's the least you can do for me."

Cerebrally Challenged

A truck driver had to deliver 500 penguins to the state zoo. As he was driving through the desert, the truck broke down. After waiting by the side of the road for about three hours he waved another truck down and offered the driver $5000 to take the penguins to the state zoo for him.

The next day the first truck driver arrived in town and saw the second truck driver crossing the road with 500 penguins walking single file behind him. The first truck driver jumped out of his truck and said, "What's going on? I gave you $5000 to take these penguins to the zoo!" The second truck driver replies, "I did take them to the zoo.

"And I had so much money left over that now we're going to see a movie."

⬇ ▭ Idiot Spotting

IDIOTS IN CUSTOMER SERVICE
This week, all our office phones went dead and I had to contact the telephone repair people. They promised to be out between 8:00 a.m. and 7:00 p.m. When I asked if they could give me a smaller time window, the pleasant gentleman asked, "Would you like us to call you before we come?" I replied that I didn't see how he would be able to do that, since our phones weren't working. He also requested that we report future outages by email. (Does YOUR email work without a telephone line?)

IDIOTS AT WORK
I was signing the receipt for my credit card purchase when the clerk noticed I hadn't signed my name on the back of the credit card. She informed me that she could not complete the transaction unless the card

was signed. When I asked why, she explained that it was necessary to compare the signature. I had just signed on the receipt. So I signed the credit card in front of her. She carefully compared the signature to the one I had just signed on the receipt. As luck would have it, they matched.

IDIOTS IN THE NEIGHBOURHOOD
I live in a semi-rural area. We recently had a new neighbour call the local township administrative office to request the removal of the Deer Crossing sign on our road. The reason: too many deer were being hit by cars and he didn't want them to cross there anymore.

IDIOTS IN FOOD SERVICE
My daughter went to a local Taco Bell and ordered a taco. She asked the person behind the counter for "minimal lettuce". He said he was sorry, but they only had iceberg.

IDIOTS IN THE AIR
I was at the airport, checking in at the gate when an airport employee asked, "Has anyone put anything in your baggage without your knowledge?" To which I replied, "If it was without my knowledge, how would I know?" He smiled knowingly and nodded, "That's why we ask."

In the Psychiatrist's Office

A middle-aged man walked into a psychologist's office wearing a dancer's tutu, flippers and a scuba mask. The psychologist, humouring him, asked, "What seems to be the problem?" The man answered, "Well, doc, I'm worried about my brother …"

The Fishermen

Tony and Harold, two avid fisherman and well-known drunks, were out in a boat on their favourite lake one day drowning some worms and polishing off some brews. Suddenly, Tony got what he thought was a nibble. Reeling it in he found a bottle with a cork in it. Naturally curious, he uncorked the bottle and a large genie appeared.

The genie said, "I will grant you one wish." Tony thought for a second and said, "I wish this whole lake was beer." Poof! His wish came true. The lake was now filled with their favorite brew. Harold looked at Tony in disgust and said,

"You asshole, now we have to piss in the boat."

His Big Break

An out-of-work actor gets a call from his agent one day.

"I've got you a job" says his agent.

"That's great," says the actor, "what is it?"

"Well," says his agent "it's a one-liner."

"That's okay," replies the actor, "I've been out of work for so long I'll take anything; what's the line?"

"'Hark I hear the cannons roar,'" says the agent.

"I love it," says the actor. "When's the audition?"

"Wednesday," says the agent.

Wednesday comes and the actor arrives at the audition. He marches on stage and shouts: "Hark I hear the cannons roar."

"Brilliant," says the director, "you've got the job, be here at 9 p.m. Saturday evening." The actor is so chuffed he got the job that he goes on a major bender.

He wakes up at 8:30 on Saturday evening and runs to the theatre continually repeating his line: "Hark I hear the cannons roar. Hark I hear the cannons roar. Hark I hear the cannons roar." He arrives at the stage entrance out of breath and is stopped by the bouncer.

"Who are you?" asks the bouncer.

"I'm 'Hark I hear the cannons roar.'"

"You're 'Hark I hear the cannons roar'? You're late, get up to make-up straight away. So he runs up to make-up.

"Who are you?" asks the make-up girl. "I'm 'Hark I hear the cannons roar.'"

"You're 'Hark I hear the cannons roar'? You're late, sit down here." And she applies the make-up. "Now quick, get down to the stage, you're about to go on." So he dashes down to the stage.

"Who are you?" asks the stage manager.

"I'm 'Hark I hear the cannons roar.'"

"You're 'Hark I hear the cannons roar'? You're late, get on there, the curtain's about to go up." So he tears onto the stage. The curtains rise, the house is full. Suddenly there is an almighty bang behind him, and the actor shouts ...

"WHAT THE FUCK WAS THAT?"

Christmas

On Santa's Lap

A little girl was waiting in line to see Santa. When her turn came she climbed up on Santa's lap and Santa asked, "What would you like Santa to bring you for Christmas?" The little girl replies, "I want a Barbie and G.I. Joe." Santa looked at the little girl for a moment and said, "I thought Barbie comes with Ken."

"No," said the little girl.

"She comes with G.I. Joe, she fakes it with Ken."

Sandra Claus

I hate to be the one to defy sacred myth, but I believe he's a she. Think about it. Christmas is a big, organized, warm, fuzzy, nurturing, social deal, and I have a tough time believing a guy (and a "straight" guy at that!) could possibly pull it all off! For starters, the vast majority of men don't even think about selecting gifts until Christmas Eve. Once at the mall, they always seem surprised to find only Ronco products, socket wrench sets, and mood rings left on the shelves. On this count alone, I'm convinced Santa is a woman. Surely, if he were a man, everyone in the universe would wake up on Christmas morning to find a rotating musical Chia Pet under the tree, still in the shopping bag. Another problem for a he-Santa would be getting there. First of all, there would be no reindeer because they would all be dead, gutted and strapped on to the rear bumper of the sleigh amid wide-eyed, desperate claims that buck season had been extended. Blitzen's rack would already be on the way to the taxidermist. Even if the male Santa *did* still have reindeer, he'd also have the transportation problems because he would inevitably get lost up there in the snow and clouds and then refuse to stop and ask for directions. Other reasons why Santa can't possibly be a man:

1. Men can't pack a bag.

2. Men would rather be dead than caught wearing red velvet.

3. Men would feel their masculinity is threatened having to be seen with all those elves.

4. Men don't answer their mail.

5. Men would refuse to allow their physique to be described, even in jest, as anything remotely resembling a "bowl full of jelly".

6. Men aren't interested in stockings unless somebody's wearing them.

7. Having to do the "Ho Ho Ho" thing would seriously inhibit their ability to pick up women.

8. Finally, being responsible for Christmas would require a commitment.

Inner City Carols

(To the tune of "Deck The Halls")

See that drag queen his name's Molly,
Fa La-La La-La, La-La La La;
For 50 bucks he'll make you jolly,
Fa La-La La-La, La-La La La;
See him in his gay apparel,
Fa La-La La-La, La-La La La;
You should meet his brother Carol,
Fa La-La La-La, La-La La La.

(To the tune of "We Wish You A Merry Christmas")

> We wish you a happy hearing,
> We wish you a happy hearing,
> We wish you a happy hearing,
> and we hope you make bail!

(To the tune of "Rudolph The Red-Nosed Reindeer")

> Rudolph the red-nosed wino,
> Had a very shiny nose,
> And if you got too close to him,
> He would take off all his clothes.
> All of the other winos,
> Used to laugh and call him names,
> They never let poor Rudolph,
> Join in any wino games.
> Then one foggy Christmas Night,
> Rudolph froze to death in an alley.
> End of story.

(Then there's my favourite rendition of an old holiday classic ...)

> 'Twas the night before Christmas,
> And all through the house,
> Not a creature was stirring,
> So I took their stereo.

Turkey Preparation

"May I take your Christmas lunch order, sir?" the waiter asked.

"Yes, but first I'd like to know how do you prepare your turkeys?"

"Nothing special sir," he replied.

"We just tell them straight out that they're going to die."

Christmas Party

A guy woke up in the morning after a fantastic Christmas party. He had a massive hangover and couldn't remember anything he did after arriving at the party the night before. He picked up his dressing gown from the floor and put it on. He noticed something in one of the pockets, fished it out and discovered it was a bra.

"Bloody hell, what happened last night?" he wondered. He walked towards the bathroom and found a pair of panties in the other pocket of his gown. Again he thought, "What happened last night, what have I done? Must have been a wild party."

He opened the bathroom door, walked in and had a look in the mirror. He noticed a little string hanging out of his mouth and thought,

"If there's a God, please let this be a teabag."

A New York City Before Christmas

'Twas the night before Christmas
da whole house was mellow
not a creature was stirrin'
I'd a gun unda my pillow

When up on da roof
I hoid somet'in pound
I sprung to da window
to scream "KEEP IT DOWN!"

When what to my
wanderin' eyes should appear
but dat hairy elf, Vinnie
and eight friggin' reindeer

Wit a bad hackin' cough
and da stench o' boiped beer
I knowed in a moment
Yo, da Kringle dude wuz here!

Wit a slap to dere snouts
and a yank on dere manes
he cursed and he shouted
and called dem by name

Yo Tony, Yo Frankie
Yo Sally, Yo Vito
Ay Joey, Ay Paulie
Ay Pepe, Ay Guido

As I drew out my gun
and hid by da bed
down came his friggin' boot
on da top o' my head

His eyes wuz all bloodshot
his B.O. was scary

his breath was like sewage
he had a mole dat wuz hairy

He spit in my eye
and he twisted my head
he soon let me know
To consider myself dead

Den pointin' a fat finga
right unda my nose
he let out some gas
and up da chimney he rose

He sprang to his sleigh
obscenities a-screamin'
and away dey all flew
before he troo dem a beatin'

But I hoid him exclaim –
or better yet, grump –
"Merry Christmas to all
and bite me, ya chump!"

The Truth About Rudolph

According to the Alaska Department of Fish and Game, while both male and female reindeer grow antlers in the summer each year, male reindeer drop their antlers at the beginning of winter, usually late November to mid-December. Female reindeer retain their antlers till after they have given birth in the spring.

Therefore, if we are to go by every available depiction of Santa's reindeer, every single one of them – from Rudolph to Blitzen – had to be a girl.

We should've known. Only women, while pregnant, would be able to drag a fat man in a red velvet suit all around the world in one night and not get lost.

Christmas Newsletter

Dear friends,

Thought you'd like to hear the latest from our family. Well, here goes. We've all been flossing regularly. The newspaper landed in the bushes twice, but we got it out, thank goodness dad has those long arms. They put a new gas station on the corner. It's the self-serve kind so there's been a lot of talk around town about it.

The other night we took the whole family to the pancake house for dinner. We all had pancakes except for mom. She had a waffle. She's a free spirt, you know.

We're saving up to buy a goldfish and can hardly wait. Pets are very exciting. And if not, you can flush them down the toilet.

Our kid finished his milk today. No one noticed we're using margarine instead of butter. It's pretty cloudy here. Sometimes we watch TV. Other times we don't. We may go shopping this weekend at the mall. There are 41 stores there. So far we've been to 28. Thirteen to go. Unless they build more. They probably will. They always do.

That's about it for the big news.

It's been some heck of a year. How about you?

Love and all …

Bernard the Brown-Nosed Reindeer

Rudolph and Dancer were in the stables talking.

Rudolph: "I don't think much of the new trainee reindeer, Bernard."

Dancer: "Really? Why's that?"

Rudolph: "Well, for one thing, he's behind me, and two, he's not too good at stopping."

Top Ten Things to Say About an Unwanted Xmas Present

10) Hey! It's a present.

9) Well, well, well …

8) Gosh, if I hadn't recently shot up four sizes, that would fit.

7) Perfect for wearing in the basement.

6) Gosh, I hope this never catches fire!

5) If the dog buries it, I'll be furious!

4) I love it, but I fear the envy it will inspire.

3) Sadly, tomorrow I enter the witness protection programme.

2) To think I got this the year I vowed to give all my gifts to charity.

1) I really don't deserve this.

Santa's Little Elf

A man walked into a bathroom and started taking a leak. Next to him an elf was also taking a leak. The man casually looked over, took a peek and was amazed at the elf's huge member. He struck up a conversation with the elf and asked how he got this enormous penis. The elf told him that he was one of Santa's helpers and Santa himself gave it to him.

The man asked the elf how he could get a member like his. The elf explained that he could grant him three wishes and he could wish for it. So the man wished for:

1. All the money in the world.

"No problem," said the elf.

2. All the women in the world.

"No problem," said the elf.

3. A member as enormous as his.

The elf agreed to grant him his three wishes, provided the man let the elf f*** him in the arse. The man thought about all the money, all the women, plus an enormous member, weighed up the pros and cons and eventually agreed.

After the ordeal, the man asked for his three wishes. The elf turned around and said,

"You idiot, you still believe in Santa?!"

E-Animals

Revenge Is Sweet

For decades, two heroic statues, one male and one female, faced each other in a city park, until one day an angel came down from heaven.

"You've been such exemplary statues," he announced to them, "that I'm going to give you a special gift. I'm going to bring you both to life for 30 minutes, in which you can do anything you want." And with a clap of his hands, the angel brought the statues to life.

The two approached each other a bit shyly, but soon dashed for the bushes, from which shortly emerged a good deal of giggling, laughter, and shaking of branches. Fifteen minutes later, the two statues emerged from the bushes, wide grins on their faces.

"You still have 15 more minutes," said the angel, winking at them. Grinning even more widely the female statue turned to the male statue and said,

"Great! Only this time you hold the pigeon down and I'll crap on its head."

The Polar Bear

A polar bear went into a bar and said, "Can I have a gin and . . . .

. . . .

. . . .

. . . .

.... tonic please?" The barman served him, saying, "Why the large pause?" The polar bear looked down and said,

"Don't know, I've always had them."

Legs

A man who lived alone was feeling a bit lonely, so he went to the pet shop to get something to keep him company. The pet shop owner suggested an unusual pet – a talking millipede.

"OK," thought the man, "I'll give it a go." So he bought a millipede, took it home, and for lack of advance preparations made it a temporary home in a cardboard box.

That evening, testing his new pet, he leaned over the closed box and said, "I'm going to the pub for a drink, do you want to come too?" He waited a few moments but there was no reply. He tried again, "Hey, millipede, wanna come to the boozer with me???" Again, no response. Disgusted by his gullible nature, he decided to give it one more try before returning the millipede to the pet shop. So he got real close to the box and repeated rather loudly, "I SAID I'M GOING TO THE PUB FOR A DRINK. DO YOU WANNA COME?"

"For God's sake, I heard you the first time!!" snapped the millipede,

"I'm just putting my f***ing shoes on."

Aleeee-ooop!

A champion jockey was about to enter an important race on a new horse. The horse's trainer met him before the race to give him some last-minute instructions.

"All you have to remember with this horse is that every time you approach a jump, you have to shout 'ALLLLEEE-OOOP!' really loudly in the horse's ear. Providing you do that, you'll be fine." The jockey thought the trainer was mad but promised to shout the command.

The race began and they approached the first hurdle. The jockey ignored the trainer's ridiculous advice and the horse crashed straight through the centre of the jump. The race continued and as the horses approached the second hurdle, the jockey, somewhat embarrassed, whispered "Aleeee-ooop" in the horse's ear. The same thing happened – the horse crashed straight through the centre of the jump.

At the third hurdle, the jockey thought, "It's no good, I'll have to do it," and yelled, "ALLLEEE-OOOP!" really loudly. Sure enough, the horse sailed over the jump with no problems. This continued for the rest of the race, but due to the earlier problems the horse only finished third.

When the jockey finally rode the horse into the paddock, the trainer was fuming and demanded to know what went wrong. The jockey replied, "Nothing is wrong with me – it's this bloody horse. What is he – deaf or something?"

"Deaf?" the trainer replied, "DEAF??!!

"He's not deaf – he's BLIND!"

Cruising Flies

Two male flies were buzzing around, cruising for good-looking females. One spotted a real cutie sitting on a pile of cow manure and dived down towards her.

"Pardon me," he said, turning on his best charm,

"but is this stool taken?"

The Truth About Cats and Dogs

A dog thinks: "Hey, these people I live with feed me, love me, provide me with a nice, warm, dry house, pet me, and take good care of me ...

"They must be gods!"

A cat thinks: "Hey, these people I live with feed me, love me, provide me with a nice, warm, dry house, pet me, and take good care of me ...

"I must be a god!"

The Blind Man's Dog

A blind man was waiting on the street corner for traffic. Another pedestrian observed the man's dog pissing on his leg. The blind man then proceeded to reach in his pocket and started to feed the dog part of a sandwich. The pedestrian said, "You are going to reward him after he just pissed on your leg?" The blind man said, "No, I just want to find out where his head is,

"so I can kick him in the ass."

Cat in Heaven

One day, a cat died of natural causes and went to heaven, where he met the Lord.

The Lord said to the cat, "You lived a good life, and if there is any way I can make your stay in heaven more comfortable, please let me know."

The cat thought for a moment and said, "Lord, all my life I have lived with a poor family and had to sleep on a hard wooden floor."

The Lord stopped the cat, saying, "Say no more," and a wonderful, fluffy pillow appeared.

A few days later, six mice were killed in a tragic farming accident, and all of them went to heaven. Again, the Lord was there to greet them with the same offer.

The mice answered, "All our lives we have been chased. We have had to run from cats, dogs, and even women with brooms. Running, running, running; we're tired of running. Do you think we could have roller skates so that we don't have to run anymore?"

The Lord said, "Say no more," and fitted each mouse with beautiful new roller skates.

About a week later, the Lord stopped by to see the cat and found him snoozing on the pillow. The Lord gently woke the cat and asked him, "How are things since you got here?"

The cat stretched and yawned, then replied, "It is wonderful here. Better than I could have ever expected. This pillow is sooo comfy,

"and those 'Meals On Wheels' you've been sending by are the best!"

The Elephant and the Ant

A lady elephant was walking through the jungle one day, when she trod on a thorn. The thorn stuck in the bottom of her foot causing her terrible pain. As she stood there groaning in agony, an ant walked past.

"Help, Help!" cried the elephant to the ant. "I have a thorn stuck in my foot, please get it out for me, I'll do anything." The ant considered for a moment and declared that he would only remove the thorn if the elephant agreed to have sex with him.

"Anything – anything at all!" So the ant removed the thorn from the elephant's foot and proceeded to mount her to claim his reward.

A monkey in the tree above them had watched the whole exchange and laughed so hard that he fell out of the tree and landed smack on the elephant's back.

"Ow!" squealed the elephant wincing.

"Suffer, bitch, suffer!" cried the ant.

The Talented Duck

A duck walked into a bar and ordered a beer.

"Hey, you're a duck," said the barman.

"Nothing wrong with your eyesight," observed the duck.

"Yeah, but I mean – you can TALK!" said the barman.

"Guess your ears are fine, too," answered the duck. "Now, can I have a beer please?" The barman served the duck a pint and asked him what he was doing in the area.

"Oh," said the duck. "I work on the building site over there. We'll be here for a couple of weeks, and I'll be in each lunchtime for a pint."

Sure enough, each day the duck waddled over from his job at the building site and had his lunchtime lager. Next week, the circus came to town on its annual round. The circus owner came in for a pint, and the barman told him about the talking duck.

"You should get it into your circus," he said. "Make a lot of money out of a talking duck. I'll speak to him about it."

The following day, the duck came in at lunchtime. The barman said, "You know, the circus is in town, and yesterday I was chatting to the owner. He's very interested in you."

"Really?" said the duck.

"Yeah. You could make a lot of money there. I can fix it up for you easily. For a small percentage."

"Hang on," said the duck. "You did say a CIRCUS, didn't you?"

"That's right."

"That's one of those tent things, isn't it? With a big pole in the middle?"

"Yeah!"

"That's canvas, isn't it?" said the duck.

"Of course," replied the barman. "I can get you a job there starting tomorrow. The circus owner's dead keen." The duck looked very puzzled.

"What the fuck would he want with a plasterer?"

The Goat in the Hole

Two guys were walking through the woods when they came across a big deep hole.

"Wow … that looks deep."

"Sure does, toss a few pebbles in there and see how deep it is." They picked up a few pebbles, threw them in and waited … no noise.

"Jeeez. That is REALLY deep! Here … throw one of these great big rocks down there. Those should make a noise." They picked up a couple of football-sized rocks and tossed them into the hole and waited … and waited. Nothing.

They looked at each other in amazement. Then one of them said determinedly, "Hey, over here in the weeds, there's a railroad tie. Help me carry it over here. When we toss THAT sucker in, it's GOTTA make some noise." The two dragged the heavy tie over to the hole and heaved it in. Not a sound comes from the hole.

Suddenly, out of the nearby woods, a goat appeared, running like the wind. It rushed towards the two men, then right past them, running as fast as its legs would carry it. Suddenly it leapt in the air and into the hole. The two men were astonished with what they'd seen. Then, out of the woods came a farmer who spotted the men and ambled over.

"Hey! You two guys seen my goat out here?"

"You bet we did! Weirdest thing I ever seen! It came running like crazy and just jumped into this hole!"

"Nah," said the farmer, "That couldn't have been MY goat.

"My goat was chained to a railroad tie."

The Piano-Playing Dog

A guy walked into a bar with a small dog.

"Get out of here with that dog!" said the bartender.

"But this isn't just any dog … this dog can play the piano!" said the man. The bartender replied, "Well, if he can play that piano, you both can stay … and have a drink on the house!"

So the guy sat the dog at the piano, and the dog started playing ragtime, then a little swing, then some Gershwin. The bartender was amazed and the patrons were thoroughly enjoying the music.

Suddenly a bigger dog ran in, grabbed the small dog by the scruff of the neck, and dragged him out. The bartender asked the guy, "What was that all about?" The guy replied, "Oh, that was his mother …

"she wants him to be a doctor."

Got Any Bread?

A duck walked into a bar, hopped on the bar stool and fixed the luscious barmaid with a beady gaze before quacking, "Got any bread?" The barmaid was having a bad day and replied testily, "Sorry, duck face, we don't serve bread – we serve drinks!" The duck cocked his head to one side.

"Got any bread?" he quacked again. The barmaid bit her lip in frustration, "Not only do we not serve bread we also don't serve ducks!" The duck fluttered his feathers.

"Got any bread?" The barmaid took a deep breath, swelling her impressive bust, and said, "No, we do not serve bread!"

"Got any bread?" The barmaid bunched her hands into fists and hissed through her teeth, "If you ask for bread once more I'll nail your bloody beak to the bar!" The duck cocked his head to one side.

"Got any nails?"

"No!" The barmaid screamed.

"Got any bread?"

🖫📷 A Bump in the Carpet

A carpet layer had just finished installing carpet for a lady. He stepped out for a smoke, only to realize that he had lost his cigarettes. In the middle of the room, under the carpet, was a bump.

"No sense pulling up the entire floor for one pack of smokes," he said to himself. He got out his hammer and flattened the hump. As he was cleaning up, the lady came in.

"Here," she said, handing him his pack of cigarettes. "I found them in the hallway."

"Now," she said, "if only I could find my parakeet."

🔽 ⬛ The Camel Clock

A tourist couple, Morris and Becky, both sociologists, were walking the streets of a small town in Jordan. It was nearing the middle of the day and they didn't want to miss lunch at their ramshackle hotel – it was the only one in town and it always served meals promptly. They came upon an old herder perched on a stool beside his camel.

"Excuse me, sir," Morris asked, "but could you tell me the time?" The old man glanced at them, spat in the dirt, then turned and reached under his camel … and hefted the animal's testicles. After a moment, he released them.

"It is ten minutes before noon," he replied. The tourists exchanged confused looks, thanked the man and hurried back to their hotel, arriving just in time for the meal.

Later that day, the wandering couple found themselves again on the same street and spied the old herder perched beside his camel, apparently unmoved. Curious as to how he could tell the time by fondling his animal's balls they approached him and asked again, "Sir, can you tell us the time?"

They watched closely as he again reached up and grabbed the camel's jewels, seemingly judging their weight, then pronounced, "It is half past four." The couple excitedly exchanged looks. Becky, the wife, blurted, "Oh, sir! That is an amazing ability you have! Could you show us how you do it?"

"Surely," the herder responded tiredly, and motioned them to squat beside him. "Now, grasp his jewels gently and lift them up to his belly." The woman did so while her husband watched.

"What now?" she inquired.

"Now," said the old man, "look over there – can you now see the clock in the far tower? When the big hand is on the …"

Province of Inhambane
Ministry of Fish and Wildlife
MOZAMBIQUE

WARNING

Due to the rising frequency of human-lion encounters, the Ministry Fish and Wildlife, Inhambane Branch, Mozambique is advising hikers, hunters, fishermen, and any motorcyclists that use the out-of-doors in a recreational or work related function to take extra precautions while in the bush.

We advise the outdoorsman to wear little noisy bells on clothing so as to give advanced warning to any lions that might be close by so you don't take them by surprise.

We also advise anyone using the out-of-doors to carry "Pepper Spray" with him or her in case of an encounter with a lion.

Outdoorsmen should also be on the watch for fresh lion activity, and be able to tell the difference between lion cub shit and big lion shit. Lion cub shit is smaller and contains lots of berries and dassie fur. Big lion shit has bells in it, and smells like pepper.

Enjoy your stay in
MOZAMBIOUE

The Seeing-Eye Chihuahua

Two guys were sitting on a park bench with their dogs, one with a Doberman pinscher and one with a chihuahua.

"Let's go over to that restaurant and get something to eat," said the guy with the Doberman pinscher.

"We can't go in there, we've got dogs with us," said the second guy.

"Just follow my lead."

They walked over to the restaurant, and the guy with the Doberman pinscher put on a pair of dark glasses, and started to walk in. He was stopped by the man at the door who said, "Sorry, Mac, no pets allowed." The first guy said, "You don't understand. This is my seeing-eye dog."

"A Doberman pinscher?" said the doorman.

"Yes, they're using them now, they're very good," said the guy with the Doberman, so the doorman let him in.

The guy with the chihuahua figured, "What the heck," put on a pair of dark glasses and started to walk in. The man at the door said, "Sorry, pal, no pets allowed."

"You don't understand," said the guy with the chihuahua. "This is my seeing-eye dog." The man at the door says, "A chihuahua?" The guy with the chihuahua says,

"You mean they gave me a chihuahua?"

Light Bulbs

The old dog–light bulb conundrum:

Golden retriever: The sun is shining, the day is young, we've got our whole lives ahead of us, and you're inside worrying about a stupid burned-out light bulb?

Border collie: Just one? If you like I'll replace any wiring that's not up to code.

Dachshund: I can't reach the stupid lamp!

Toy poodle: I'll just blow in the Border collie's ear and he'll do it. By the time he finishes rewiring the house, my nails will be dry.

Rottweiler: Go Ahead! Make me!

Shi-tzu: Puh-leeze, dah-ling. Let the servants …

Lab: Oh, me, me!!! Pleeeeeeze let me change the light bulb! Can I? Can I? Huh? Huh? Can I?

Malamute: Let the Border collie do it. You can feed me while he's busy.

Cocker Spaniel: Why change it? I can still pee on the carpet in the dark.

Doberman pinscher: While it's dark, I'm going to sleep on the couch.

Mastiff: Mastiffs are NOT afraid of the dark.

Hound dog: ZZZZZZZZZZZZZZZZZZZZZZZ.

Chihuahua: *Yo quiero Taco Bulb.*

Irish wolfhound: Can somebody else do it? I've got a hangover.

Pointer: I see it, there it is, right there …

Greyhound: It isn't moving. Who cares?

Australian shepherd: Put all the light bulbs in a little circle …

Old English sheepdog: Light bulb? Light bulb? That thing I just ate was a light bulb?

Rollo

Paul got off the elevator on the 40th floor and nervously knocked on his blind date's door. She opened it and was as beautiful and charming as everyone had said.

"I'll be ready in a few minutes," she said. "Why don't you play with Rollo while you're waiting? He does wonderful tricks. He rolls over, shakes hands, sits up and if you make a hoop with your arms, he'll jump through."

The dog followed Paul onto the balcony and started rolling over. Paul made a hoop with his arms and Rollo jumped through and went right over the balcony railing. Just then Paul's date walked out.

"Isn't Rollo the cutest, happiest dog you've ever seen?

"To tell the the truth," he replied,

"He seemed a little depressed to me."

Funny Already

First Jewish President

The first Jewish President of the United States calls his mother in Queens and invites her to come down for Thanksgiving. She says, "I'd like to, but it's so much trouble … I mean, I have to get a cab to the airport, and I hate waiting on Queens Blvd …" He replies, "Mom! I'm the President! You won't need a cab – I'll send a limousine for you!" His mother replies, "I know, but then I'll have to get my ticket at the airport, and try to get a seat on the plane, and I hate to sit in the middle … it's just too much trouble."

"Mom!" he replies, "I'm the President of the United States! I'll send Air Force One for you – it's my private jet!" To which she replies, "Oh, well, but then when we land, I'll have to carry my luggage through the airport, and try to get a cab … it's really too much trouble." He replies, "Mom! I'm the President! I'll send a helicopter for you! You won't have to lift a finger."

"Yes, that's nice," she says, "but, you know, I still need a hotel room, and the rooms are so expensive, and I really don't like the rooms …"

"Mom!" he exclaims in exasperation, "I'm the President! You'll stay at the White House!"

"Well … all right … I guess I'll come."

The next day, she's on the phone with her friend Beckie.

"Hello, Sylvia … so what's new?" asks Beckie. Sylvia replies, "I'm visiting my son for Thanksgiving!"

"The doctor?" asks Beckie.

"No … the other one."

A Nice Jewish Dog

A guy got a new dog, a nice Jewish dog, and called him Irving. He couldn't wait to show him off to his neighbour, so when the neighbour finally came over, the guy called Irving into the house, bragging about how smart he was.

The dog quickly came running and stood looking up at his master, tail wagging excitedly, mouth open, tongue hanging out, eyes bright with anticipation. The guy pointed to the newspaper by the door and gave the command, "Okay, Irving, fetch!"

Immediately, the dog climbed on to the couch and sat, his tail wagging furiously. Then all of a sudden, he stopped. His doggie smile disappeared. He started to frown and put on a sour face. Looking up at his master, he whined, "You think this is easy, wagging my tail all the time? Oy ... This constant wagging of the tail puts me in such pain, you should only know! And you think it's easy eating that dreck you call designer dog food. Forget it ... it's too salty and it gives me gas. And also the runs, but what do you care? Why don't you try it if you think it's so good? You try it. Dreck I say! Then you push me out the door to take care of my business, twice a day. It's disgusting I tell you! And when was the last time you took me for a nice long walk? I can't remember when!"

The neighbour was absolutely amazed ... stunned. In astonishment, he said, "I can't believe it. Irving can speak. Your dog actually talks. Here he is sitting on the sofa talking to us."

"I know, I know," said the owner. "He's not yet fully trained yet.

"He thought I said 'Kvetch'."

Vus Tutzuch?

Bush, newly elected, called in the head of the CIA and asked, "How come the Jews know everything before WE do?" The CIA chief replied, "It's because the Jews have this expression 'Vus tutzuch?' ['What's doing?']. They just ask each other and they know everything!"

George Bush decided that in order to see it and to believe it, he should go undercover himself. So Bush got dressed up (the hat, beard, long peius etc.) as an orthodox Jew, was secretly flown, under radar, in an unmarked plane to New York, was picked up in an unmarked car and dropped off in Brooklyn's most Jewish neighbourhood.

Soon this little old Jewish man came shuffling along and George Bush whispered to him, "Vus tutzuch?" The old guy whispered back,

"Did you hear President Bush is in Brooklyn?"

Two Beggars

Two beggars were sitting on a bench in Mexico City, one holding a large cross and the other a large Star of David. Both were holding big hats to collect contributions.

People walking by lifted their noses at the man with the Star of David and, almost for spite, dropped large amounts of money in the hat held by the man with the cross. Soon the hat of the man with the cross was filled and the hat of the man with the Star of David was empty.

A priest, who had been watching, approached the men. He turned to the man with the Star of David and said, "Young man, do you realize this is a Catholic country? You'll never get any contributions holding a Star of David." And he walked off.

The man with the Star of David turned to the man with the cross and said,

"Moshe, can you imagine, this guy is trying to tell us how to run our business?"

Guru's Mother

Goldie Cohen, an elderly Jewish lady from New York, went to her travel agent.

"I vont to go to India," she said.

"But, Mrs Cohen, why India? It's filthy, much hotter than New York, it's full of poor, dirty people."

"I vont to go to India."

"But it's a long journey, and those trains, how will you manage? What will you eat? The food is too hot and spicy for you. You can't drink the water. You must not eat fresh fruit and vegetables. You'll get sick: the plague, hepatitis, cholera, typhoid, malaria, God only knows. What will you do? Can you imagine the hospital, no Jewish doctors? Why torture yourself?"

"I vont to go to India."

So the necessary arrangements were made, and off she went. She arrived in India and, undeterred by the noise, smell and crowds, made her way to an ashram. There she joined the seemingly never-ending line of people waiting for an audience with the guru. An aide tells her that it will take at least three days of standing in line to see the guru.

"Dotz OK."

Eventually she reached the hallowed portals. There she was told firmly that due to the long lines she would only be allowed to say SIX words to the guru.

"Fine."

She was ushered into the inner sanctum where the wise guru was seated, ready to bestow spiritual blessings upon his eager initiates. Just before she reached the holy of holies she was once again reminded:

"Remember, just SIX words."

Unlike the other devotees, she did not prostrate herself at his feet. She stood directly in front of him, crossed her arms over her chest, fixed her gaze on his, and said,

"Sheldon, it's your mother. Come home."

Mama's Strudel

Saul has been lying ill for weeks. Eventually he slips into a coma, and everyone fears the worst. The family is called: the son from Miami, the daughter from Bridgewater, the aunts, the uncles. All sit waiting for the end.

Suddenly a miracle! Saul opens his eyes. Weakly he motions for his son to approach so he can talk to him. Saul is weak from illness and so his voice is very faint as he says, "I've been ill?"

"Yes, papa," replies the son with tears choking his voice, "very ill." Saul nods and speaks again.

"I had a dream. I was nearing death when I suddenly smelled the aroma of your mother's apple strudel. I love that strudel. As wonderful a cook as my Sadie is, that strudel is her masterpiece." He lays back against the pillow weak from the exertion of speaking.

"What a wonderful dream, papa. But the smell is real. Mama just took the strudel out of the oven to cool."

"A miracle!" cries Saul as he tries to rise, and weakly falls against the pillows. He turns to his son and says, "I'm still too weak to get up. Go to the kitchen and get for me a piece of Sadie's strudel." The son obediently rises and leaves the room to fulfil his father's request ... only to return a few moments later empty-handed. He sits again by his father's side. Saul looks at him and says, "Nu? Where is the strudel?" The son replies, "I'm sorry, papa.

"Mama says it's for AFTER the funeral!"

My Wonderful Son

Three Jewish mothers were sitting on a park bench in Miami Beach talking about how much their sons love them.

Sadie said, "You know the Chagall painting hanging in my living room? My son, Arnold, bought that for me for my 75th birthday. What a good boy he is and how much he loves his mother."

Minnie said, "You call that love? You know the Eldorado Cadillac I just got for Mother's Day? That's from my son Bernie. What a doll."

Shirley said, "That's nothing. You know my son Stanley? He's in analysis with a psychoanalyst on Park Avenue. Five sessions a week.

"And what does he talk about? Me."

Jewish Mother-in-Law

A young Jewish man excitedly told his mother he'd fallen in love and was going to get married. He said, "Just for fun, Ma, I'm going to bring over three women and you try and guess which one I'm going to marry." The mother agrees.

The next day, he brought three beautiful women into the house, sat them down on the couch and had them chat for a while. Then he said, "Okay, Ma. Guess which one I'm going to marry." She immediately replied, "The redhead in the middle."

"That's amazing, Ma. You're right. How did you know?"

"I don't like her."

Two Bagels

It was a terrible night, blowing cold and rain in a most frightful manner. The streets were deserted and the local baker was just about to close up shop when a little Jewish man slipped through the door. He carried an umbrella, blown inside out, and was bundled in two sweaters and a thick coat. But even so he still looked wet and bedraggled.

As he unwound his scarf he said to the baker, "May I have two bagels to go, please?" The baker said in astonishment, "Two bagels? Nothing more?"

"That's right," answered the little man. "One for me and one for Bernice."

"Bernice is your wife?" asked the baker.

"What do you think," snapped the little man,

"my mother would send me out on a night like this?"

The Shortlist Interview

There were four people who were in the final stages of interviewing for a prestigious job. One was Christian, one was Catholic, one was a Buddhist and the fourth was Jewish. The company decided to fly them all in for dinner and a final interview.

Over dinner at a fine restaurant, the president of the company told them that all were very worthy applicants, and that he wished he could hire them all, but that they only had enough money budgeted to hire one person. He told them that he would call each of them in one at a time for a final interview the next day, and that he would ask each one of them the same question. Whoever answered the question the best would be the one hired. All the applicants agreed that this was fair.

The next day the first applicant, the Christian, was called in. The president posed the question, "What is the fastest thing in the world?" The Christian thought for a moment and replied, "That would have to be a thought."

"Why do you say that?" asked the president.

"Well, a thought takes no time at all – it is in your mind in an instant, then gone again."

"Ahh, very good. Thank you," replied the president.

Next the same question was posed to the Catholic woman.

"What is the fastest thing in the world?" She paused and replied, "That would have to be a blink."

"Why?" asked the president.

"Because you don't even think about a blink, it's just a reflex. You do it in an instant." The president thanked her, then called in the next person.

The Buddhist was asked what the fastest thing in the world was, and after hesitating for a brief moment, he replied, "I would have to say electricity. Why? Because a man can flip a switch, and immediately, three miles away a light will go on."

"I see, very good," replied the president. Then, the Jewish man was called in. He, too, was asked, "What is the fastest thing in the world?"

"That's easy …" he replied, "that would have to be diarrhoea!" Rather stunned, the president asked, "Why do you say that?"

"Well, last night after dinner, I was lying in my bed and I got the worst stomach cramps …

"and before I could THINK, BLINK, or TURN ON THE LIGHTS …"

🖫 🖳 Dirty Dancing

A modern Orthodox couple, preparing for their wedding, meets with their rabbi for their final session. The rabbi asks if they have any last questions before they leave. The man asks, "Rabbi, is it true that men and women still don't dance together?"

"Yes," says the rabbi. "For modesty reasons, men and women dance separately."

"So at our wedding, I can't dance with my own wife?"

"No," answered the rabbi.

"Well, okay," says the man, "but what about sex?"

"Fine," replies the rabbi. "A mitzvah within the marriage, to have Jewish children!"

"What about different positions?" asks the man.

"No problem," says the rabbi. "It's a mitzvah!"

"Women on top?" the man asks.

"Why not?" is the response. "Sex in a marriage is a mitzvah!"

"Without clothes?"

"Of course! It's a mitzvah!"

"Even on the table?"

"Of course! It's a mitzvah!"

"Well, what about standing up?"

"NO, NO, NO!" says the rabbi.

"Why not?" asks the man.

"Could lead to dancing."

📥 ✉ They Said It

I don't want to achieve immortality through my work. I want to achieve immortality through not dying.
* Woody Allen

My father never lived to see his dream come true of an all-Yiddish-speaking Canada.
* David Steinberg

Too bad that all the people who know how to run this country are busy driving taxis and cutting hair.
* George Burns

I once wanted to become an atheist but I gave up. They have no holidays.
* Henny Youngman

Don't be humble; you are not that great.
* Golda Meir

It's so simple to be wise. Just think of something stupid to say and then don't say it.
* Sam Levenson

I went on a diet, swore off drinking and heavy eating, and in 14 days I had lost exactly two weeks.
* Joe E. Lewis

I have enough money to last me the rest of my life unless I buy something.
* Jackie Mason

Most Texans think Hanukkah is some sort of duck call.
* Richard Lewis

The time is at hand when the wearing of a prayer shawl and skullcap will not bar a man from the White House, unless, of course, the man is Jewish.
* Jules Farber

Even if you are Catholic, if you live in New York you're Jewish. If you live in Butte, Montana, you are going to be goyish even if you are Jewish.
* Lenny Bruce

The remarkable thing about my mother is that for 30 years she served us nothing but leftovers. The original meal has never been found.
* Calvin Trillin

Let me tell you the one thing I have against Moses. He took us 40 years into the desert in order to bring us to the one place in the Middle East that has no oil.
* Golda Meir

Even a secret agent can't lie to a Jewish mother.
* Peter Malkin

Humility is no substitute for a good personality.
* Fran Lebowitz

My idea of an agreeable person is a person who agrees with me.
* Benjamin Disraeli

God will pardon me. It's His business.
* Heinrich Heine

Bankruptcy is a legal proceeding in which you put your money in your pants pocket and give your coat to your creditors.
* Sam Goldwyn

A spoken contract isn't worth the paper it's written on.
* Sam Goldwyn

A politician is a man who will double-cross that bridge when he comes to it.
* Oscar Levant

Liberals feel unworthy of their possessions. Conservatives feel they deserve everything they've stolen.
* Mort Sahl

I don't want any yes-men around me. I want everybody to tell me the truth, even if it costs them their jobs.
* Sam Goldwyn

Making Mom Happy

After many years of waiting, a Jewish mother received the phone call she never thought she'd get from her openly gay son.

"Mom, I've met a wonderful girl. I'm going straight, and we're going to get married." Mom was overjoyed, but couldn't really believe things were that good.

"I suppose it's too much to ask that she's Jewish?" Her son says, "Mom, not only is she Jewish, but she happens to be from a very wealthy and prominent Beverly Hills family." Mom is beside herself with joy, and says, "You don't know how happy you've made me. What's her name?" The son says, "Monica Lewinsky." Mom is silent for a moment, and then she says,

"What happened to that nice Catholic boy you used to date?"

The Card Game

Six Jewish men were playing poker when Meyerwitz lost $500 on a single hand, clutched his chest and dropped dead at the table. Showing respect for their fallen comrade, the other five completed their playing time standing up.

When the game was over Finkelstein looked around and asked, "Now, who is going to tell the wife?"

They drew straws. Goldberg, who was always a loser, picked the short one. They told him to be discreet, be gentle, not to make a bad situation any worse than it was.

"Gentlemen! Discreet? I'm the most discreet mensch you will ever meet. Discretion is my middle name, leave it to me."

Goldberg schlepped over to the Meyerwitz house and knocked on the door. The wife answered and asked what he wanted. Goldberg declared, "Your husband just lost $500, and is afraid to come home."

"TELL HIM HE SHOULD DROP DEAD!" she hollered.

Goldberg said, "I'll tell him."

Jewish Holidays

Jewish holidays can be summed up in three sentences:
1. They tried to kill us.
2. We survived.
3. Let's eat.

How Can You Tell?

A guy from Brooklyn was in Hong Kong. While passing through a Jewish neighbourhood he was surprised to see a synagogue. He went in and sure enough, he saw a Chinese rabbi and a Chinese congregation. The service was touching.

As the service ended, the rabbi stood at the door greeting his congregants. When our Brooklyn friend came up, the Chinese rabbi said, "You're a Jew?"

"Yes, I'm Jewish," replied the Brooklynite.

"Funny," said the Chinese rabbi.

"You don't look it."

Gender Wars

Caress, praise, pamper, relish, savour, massage, make plans, fix, empathize, serenade, compliment, support, feed, tantalize, bathe, humour, placate, stimulate, jiffylube, stroke, console, purr, hug, coddle, excite, pacify, protect, phone, correspond, anticipate, nuzzle, smooch, toast, minister to, forgive, sacrifice, ply, accessorize, leave, return, beseech, sublimate, entertain, charm, lug, drag, crawl, show equality for, spackle, oblige, fascinate, attend, implore, bawl, shower, shave, trust, grovel, ignore, defend, coax, clothe, brag about, acquiesce, aromate, fuse, fizz, rationalize, detoxify, sanctify, help, acknowledge, polish, upgrade, spoil, embrace, accept, butter up, hear, understand, jitterbug, locomote, beg, plead, borrow, steal, climb, swim, nurse, resuscitate, repair, patch, crazy-glue, respect, entertain, calm, allay, kill for, die for, dream of, promise, deliver, tease, flirt, commit, enlist, pine, cajole, angelicize, murmur, snuggle, snoozle, snurfle, elevate, enervate, alleviate, spotweld, serve, rub, rib, salve, bite, taste, nibble, gratify, diddle, doodle, hokey-pokey, hanky-panky, crystal blue persuade, flip, flop, fly, don't care if I die, swing, slip, slide, slather, mollycoddle, squeeze, moisturize, humidify, lather, tingle, slam-dunk, wet, slicken, undulate, gelatinize, brush, tingle, dribble, drip, dry, knead, fluff, fold, blue-coral wax, ingratiate, indulge, wow, dazzle, amaze, flabbergast, enchant, idolize, worship …

📥 🖾 How to Satisfy a Man Every Time

Show up naked.

 Gender

From the Washington Post, in which it was postulated that English should have male and female nouns. Readers were asked to assign a gender to nouns of their choice and explain their reasoning.

SWISS ARMY KNIFE: male, because even though it appears useful for a wide variety of tasks, it spends most of its time just opening bottles.

KIDNEYS: female, because they always go to the bathroom in pairs.

TYRES: male, because they go bald and are often over-inflated.

HOT-AIR BALLOON: male, because to get it to go anywhere you have to light a fire under it ... and, of course, there's the hot-air part.

SPONGES: female, because they are soft and squeezable and retain water.

WEB PAGE: female, because it is always getting hit on.

SHOE: male, because it is usually unpolished, with its tongue hanging out.

COPIER: female, because once turned off it takes a while to warm up – because it is an effective reproductive device when the right buttons are pushed – because it can wreak havoc when the wrong buttons are pushed.

ZIPLOC BAGS: male, because they hold everything in, but you can always see right through them.

SUBWAY: male, because it uses the same old lines to pick people up.

HOURGLASS: female, because over time the weight shifts to the bottom.

HAMMER: male, because it hasn't evolved much over the last 5000 years, but it's handy to have around.

REMOTE CONTROL: female … Ha! … you thought I'd say male. But consider: it gives man pleasure; he'd be lost without it; and while he doesn't always know the right buttons to push, he keeps trying.

Wearing the Trousers

A young couple, just married, were in their honeymoon suite on their wedding night. As they were undressing for bed, the husband, who was a big burly man, tossed his trousers to his bride and said, "Here, put these on." She put them on and the waist was twice the size of her body.

"I can't wear your trousers," she said.

"That's right," said the husband, "and don't you ever forget it. I'm the man who wears the trousers in this family." With that she flipped him her knickers and said, "Try these on." He tried them on and found he could only get them as far as his knees.

"Hell," he said, "I can't get into your knickers!"

She replied, "That's right, and that's the way it's going to stay until your attitude changes."

He Said, She Said

1) He said: "Two inches more, and I would be king."
She said: "Two inches less, and you'd be queen."

2) On wall in ladies' room: "My husband follows me everywhere."
Written just below it: "I do not."

3) He said: "Shall we try a different position tonight?"
She said: "That's a good idea. You stand by the ironing board while I sit on the sofa and fart."

4) Priest: "I don't think you will ever find another man like your late husband."
She said: "Who's gonna look?"

Mathematics

A professor of mathematics sent a fax to his wife:

Dear Wife:
You must realize that you are 54 years old, and I have certain needs which you are no longer able to satisfy. I am otherwise happy with you as wife, and I sincerely hope you will not be hurt or offended to learn that by the time you receive this letter, I will be at the Grand Hotel with my 18-year-old teaching assistant. I'll be home before midnight.

Your Husband

When he arrived at the hotel, there was a faxed letter waiting for him that read as follows:

Dear Husband:
You, too, are 54 years old and by the time you receive this letter, I will be at the Breakwater Hotel with the 18-year-old pool boy. Being the brilliant mathematician that you are, you can easily appreciate the fact that 18 goes into 54 a lot more times than 54 goes into 18. Therefore, my love, don't wait up.

Your Wife

Men and Women

WOMEN

Women have strengths that amaze men. They carry children, they carry hardships, they carry burdens, but they hold happiness, love and joy. They smile when they want to cry. They cry when they are happy, and laugh when they are nervous. Women have special qualities. They volunteer for good causes. They are angels of mercy in hospitals. They are child-care workers, executives, stay-home mothers, aerobic babes and your neighbours. Women want to be the best for their family, their friends and themselves. They cry when their children excel and cheer when their friends get awards. They are happy when they hear about a birth or marriage. Their hearts break when a friend dies. A woman's touch can cure any ailment. They know that a hug and a kiss can heal a broken heart. The heart of a woman is what makes the world spin!

MEN

Men are good for lifting heavy stuff. And the occasional shag.

Gender Definitions

"THINGY"
Female: Any part under a car's hood.
Male: The strap fastener on a woman's bra.

"VULNERABLE"
Female: Fully opening up oneself emotionally to another.
Male: Playing football without a helmet.

"COMMUNICATION"
Female: The sharing of thoughts and feelings with one's partner.
Male: Leaving a note before suddenly taking off for a weekend with the boys.

"BUTT"
Female: The body part that "looks bigger" no matter what is worn.
Male: What you slap when someone scores a touchdown, home run, or goal. Also good for mooning.

"COMMITMENT"
Female: A desire to get married and raise a family.
Male: Trying not to pick up other women while out with girlfriend.

"ENTERTAINMENT"
Female: A good movie, concert, play or book.
Male: Anything that can be done while drinking.

"FLATULENCE"
Female: An embarrassing by-product of digestion.
Male: An endless source of entertainment, self-expression, and male bonding.

New Elements

Element: WOMAN
Symbol: Wo
Atomic weight: 120 (more or less)
Physical properties: Generally round in form. Boils at nothing and may freeze anytime. Melts whenever treated properly. Very bitter if not used well.
Chemical properties: Very active. Possesses strong affinity to gold, silver, platinum, and precious stones. Violent when left alone. Able to absorb

great amount of exotic food. Turns slightly green when placed beside a better specimen. Ages rapidly.

Usage: Highly ornamental. An extremely good catalyst for disintegration of wealth. Probably the single most powerful income-reducing agent known.

Caution: Highly explosive in inexperienced hands.

Element: MAN
Symbol: XY
Atomic weight: 180 (+/-100)

Physical properties: Solid at room temperature, but easily gets bent out of shape. Fairly dense and sometimes flaky. Difficult to find a pure sample. Due to rust, ageing samples are unable to conduct electricity as easily as young, fresh samples.

Chemical properties: Attempts to bond with Wo any chance it can get. Also, tends to form strong bonds with itself. Becomes explosive when mixed with Kd (element KID) for a prolonged period of time. Neutralize by saturating with alcohol.

Usage: None really, except methane production. Good samples are able to produce large quantities on command.

Caution: In the absence of Wo, this element rapidly decomposes and begins to smell.

Giggles for Girls

Delia Vs. Real Woman

> Delia's way #1: Stuff a miniature marshmallow in the bottom of a sugar cone to prevent ice cream drips.
> The Real Woman's Way: Just suck the ice cream out of the bottom of the cone, for God's sake, you're probably lying on the couch with your feet up eating it anyway.

> Delia's way #2: To keep potatoes from budding, place an apple in the bag with the potatoes.
> The Real Woman's Way: Buy Smash and keep it in the cupboard for up to a year.

> Delia's way #3: When a cake recipe calls for flouring the tin, use a bit of the dry cake mix instead and there won't be any white mess on the outside of the cake.
> The Real Woman's Way: Go to the bakers. They'll even decorate it for you.

> Delia's way #4: If you accidentally over-salt a dish while it's still cooking, drop in a peeled potato and it will absorb the excess salt for an instant "fix me up".
> The Real Woman's Way: If you over-salt a dish while you're cooking, that's tough. Please recite with me the Real Woman's motto: "I made it and you will eat it and I don't care how bad it tastes."

> Delia's way #5: Wrap celery in foil when putting in the fridge and it will keep for weeks.
> The Real Woman's Way: Celery? Never heard of the stuff.

> Delia's way #6: Brush some beaten egg white over pie crust before baking to yield a beautiful glossy finish.
> The Real Woman's Way: The Fray Bentos pie directions do not include brushing egg whites over the crust and so I don't do it.

> Delia's way #7: If you have a problem opening jars, try using rubber gloves. They give a non-slip grip that makes opening jars easy.
> The Real Woman's Way: Go ask the very gorgeous neighbour to do it.

> Delia's way #8: Don't throw out all that leftover wine. Freeze into ice cubes for future use in casseroles and sauces.
> The Real Woman's Way: Leftover wine?

> Delia's way #9: When catering for an evening buffet, calculate food portions and timings a week in advance, so that you're not rushing on the night.
> The Real Woman's Way: Nip into Marks & Sparks on the way home that evening, and buy everything in packets.

> Delia's way #10: When you have finished the preparation for your buffet, wash up and treat yourself to a glass of wine.
> The Real Woman's Way: Hide the packets and drain the last of that "pre-dinner" wine bottle ...

Hell Hath No Fury

A wife came home from work just in time to find her husband in bed with another woman. With super-human strength, born of fury, she dragged him down the stairs, out the back door, and into the tool shed in the backyard where she put his penis in a vice. She secured it tightly and removed the handle.

Next she picked up a hacksaw. The husband was terrified, and screamed, "Stop! Stop! You're not going to cut it off, are you?" The wife, with a gleam of revenge in her eye, put the hacksaw in her husband's hand and said, "Nope. I'm going to set the shed on fire.

"You do whatever you have to."

Phrasebook for PC Women

He does not have a beer gut,
He has developed a Liquid Grain Storage Facility.

He is not quiet,
He is a Conversational Minimalist.

He is not stupid,
He suffers from Minimal Cranial Development.

He does not get lost all the time,
He discovers Alternative Destinations.

He is not balding,
He is in Follicle Regression.

He is not a cradle robber,
He prefers Generational Differential Relationships.

He does not get falling-down drunk,
He becomes Accidentally Horizontal.

He is not short,
He is Anatomically Compact.

He does not have a rich daddy,
He is a Recipient of Parental Asset Infusion.

He does not constantly talk about cars,
He has a Vehicular Addiction.

He does not have a hot body,
He is Physically Combustible.

He is not unsophisticated,
He is Socially Challenged.

He does not eat like a pig,
He suffers from Reverse Bulimia.

He is not a bad dancer,
He is Overly Caucasian.

He does not hog the blankets,
He is Thermally Unappreciative.

He is not a male chauvinist pig,
He has Swine Empathy.

He does not undress you with his eyes,
He has an Introspective Pornographic Moment.

Getting What You Want

Every day little Johnny walks home from school past a fourth-grade girl's house. One day he is carrying a football and he stops to taunt the little girl. He holds up the football and says, "Hey Mary! See this football? Football is a boys' game and girls can't have one!" Little Mary runs into the house crying and tells her mother about the encounter. Her mother immediately runs out and buys the girl a football.

The next day, Johnny is riding home on his bike and little Mary shows him the football and yells, "Nyah nyah nyah nyah nyah!" Little Johnny gets mad and points to his bike.

"See this bike? This is a boys' bike and girls can't have 'em!"

The next day, Johnny comes by and little Mary is riding a new boys' bike. Now he is really mad. So he immediately drops his pants, points at his most private of private parts and says, "You see THIS? Only BOYS have these and not even YOUR mother can go out and buy you one!"

The next day as Johnny passes the house he asks little Mary, "Well, what do you have to say NOW?" She pulls up her dress and replies, "My mother told me that as long as I have one of these …

"I can have as many of THOSE as I want!"

Something Cheap

After being away on business, Tim thought it would be nice to bring his wife a little gift.

"How about some perfume?" he asked the cosmetics clerk. She showed him a bottle costing $50.

"That's a bit much," said Tim, so she returned with a smaller bottle for $30.

"That's still quite a bit," Tim complained. Growing annoyed, the clerk brought out a tiny $15 bottle.

"What I mean," said Tim, "is I'd like to see something really cheap."

The clerk handed him a mirror.

Bell 4

A fireman came home from work one day and said to his wife, "You know, we have a wonderful system at the fire station. Bell 1 rings and we all put on our jackets; Bell 2 rings and we all slide down the pole; Bell 3 rings and we're on the fire truck ready to go. From now on when I say 'Bell 1', I want you to strip naked; when I say 'Bell 2', I want you to jump in bed and when I say 'Bell 3', we are going to make love all night."

The next night he came home from work and yelled, "Bell 1!" His wife promptly took all her clothes off. Then he yelled "Bell 2!" and his wife jumped into bed. When he yelled "Bell 3!" they began making love.

After a few minutes his wife yelled, "Bell 4!"

"What the hell is Bell 4?" asked the husband.

"ROLL OUT MORE HOSE," she yelled, "YOU'RE NOWHERE NEAR THE FIRE!"

A Dictionary for Mothers

AMNESIA: Condition that enables a woman who has gone through labour to make love again.

DUMBWAITER: One who asks if the kids would care to order dessert.

FAMILY PLANNING: The art of spacing your children the proper distance apart to keep you on the edge of financial disaster.

FEEDBACK: The inevitable result when your baby doesn't appreciate the strained carrots.

FULL NAME: What you call your child when you're mad at him.

GRANDPARENTS: The people who think your children are wonderful even though they're sure you're not raising them right.

HEARSAY: What toddlers do when anyone mutters a dirty word.

IMPREGNABLE: A woman whose memory of labour is still vivid.

INDEPENDENT: How we want our children to be as long as they do everything we say.

OW: The first word spoken by children with older siblings.

PUDDLE: A small body of water that draws other small bodies wearing dry shoes into it.

SHOW OFF: A child who is more talented than yours.

STERILIZE: What you do to your first baby's dummy by boiling it and to your last baby's dummy by blowing on it.

TOP BUNK: Where you should never put a child wearing Superman pyjamas.

TWO-MINUTE WARNING: When the baby's face turns red and she begins to make those familiar grunting noises.

VERBAL: Able to whine in words

WHODUNIT: None of the kids that live in your house ...

Fully Equipped

A couple went on vacation to a fishing resort up north. The husband liked to fish at the crack of dawn. The wife liked to read.

One morning the husband returned after several hours of fishing and decided to take a short nap. Although she wasn't familiar with the lake, the wife decided to take the boat. She rowed out a short distance, anchored, and returned to reading her book. Eventually the sheriff came along in his boat. He pulled up alongside her and said, "Good morning, ma'am. What are you doing?"

"Reading my book," she replied, thinking to herself, "Isn't it obvious?"

"You're in a restricted fishing area," he informed her.

"But officer, I'm not fishing as you can see."

"Yes, but you have all the equipment. I'm afraid I'll have to take you in and write you up."

"If you do that, I'll have to charge you with rape," snapped the irate woman.

"But, I haven't even touched you," groused the sheriff.

"Yes, that's true," she replied,

"but you do have all the equipment."

Because I'm a Man ...

> Because I'm a man, when I lock my keys in the car, I will fiddle with a wire clothes hanger and ignore your suggestions that we call a road service until long after hypothermia has set in.

> Because I'm a man, when the car isn't running very well, I will pop the hood and stare at the engine as if I know what I'm looking at. If another man shows up, one of us will say to the other, "I used to be able to fix these things, but now with all these computers and everything, I wouldn't know where to start." We will then drink beer.

> Because I'm a man, when I catch a cold, I need someone to bring me soup and take care of me while I lie in bed and moan. You never get as sick as I do, so for you this isn't a problem.

> Because I'm a man, when one of our appliances stops working, I will insist on taking it apart, despite evidence that this will just cost me twice as much once the repair person gets here and has to put it back together.

> Because I'm a man, I must hold the television remote control in my hand while I watch TV. If the thing has been misplaced, I may miss a whole show looking for it (though one time I was able to survive by holding a calculator).

> Because I'm a man, I don't think we're all that lost, and no, I don't think we should stop and ask someone. Why would you listen to a complete stranger? I mean, how the hell could he know where we're going anyway?

> Because I'm a man, there is no need to ask me what I'm thinking about.

The answer is always either sex or sports. I have to make up something else when you ask, so don't bother.

> Because I'm a man, you don't have to ask me if I liked the movie. Chances are, if you cried at the end of it, I didn't.

> Because I'm a man, I think what you're wearing is fine. I thought what you were wearing five minutes ago was fine, too. Either pair of shoes is fine. With the belt or without it – looks fine. Your hair is fine. You look fine. Can we just go now?

> Because I'm a man, and this is, after all, the 21st century, I will share equally in the housework. You just do the laundry, the cooking, the gardening, the cleaning, the vacuuming, the shopping and the dishes, and I'll do the rest.

Good News, Bad News

One day the Lord came to Adam to pass on some news.

"I've got some good news and some bad news," the Lord said. Adam looked at the Lord and said, "Well, give me the good news first."

Smiling, the Lord explained, "I've got two new organs for you, one is called a brain. It will allow you to be very intelligent, create new things, and have intelligent conversations with Eve. The other organ I have for you is called a penis. It will allow you to reproduce your now intelligent life form and populate this planet. Eve will be very happy that you now have this organ to give her children."

Adam, very excited, exclaimed, "These are great gifts you have given to me. What could possibly be bad news after such great tidings?"

The Lord looked upon Adam and said with great sorrow, "The bad news is that when I created you,

"I only gave you enough blood to operate one of these organs at a time."

Olympic Condoms

A man was out shopping and discovered a new brand of so-called "Olympic Condoms". Impressed by their apparent implication, he bought a pack. Upon getting home he announced to his wife the purchase he just made.

"Olympic condoms?" she asked. "What makes them so special?"

"There are three colours," he replied, "gold, silver and bronze."

"What colour are you going to wear tonight?" she asks cheekily.

"Gold of course," says the man proudly. His wife responds, "Really? Why don't you wear silver?

"It would be nice if you came second for a change!"

Nice Men

1. The nice men are ugly.

2. The handsome men are not nice.

3. The handsome, nice men are gay.

4. The handsome, nice and heterosexual men are married.

5. The men who are not so handsome, but are nice men, have no money.

6. The men who are not so handsome, but are nice men with money think we are only after their money.

7. The handsome men without money are after our money.

8. The handsome men, who are not so nice and somewhat heterosexual, don't think we are beautiful enough.

9. The men who think we are beautiful, who are heterosexual, somewhat nice and have money, are cowards.

10. The men who are somewhat handsome, somewhat nice and have some money and thank God are heterosexual, are shy and NEVER MAKE THE FIRST MOVE!!!!

11. The men who never make the first move automatically lose interest in us when we take the initiative.

Three Bears

It's a sunny morning in the Big Forest and the Bear family is just waking up. Baby Bear goes downstairs and sits in his small chair at the table. He looks into his small bowl. It's empty!

"Who's been eating my porridge?" he squeaks. Daddy Bear arrives at the table and sits in his big chair. He looks into his big bowl. It is also empty.

"Who's been eating my porridge?" he roars. Mummy Bear puts her head through the serving hatch from the kitchen and yells, "For Pete's sake, how many times do we have to go through this? ... It was Mummy Bear who got up first. ... It was Mummy Bear who woke everybody else in the house up. ... It was Mummy Bear who unloaded the dishwasher from last night and put everything away. ... It was Mummy Bear who went out into the cold early morning air to fetch the newspaper. ... It was Mummy Bear who set the table. ... It was Mummy Bear who put the cat out, cleaned the litter box and filled the cat's water and food dish. ... And now that you've decided to come downstairs and grace me with your presence, listen good, because I'm only going to say this one more time ...

"I HAVEN'T MADE THE F**KING PORRIDGE YET!!!!"

Delia-Free Zone

Two confirmed bachelors sat talking. Their conversation drifted from politics to cooking.

"I got a cookbook for Christmas once," said the first, "but I could never do anything with it."

"Too much fancy cooking in it, eh?" asked the second.

"You said it. Every one of the recipes began the same way – 'Take a clean dish ... '"

How to Spot a Bachelor

A guy went into a supermarket and bought:

* one can of beans,
* one bag of potato chips,
* one pack of burgers,
* one tub of ice cream,
* one cake,
* one yoghurt,
* one pint of milk.

He took them over to the checkout, and the girl looked at what he had bought and asked if he was single. The guy replied sarcastically, "Yes. However how did you guess?"

The girl said, "You're an ugly bastard."

📥 📧 Good/Bad/Ugly

Good: Your hubby and you agree, no more kids.
Bad: You can't find your birth control pills.
Ugly: Your daughter borrowed them.

Good: Your son studies a lot in his room.
Bad: You find several porn movies hidden there.
Ugly: You're in them.

Good: Your husband understands fashion.
Bad: He's a cross-dresser.
Ugly: He looks better than you.

Good: Your son's finally maturing.
Bad: He's involved with the woman next door.
Ugly: So are you.

Good: You give the birds and bees talk to your daughter.
Bad: She keeps interrupting.
Ugly: With corrections.

Good: Your husband's not talking to you.
Bad: He wants a divorce.
Ugly: He's a lawyer.

📥 📧 Lie Back and Think of ...

An escaped convict broke into a house and tied up a young couple who had been sleeping in the bedroom. As soon as he had a chance, the husband turned to his voluptuous young wife, bound up on the bed in a skimpy nightgown, and whispered, "Honey, this guy hasn't seen a woman in years. Just cooperate with anything he wants. If he wants to have sex with you, just go along with it and pretend you like it. Our lives depend on it!"

"Dear," the wife hissed, spitting out her gag, "I'm so relieved you feel that way,

"because he just told me he thinks you have a nice, tight butt!"

Yet More New Barbies

*Birkenstock Barbie: Finally, a Barbie doll with horizontal feet and comfortable sandals. Made from recycled materials.

*Bisexual Barbie: Comes in a package with Skipper and Ken.

*Bite-the-Bullet Barbie: An anthropologist Barbie with pith helmet, camera, detachable limbs, fake blood, and the ability to perform surgery on herself in the Outback.

*Blue-Collar Barbie: Comes with overalls, protective goggles, lunch pail, UAW membership, pamphlet on union organizing and pay scales for women as compared to men. Waitressing outfits and cashier's aprons may be purchased separately for Barbies holding down two jobs in order to make ends meet.

*Our Barbies Ourselves: Anatomically correct Barbie, both inside and out; comes with spreadable legs, her own speculum, magnifying glass, and detailed diagrams of female anatomy so that little girls can learn about their bodies in a friendly, non-threatening way. Also includes tiny Kotex, booklets on sexual responsibility. Accessories such as contraceptives, sex toys, expanding uterus with fetuses at various stages of development and breast pump are all optional, underscoring that each young woman has the right to do what she chooses with her own Barbie.

*Rebbe Barbie: So why not? Women rabbis are on the cutting edge of Judaism. Rebbe Barbie comes with tiny yarmulke, prayer shawl, teffilin, silver kaddish cup, Torah scrolls. Options include a tiny mezuzah for doorway of Barbie townhouse. Accessories include garb suitable for most Christian and Eastern faiths. So why not already?

*Homegirl Barbie: A truly fly Barbie in midriff-baring shirt and baggy jeans, complete with gold jewellery, hip-hop accessories and plenty of attitude. Pull cord and she says things like "I don't THINK so!", "Dang, get outta my face" and "You GO girl!" Teaches girls not to take shit from men and condescending white people.

*Transgender Barbie: Formerly known as G.I. Joe.

*Robotic Barbie: Hey kids! Experiment with an autonomous two-legged walking machine! After falling over, she says "Control theory is hard. Damn these spike heels anyway!"

*Dinner Roll Barbie: A Barbie with multiple love handles, double chin, a real curvy belly, and voluminous thighs to show girls that voluptuousness is also beautiful. Comes with a miniature basket of dinner rolls, Bucket-O'-Fried Chicken, tiny Entenmann's walnut coffee ring, a brick of Sealtest ice cream, three bags of potato chips, a t-shirt reading "Only the Weak Don't Eat" and, of course, an appetite.

Man Talks to God

A man was talking to God and asked him, "God, why did you make women so beautiful?"

"So that you would find them attractive," says God. Then the man asks, "God, but why did you have to make them so dumb?"

"So that they would find you attractive!"

What She Does All Day

One day a man came home from work to find total mayhem. The kids were outside still in their pyjamas playing in the mud and muck. There were empty food boxes and wrappers all around.

As he proceeded into the house, he found an even bigger mess. Dishes on the counter, dog food spilled on the floor, a broken glass under the table, and a small pile of sand by the back door. The family room was strewn with toys and various items of clothing, and a lamp had been knocked over.

He headed up the stairs, stepping over toys, to look for his wife. He was becoming worried that she might be ill, or that something had happened to her.

He found her in the bedroom, still in bed with her pyjamas on, reading a book. She looked up at him, smiled, and asked how his day had been. He looked at her bewildered and asked, "What happened here today?" She again smiled and answered, "You know every day when you come home from work and ask me what I do all day?"

"Yes."

"Well, today I didn't do it!"

Looking for a Card

At the card shop a woman was spending a long time looking at the cards, finally shaking her head, "No." An assistant came over and asked, "May I help you?"

"I don't know," said the woman.

"Do you have any 'Sorry I laughed at your cock' cards?"

Social Security Sex

Kathy and Suzy were having a conversation during their lunch break. Kathy asked, "So, Suzy, how's your sex life these days?" Suzy replies, "Oh, you know. It's the usual, social security kind."

"Social security?" Kathy asked quizzically.

"Yeah, you get a little each month, but it's not enough to live on."

God Bless America

THE BRAINS TRUST PRESENTS: PRETZEL EATING IN SAFETY AND COMFORT (A Guide for the Dangerously Stupid)

Congratulations on purchasing a bag of "Mr Salty" Pretzels. Correctly used, these salty snacks should provide minutes of healthy enjoyment. However, in order to derive optimum pleasure, and minimal injury, we do recommend that the following procedure is studied and followed.

YOU WILL NEED
1 x comfortable chair
1 x bag of pretzels (contents approximately 24 pretzels)
1 x television receiving equipment, tuned to the sporting event of your choice
Up to three dogs – cats or other pets are NOT RECOMMENDED and could be DANGEROUS

STEP 1: OPENING THE BAG
This is a relatively simple procedure, but care needs to be taken nonetheless, so follow the steps carefully.

1. Take hold of the TOP of the bag at EITHER SIDE between FOREFINGER AND THUMB, taking care not to slash your wrists open on the surprisingly sharp plastic edges.

2. Draw the edges of the bag apart with a smooth, firm motion.

3. If you SHOULD LOSE YOUR GRIP on the bag, take extreme care not to smack yourself in the face with your flailing hand as this can result in

OBVIOUS BRUISING. Instead, you are advised to throw yourself into the safe haven of the COMFORTABLE CHAIR until the hand-danger is passed. On NO ACCOUNT throw yourself into the safe haven of THE FLOOR, THE TELEVISION, THE DOGS, THE WINDOW, THE OVEN, THE LIGHT FITTINGS or THE ROTATING BLADES OF A NEARBY HELI-COPTER as severe injury and embarrassment may result.

If you have an open bag of pretzels before you, you may now proceed to step 2. Otherwise, simply repeat step 1 until full openness is achieved.

STEP 2: REMOVING PRETZEL FROM BAG
1. Set the bag upon your lap, making sure it is reasonably stable.

2. GENTLY insert one hand into the bag. IT MAY BE NECESSARY TO WITHDRAW EYES FROM TELEVISION IN ORDER TO ACCOMPLISH THIS SAFELY. You may prefer to wait until a commercial break or other interval in the action. You should also ensure that you are not over-excited by the sporting events in progress before attempting this manoeuvre.

3. CLOSE YOUR FINGER AND THUMB over a single pretzel. DO NOT attempt to select MULTIPLE PRETZELS. Not only is this an extremely advanced manoeuvre and highly risky in itself, but it will unnecessarily complicate step 3 and will almost certainly lead to brain injury, death and further embarrassment. If you FAIL to secure a pretzel, open the finger and thumb, then close again in a different position – although STILL WITHIN THE BAG – until a pretzel is secured.

4. WITHDRAW HAND FROM BAG taking care not to break pretzel, drop pretzel, lacerate hand on edges of bag, grind pretzel into own eye, smack head on door jamb, press thigh against red-hot coals, or drive meat skewers through fleshy parts of upper arm.

With the pretzel now secured in the hand, the operation is nearly complete. However, you cannot afford to let your guard down.

STEP 3: TRANSPORTING PRETZEL TO MOUTH

1. Delicate hand–eye coordination is required. KEEPING YOUR EYES FIXED ON THE PRETZEL, first WITHDRAW your hand. Should the pretzel DROP at this point, you will have to repeat step 2.

2. RAISE PRETZEL TOWARDS FACE – avoiding eyes, ears, nostrils, hotline to Moscow and nuclear button in the process.

3. OPEN MOUTH – this step is vital and EASILY FORGOTTEN IN THE HEAT OF THE MOMENT.

4. PLACE PRETZEL JUST INSIDE MOUTH. Do not attempt to force pretzel in. Pretzel should fit easily inside, and need not be entirely encased in mouth orifice. If pretzel does not fit easily, check that mouth is open and that pretzel is in mouth, rather than ear. A small mirror may be helpful.

5. RELEASE PRETZEL AND WITHDRAW FINGERS FROM MOUTH. Failure to perform this easily overlooked step can lead to crippling injuries. If you are in any doubt, consult mirror once more. Pretzel will probably be just visible inside mouth and FINGERS SHOULD BE WELL CLEAR before step 4 commences.

You are nearly ready to enjoy your pretzel – however, the last step is by far the most dangerous, and EXTREME CARE should be taken. Inexperienced eaters of pretzels may care to practise without pretzels in order to have confidence in steps 1 to 3 before proceeding to the pretzel "fire fight" which is step 4.

STEP 4: EATING THE PRETZEL

1. Begin to move jaws up and down in a rhythmic fashion. AT LEAST 20 ITERATIONS ARE RECOMMENDED. "MR SALTY" CANNOT BE HELD RESPONSIBLE FOR INJURY, WOUNDING, DEATH, INTERNATIONAL INCIDENTS OR WARFARE RESULTING FROM FAILURE TO FOLLOW THIS DIRECTIVE.

2. As pretzel structure begins to break down, guide resulting substance to rear of mouth. DO NOT ATTEMPT TO BREATHE – BUT DO NOT LINGER AT THIS POINT EITHER. All your concentration must now be brought to bear on guiding the pretzel safely down the oesophagus, without inhaling and without passing out due to lack of oxygen.

3. As pretzel remnants reach back of throat, swallow quickly THEN RE-COMMENCE BREATHING.

Congratulations – you may now repeat from step 1, until bag is empty or belly is full.

TROUBLESHOOTING GUIDE
1. Pretzels taste "plasticky" – you are eating the bag.

2. Pretzels taste "furry" and dogs are yelping – you are eating the dogs.

3. Pretzels taste revolting – this is normal.

4. Fingers cannot grasp pretzel – bag is closed or is empty.

5. Pretzels are all over floor – bag is upside down, or has been opened with undue force. Deploy dogs and request fresh bag.

6. Pretzels cannot be seen – light is off or eyes are closed.

7. Pretzels are tasteless and eyes are full of grit – you have placed pretzel in eye instead of mouth.

8. Pretzels are tasteless and I am deaf – you have placed pretzel in ear instead of mouth.

9. I am lying on the floor and the dogs are staring at me – you have attempted to breathe while chewing and/or have failed to chew pretzel thoroughly.

10. Sirens are going off, Mr Rumsfeld is shouting and Mr Cheney is clutching at his chest – you have confused bag of pretzels with nuclear alert. Go back to watching television.

NB: If you are not President of the United States of America, the most powerful individual in the Western world and controller of the world's largest nuclear arsenal and/or you have two brain cells to rub together, you can safely ignore these instructions.

Arsehole Surgery

A journalist overheard the following conversation at a global convention for the world's top surgeons.

Israeli surgeon: "Our methods are so advanced that we can remove a leg from a patient and within three months they are hopping around looking for work again."

Italian surgeon: "That's nothing. We can transplant a liver to a patient and have them looking for work within two months."

British surgeon: "You think that's good? We can remove a kidney from one patient, transplant it into another and have them BOTH looking for work within four weeks!"

American surgeon: "I admire your skills and national pride but consider this: we can remove an arsehole from Texas, transplant it into the Whitehouse and have the whole country looking for work within a week!"

New Hollywood Movie

Universal Pictures announced today that they plan to make a film of the momentous football match that took place on Saturday.

"Five-One" is the tentative title of what could be next year's big summer hit, depicting the American national soccer team's stunning victory over Germany. Nicolas Cage heads an all star cast as the captain of the brave US soccer team haunted by the trauma of losing in the 2000 World Cup final on penalties and the death of his wife in a riot caused by English football hooligans, who finds love in the arms of a female sports journalist played by Julia Roberts. Mel Gibson is the no-nonsense Swedish coach who leads them to glory, with Keanu Reeves, Ben Affleck, Matt Damon and Will Smith playing some of Cage's heroic team mates. Jeremy Irons is set to star as Sir Nigel Villiers-Smythe, the dastardly Englishman who coaches the German team and forces them to play with poison-tipped studs to try and cheat the heroic American team out of victory.

Director Steven Spielberg defended the film-makers' decision to focus on the American contribution to the victory over Germany and introduce inaccurate and even imagined events in the story, saying, "Obviously we've had to take some artistic licence to make the story work on film, but I hope that what we produce will be true to the spirit of what happened on that famous night."

The Way It Is

God bless America, land of free, home of the blame!

*If a woman burns her thighs on the hot coffee she was holding in her lap while driving, she blames the restaurant.

*If your teenage son kills himself, you blame the rock 'n' roll musician he liked.

*If you smoke three packs a day for 40 years and die of lung cancer, your family blames the tobacco company.

*If your daughter gets pregnant by the football captain, you blame the school for poor sex education.

*If your neighbour crashes into a tree while driving home drunk, you blame the bartender.

*If your cousin gets AIDS because the needle he used to shoot heroin was dirty, you blame the government for not providing clean ones.

*If your grandchildren are brats without manners, you blame television.

*And if your friend is shot by a deranged madman, you blame the gun manufacturer.

How to Be a Good Republican

1) You have to believe that the nation's eight-year unprecedented prosperity was due to the work of Ronald Reagan and George Bush, but that today's gas prices are all Clinton's fault.

2) You have to believe that those privileged from birth achieve success all on their own.

3) You have to be against government programmes, but expect your social security cheques on time.

4) You have to believe that government should stay out of people's lives, yet want government to regulate only opposite-gender marriages, what a woman does with her uterus, and what your official language should be.

5) You have to believe that pollution is OK so long as it makes a profit.

6) You have to believe in prayer in schools, as long as you don't pray to Allah or Buddha or the Goddess.

7) You have to believe that only your own teenagers are still virgins.

8) You have to believe that a woman cannot be trusted with decisions about her own body, but that large multi-national corporations should have no regulation or interference whatsoever.

9) You love Jesus and Jesus loves you – and, by the way, Jesus shares your hatred of AIDS victims, homosexuals and Bill and Hillary Clinton.

10) You have to believe that society is colour-blind and growing up black in America doesn't diminish your opportunities, but you wouldn't vote for a black candidate for president.

11) You have to believe that it was great to allow Ken Starr to spend $90 million dollars to attack Clinton because no other US presidents have been unfaithful to their wives.

12) You have to believe that a waiting period for purchasing a handgun is bad because quick access to a new firearm is an important concern for all Americans.

13) You have to believe it is wise to keep condoms out of schools, because we all know if teenagers don't have condoms they won't have sex.

14) You have to believe that the ACLU is bad because it defends the institution, while the NRA is good because it defends the Constitution.

15) You have to believe that socialism hasn't worked anywhere, and that Europe doesn't exist.

16) You have to believe the AIDS virus is not important enough to deserve Federal funding proportionate to the resulting death rate and

that the public doesn't need to be educated about it, because if we ignore it, it will go away.

17) You have to believe that biology teachers are corrupting the morals of sixth graders if they teach them the basics of human sexuality, but the Bible, which is full of sex and violence, is good reading.

18) You have to believe that Communist Chinese missiles have killed more Americans than handguns, alcohol, and tobacco.

19) You have to believe that even though governments have supported the arts for 5000 years and that most of the great works of Renaissance art were paid for by governments, the US government should shun any such support. After all, the rich can afford to buy their own and the poor don't need any.

20) You have to believe that the timber from the last one per cent of old-growth US forests is well worth the destruction of those forests and the extinction of the species of plants and animals in them because it allows logging companies to add to their profit margin.

21) You have to believe that we should forgive and pray for Newt Gingrich, Henry Hyde, and Bob Livingston for their marital infidelities, but that bastard Clinton should have been impeached.

Guffaws for Guys

We All Know Pubs Like This

An 18th-century traveller in England, exhausted and famished, came to a roadside inn with a sign reading "The George and Dragon". He knocked. The innkeeper's wife stuck her head out of a window.

"Could ye spare some victuals?" The woman glanced at his shabby, dirty clothes.

"No!" she shouted.

"Could I have a pint of ale?"

"No!" she shouted.

"Could I at least use your privy?"

"No!" she shouted again. The traveller said, "Might I please …?"

"What now?" the woman screeched, not allowing him to finish.

"D'ye suppose," he asked, "that I might have a word with George?"

PMS in the Bible

A preacher was telling his congregation that anything they could think of, old or new, was discussed somewhere in the Bible and that the entirety of the human experience could be found there.

After the service, he was approached by a woman who said, "Preacher, I don't believe the Bible mentions PMS." The preacher replied that he was sure it must be there somewhere and that he would look for it.

The following week after service, the preacher called the woman aside and showed her a passage which read …

"And Mary rode Joseph's ass all the way to Bethlehem."

PMS: Advice for Men

Every "Hormone Hostage" knows that there are days in the month when all a man has to do is open his mouth and he takes his life in his hands. This is a handy guide that should be as common as a driver's licence in the wallet of every husband, boyfriend or significant other.

DANGEROUS: What's for dinner?
SAFER: Can I help you with dinner?
SAFEST: Where would you like to go for dinner?

DANGEROUS: Are you wearing THAT?
SAFER: You look good in brown.
SAFEST: Wow! Look at you!

DANGEROUS: What are you so worked up about?
SAFER: Could we be overreacting?
SAFEST: Here's £50.

DANGEROUS: Should you be eating that?
SAFER: You know, there are a lot of apples left.
SAFEST: Can I get you a glass of wine with that?

DANGEROUS: What did you DO all day?
SAFER: I hope you didn't overdo it today.
SAFEST: I've always loved you in that dressing gown.

Ultimate Bloke Test

1. Alien beings from a highly advanced society visit the Earth, and you are the first human they encounter. As a token of intergalactic friendship,

they present you with a small but incredibly sophisticated device that is capable of curing all disease, providing an infinite supply of clean energy, wiping out hunger and poverty, and permanently eliminating oppression and violence all over the entire Earth. You decide to:

a) present it to the president of the United States

b) present it to the secretary general of the United Nations

c) take it apart

2. As you grow older, what lost quality of your youthful life do you miss the most?

a) innocence

b) idealism

c) cherry bombs

3. When is it okay to kiss another male?

a) when you wish to display simple and pure affection without regard for narrow-minded social conventions

b) when he is the Pope (not on the lips)

c) when he is your brother and you are Al Pacino and this is the only really sportsman-like way to let him know that, for business reasons, you have to have him killed

4. In your opinion, the ideal pet is:

a) a cat

b) a dog

c) a dog that eats cats

5. You have been seeing a woman for several years. She's attractive and intelligent, and you always enjoy being with her. One leisurely Sunday afternoon the two of you are taking it easy. You're watching a football game; she's reading the papers when she suddenly, out of the clear blue sky, tells you that she thinks she really loves you, but she can no longer bear the uncertainty of not knowing where your relationship is going.

She says she's not asking whether you want to get married; only whether you believe that you have some kind of future together. What do you say?
a) that you sincerely believe the two of you do have a future, but you don't want to rush it
b) that although you also have strong feelings for her, you cannot honestly say that you'll be ready anytime soon to make a lasting commitment, and you don't want to hurt her by holding out false hope
c) that you can't understand why Fergie goes on picking Phil Neville

6. Okay, so you have decided that you truly love a woman and you want to spend the rest of your life with her, sharing the joys and the sorrows the world has to offer, come what may. How do you tell her?
a) you take her to a nice restaurant and tell her after dinner
b) you take her for a walk on a moonlit beach, and you say her name, and when she turns to you, with the sea breeze blowing through her hair and the stars in her eyes, you tell her
c) tell her what?

7. One weekday morning your wife wakes up feeling ill and asks you to get your three children ready for school. Your first question to her is:
a) "Do they need to eat or anything?"
b) "They're in school already?"
c) "There are three of them?"

8. When is it okay to throw away a set of veteran underwear?
a) when it has turned the colour of a dead whale and developed new holes so large that you're not sure which ones were originally intended for your legs
b) when it is down to eight loosely connected underwear molecules and has to be handled with tweezers
c) it is never okay to throw away veteran underwear. A real guy checks the garbage regularly in case somebody, and we are not naming names, but this would be his wife, is quietly trying to discard his underwear

(which she is frankly jealous of because the guy seems to have a more intimate relationship with it than with her)

9. What, in your opinion, is the most reasonable explanation for the fact that Moses led the Israelites all over the place for 40 years before they finally got to the Promised Land?
a) he was being tested
b) he wanted them to really appreciate the Promised Land when they finally got there
c) he refused to ask for directions

10. What is the human race's single greatest achievement?
a) democracy
b) religion
c) remote control

Adam and Eve

After a few days in the Garden of Eden, the Lord called Adam to Him, and said, "It is time for you and Eve to begin the process of populating the Earth, so I want you to start by kissing Eve." Adam answered, "Yes Lord, but what's a 'kiss'?" So the Lord gave Adam a brief description and Adam then took Eve by the hand behind a nearby bush. A few minutes later, Adam emerged.

"Lord, that was enjoyable," said Adam.

"Yes, Adam," replied the Lord, "I thought you'd enjoy that. Now I'd like you to caress Eve."

"Lord, what's a 'caress'?" asked Adam. So the Lord gave Adam a brief description and Adam went again behind the bush with Eve. Quite a few minutes later, Adam returned, smiling, and said, "Lord, that was even better than the kiss."

And the Lord said, "You've done well, Adam, and now I want you to make love to Eve."

"Lord, what's 'making love'?" asked Adam. So the Lord again gave Adam directions, and Adam went to Eve and took her behind the bush. But this time he reappeared in two seconds …

"Lord, what's a 'headache'?"

Bloke Rules

1. Any man who takes a camera to a stag night may be legally killed and eaten by his fellow partygoers.

2. Under no circumstances may two men share an umbrella.

3. It is OK for a man to cry under the following circumstances:
a) when a heroic dog dies to save its master
b) the moment Angelina Jolie starts unbuttoning her blouse
c) after wrecking your boss's car
d) one hour, 12 minutes, 37 seconds into *The Crying Game*
e) when your date is using her teeth

4. Unless he murdered someone in your family, you must bail a friend out of jail within 12 hours.

5. Acceptable excuse for not helping a friend move:
– Your legs have been severed in a freak threshing accident.

6. Acceptable excuse for not helping a friend-of-a-friend move:
– You'd rather stay home and watch speed buggy reruns.

7. If you've known a guy for more than 24 hours, his sister is off-limits forever, unless you actually marry her.

8. The minimum amount of time you have to wait for a guy who's running late is five minutes. The maximum waiting time is six minutes.

For a girl, you have to wait ten minutes for every point of hotness she scores on the classic 1–10 scale.

9. Bitching about the brand of free beer in a mate's fridge is forbidden. Gripe at will if the temperature is unsuitable.

10. No man shall ever be required to buy a birthday present for another man (in fact, even remembering your mate's birthday is strictly optional).

11. On a road trip, the strongest bladder determines pit stops, not the weakest.

12. While your girlfriend must bond with your mates' girlfriends within 30 minutes of meeting them, you are not required to make nice with her girlfriends' significant others – low-level sports bonding is all the law requires.

13. Unless you have signed a lucrative endorsement contract, never appear in public wearing more than one swoosh.

14. When stumbling upon other guys watching a sporting event, you may always ask the score of the game in progress, but you may never ask who's playing.

15. You may fart in front of a woman only after you have brought her to climax. If you trap her head under the covers for the purpose of flatulent entertainment, she's officially your girlfriend.

16. It is permissible to quaff a fruity chick drink only when you're sunning on a tropical beach … and a topless supermodel delivers it … and it's free.

17. Only in situations of moral and/or life peril are you allowed to kick another guy in the nuts.

18. Unless you're in prison, never fight naked.

19. Friends don't let friends wear Speedos. Ever. Issue closed.

20. If a man's zipper is down, that's his problem – you didn't see nothing.

21. Women who claim they "love to watch sports" must be treated as spies until they demonstrate knowledge of the game and the ability to drink as much beer as the other sports watchers.

22. If you compliment a guy on his six-pack, you'd better be talking about his choice of beer.

23. Phrases that may not be uttered to another man while lifting weights:
a) Yeah, baby! Push it!
b) C'mon, give me one more! Harder!
c) Another set and we can hit the showers!
d) Nice arse, are you a Sagittarius?

24. Never talk to a man in the gents unless you are on equal footing: both urinating, both waiting in line, etc. For all other situations, an almost imperceptible nod is all the conversation you need.

Things That You Should Never Say to a Woman During an Argument

~ "Don't you have some laundry to do or something?"

~ "Ohh, you are so cute when you get all pissed off."

~ "You're just upset because your ass is beginning to spread."

~ "Wait a minute – I get it. What time of the month is it?"

~ "You sure you don't want to consult the great Oprah on this one?"

~ "Sorry. I was just picturing you naked."

~ "Whoa, time out. Football is on."

~ "Looks like someone had an extra bowl of bitch flakes this morning!"

~ "Is there any way we can do this via e-mail?"

~ "Who are you kidding? We both know that thing ain't loaded."

A-Level Sexism Studies
Examination Paper

Time allowed three hours. Attempt all questions.

SECTION A (50%)

1. Explain why the best women's cricket team in the world wouldn't stand a chance against you and ten of your mates.
   Include in your answer:
   a) Why they throw the ball like spastics and catch crocodile style.
   b) What you wouldn't mind doing with them in the showers after the match.

2. Pamela Anderson's tits are plastic but look good in photographs. Compare and contrast the relative merits of plastic and real tits for recreational purposes.

3. It is a long established fact that fat lasses are more grateful for it. Outline some of the reasons why this is so, and explain why all feminists are fat, ugly lesbians; or compare and contrast video lesbians with those you have encountered in real life.

4. Write a critique of the film *White Water Shafting* you watched at your mate's house while his parents were away for the weekend.

Include in your discussion a justification for such films to be considered "art-house" rather than pornographic.

5. Women drivers, eh? Discuss.

SECTION B (50%)

1. Describe an experiment to impress a girl by lighting a fart. What apparatus would you require? What risks would you run in lighting a fart and what are the benefits? Write a balanced chemical equation to describe the reaction that takes place when an eggy fart is lit in a pub with a match.

2. Name something a woman has invented.

3. On average, women live seven years longer than men yet get their pension five years earlier. Explain why this isn't fair, making reference to your lazy old granny who lived to be 100 and your poor grandad who worked 52 years down the pit and died the day before he retired.

4. Argue heatedly over the respective merits of the Lamborghini Diablo and the Ferrari Testarossa without ever having seen, let alone driven, either.

5. Discuss the philosophical implications of this statement: "If a man speaks in a forest, and no woman hears him, is he still wrong?"

Words Women Use

FINE: This is the word we use at the end of any argument that we feel we are right about but need to shut you up. Never use FINE to describe how a woman looks. This will cause you to have one of those arguments.

FIVE MINUTES: This is half an hour. It is equivalent to the five minutes that your football game is going to last before you take out the trash, so I feel that it's an even trade.

NOTHING: If you ask her what is wrong and she says NOTHING, this means something and you should be on your toes. NOTHING is usually used to describe the feeling a woman has of wanting to turn you inside out, upside down, and backwards. NOTHING usually signifies an argument that will last FIVE MINUTES and end with the word FINE.

GO AHEAD (with raised eyebrows): This is a dare. One that will result in a woman getting upset over NOTHING and will end with the word FINE.

GO AHEAD (normal eyebrows): This means "I give up" or "Do what you want because I don't care." You will get a raised eyebrow GO AHEAD in just a few minutes, followed by NOTHING and FINE and she will talk to you in about FIVE MINUTES when she cools off.

LOUD SIGH: This is not actually a word, but is still often a verbal statement much misunderstood by men. A LOUD SIGH means she thinks you are an idiot at that moment and wonders why she is wasting her time standing here and arguing with you over NOTHING.

SOFT SIGH: Again, not a word, but a verbal statement. A SOFT SIGH is one of the few things that some men actually understand. She is content. Your best bet is to not move or breathe and she may stay content.

THAT'S OKAY: This is one of the most dangerous statements that a woman can say to a man. THAT'S OKAY means that she wants to think long and hard before paying you back for whatever it is that you have done. THAT'S OKAY is often used with the word FINE and used in conjunction with a raised eyebrow GO AHEAD. At some point in the near future when she has plotted and planned, you are going to be in some mighty big trouble.

PLEASE DO: This is not a statement, it is an offer. A woman is giving you the chance to come up with whatever excuse or reason you have for doing whatever it is that you have done. You have a fair chance to tell the truth, so be careful and you shouldn't get a THAT'S OKAY.

THANKS: A woman is thanking you. Do not faint; just say "You're welcome."

THANKS A LOT: This is very different from THANKS. A woman will say, THANKS A LOT when she is really pissed off with you. It signifies that you have hurt her in some callous way, and will be followed by the LOUD SIGH. Be careful not to ask what is wrong after the LOUD SIGH, as she will only tell you NOTHING.

Chain Letter

At last, a chain letter with a point …

This chain letter was started in the hope of bringing relief to other tired and discouraged men. Unlike most chain letters, this one does not cost anything. Just send a copy of this letter to five of your friends who are equally tired and discontented. Then bundle up your wife or girlfriend and send her to the man whose name appears at the top of the list, and add your name to the bottom of the list.

When your turn comes, you will receive 15,625 women. One of them is bound to be better than the one you already have. At the writing of this letter, a friend of mine had already received 184 women, four of whom were worth keeping.

REMEMBER this chain brings luck. One man's pit bull died, and the next day he received a *Playboy* swimsuit model. An unmarried Jewish man living with his widowed mother was able to choose between a Hooters waitress and a Hollywood supermodel.

You can be lucky too, but DO NOT BREAK THE CHAIN! One man broke the chain, and got his own wife back again.

The Terrible Four Questions

Four Questions Feared by Men:

1. What are you thinking about?
2. Do you love me?
3. Do I look fat?
4. Do you think she is prettier than me?

What makes these questions so difficult is that every one is guaranteed to explode into a major argument if the man answers incorrectly (i.e. tells the truth). Therefore, as a public service, each question is analysed below, along with possible responses.

Question #1: What are you thinking about?
The proper answer to this, of course, is: "I'm sorry if I've been pensive, dear. I was just reflecting on what a warm, wonderful, thoughtful, caring, intelligent woman you are, and how lucky I am to have met you."
This response obviously bears no resemblance to the true answer, which most likely is one of the following:

a) Football.
b) Nothing.
c) How fat you are.
d) How much prettier she is than you.
e) How I would spend the insurance money if you died.

Question #2: Do you love me?
The proper response is: "YES!" or, if you feel a more detailed answer is in order, "Yes, dear."
Inappropriate responses include:
a) Oh yeah, shit-loads.
b) Would it make you feel better if I said "yes"?
c) That depends on what you mean by love.
d) Does it matter?
e) Who, me?

Question #3: Do I look fat?
The correct answer is an emphatic "Of course not!"
Among the incorrect answers are:
a) Compared to what?
b) I wouldn't call you fat, but you're not exactly thin.
c) A little extra weight looks good on you.
d) I've seen fatter.
e) Could you repeat the question? I was just thinking about how I would spend the insurance money if you died.

Question #4: Do you think she's prettier than me?
Once again, the proper response is an emphatic "Of course not!"
Incorrect responses include:
a) Yes, but you have a better personality.
b) Not prettier, but definitely thinner.
c) Not as pretty as you when you were her age.
d) Define "pretty".

e) Could you repeat the question? I was just thinking about how I would spend the insurance money if you died.

Seven Inches

A man entered his favorite ritzy restaurant, and while sitting at his regular table, noticed a gorgeous woman sitting at a table nearby, all alone. He called the waiter over and asked for their most expensive bottle of Merlot to be sent over to her, knowing that if she accepted it, she would be his.

The waiter got the bottle and quickly brought it over to the girl, saying, "This is from the gentleman over there."

She looked at the wine and decided to send a note over to the man. The note read, "For me to accept this bottle, you need to have a Mercedes in your garage, a million dollars in the bank, and seven inches in your pants."

The man read the note and sent one of his own back to her. It read, "Just so you know – I happen to have a Ferrari Testarossa, a BMW 850iL, and a Mercedes 560SEL in my garage; plus I have over 20 million dollars in the bank. But not even for a woman beautiful as you would I cut off three inches. Just send the bottle back."

A Light Bulb Joke

Q: How many women with PMT does it take to screw in a light bulb?
A: One.

ONE!! And do you know WHY it only takes ONE? Because no one else in this house knows HOW to change a light bulb. They don't even notice the bulb is BURNED OUT. They would sit in this house in the dark for

THREE DAYS before they figured it OUT. And once they figured it out they wouldn't be able to FIND the light bulbs despite the fact that they've been in the SAME CUPBOARD for the past 17 YEARS!! But if they did, by some miracle, find the light bulbs, TWO DAYS LATER the chair that they dragged from two rooms over to stand on to change the STUPID light bulb would STILL BE IN THE SAME SPOT!!!!! AND UNDERNEATH IT WOULD BE THE CRUMPLED WRAPPER THE STUPID F*&KING LIGHT BULBS CAME IN. WHY??? BECAUSE NO ONE IN THIS HOUSE EVER CARRIES OUT THE GARBAGE!

IT'S A WONDER WE HAVEN'T ALL SUFFOCATED UNDER THE PILES OF GARBAGE THAT ARE 12 FEET DEEP THROUGHOUT THE ENTIRE HOUSE. THE HOUSE !!! THE HOUSE !!!! IT WOULD TAKE AN ARMY TO CLEAN THIS ...

Male Manifesto

Dear Girls,

For too long we men have been divided and conquered in the name of equality, feminism and a host of other bobbins.

No more! The man fights back!! Tell your friends, the 90s man is dead ... Long live the Man of the 21st century.

So listen up ladies, below is how it REALLY is ...

1. If you think you might be fat, you are. Don't ask us. Just get your arse down a gym.

2. Learn to work the toilet seat: if it's up, put the bloody thing down.

3. Don't cut your hair. Ever. It causes unnecessary arguments when we dare to comment on it.

4. Birthdays, Valentines, and anniversaries are not quests to see if we can find the perfect present ... again.

5. Sometimes, we're not thinking about you. Live with it.

6. Saturday = Football. Let it be.

7. Shopping is not a sport.

8. Anything you wear is fine. Really!!!

9. Ask for what you want directly. Subtle hints don't work.

10. Face it, peeing standing up is more difficult than peeing from point-blank range. We're bound to miss sometimes.

11. Most blokes own two to three pairs of shoes, so what makes you think we'd be any good at choosing which pair, out of 30, would look good with that particular dress?

12. "Yes", "No" and "Mmm" are perfectly acceptable answers.

13. A headache that lasts for 17 months is a problem. See a doctor.

14. Your mum doesn't have to be our best friend.

15. Check your oil. It is an essential part of car maintenance.

16. The relationship is never going to be like it was the first two months we were going out.

17. Anything we said six or eight months ago is inadmissible in a subsequent argument.

18. It's not the dress that makes you look fat. It's all that bloody chocolate you eat!!

19. Telling us that the models in the men's magazines are airbrushed makes you sound jealous and petty and it's certainly not going to deter

us from reading them.

20. The male models with great bodies you see in magazines are all gay.

21. If something we said could be interpreted two ways, and one of these ways makes you sad and angry, we meant the other one.

22. Let us ogle. If we don't look at other women, how can we rate how pretty you are?

23. Whenever possible, please say whatever you have to say during the commercial breaks.

24. When we are in bed and look tired this means that we are tired and definitely does not mean that we want to discuss the relationship.

25. If you want some dessert after a meal – have some. You don't HAVE to finish it. You can just taste it if you like but don't say "No, I couldn't/shouldn't/don't want any" and then eat half of mine.

26. Dieting doesn't work without exercise.

27. If you're on a diet it doesn't mean my meals should be rabbit food as well.

28. A man's four essential food groups are: white meat, red meat, warm beer and cold lager. Please ensure all meals contain a good balance of the above in acceptable quantities – everything else falls under the category "garnish".

29. Do not question our sense of direction.

If you can learn the above, then man and woman can coexist on a level based on love and mutual respect.

The ball's in your court.

Sincerely,
The Lads

Why Fishing Is Better Than Sex

1. You don't have to hide your fishing magazines.

2. It's perfectly acceptable to pay a professional to fish with you once in a while.

3. The Ten Commandments don't say anything about fishing.

4. If your partner takes pictures or videotapes of you fishing in your boat, you don't have to worry about them showing up on the Internet if you become famous.

5. Your fishing partner doesn't get upset about people you fished with long ago.

6. It's perfectly respectable to fish with a total stranger.

7. When you see a really good fishing person, you don't have to feel guilty about imagining the two of you fishing in a boat together.

8. If your regular fishing partner isn't available, he/she won't object if you fish with someone else.

9. Nobody will ever tell you that you will go blind if you fish by yourself.

10. When dealing with a fishing professional, you never have to wonder if they are really undercover police.

11. You can have a fishing calendar on your wall at the office, tell fishing jokes, and invite co-workers to fish with you without getting sued for harassment.

12. There are no fishing-transmitted diseases.

13. If you want to watch fishing on television, you don't have to subscribe to the porno channel.

14. Nobody expects you to fish with the same partner for the rest of your life.

15. Nobody expects you to give up fishing if your partner loses interest in it.

16. Your fishing partner will never say, "Not again? We just fished last week! Is fishing all you ever think about?"

Hicks, Rednecks and Lowlife

Two rednecks, Bubba and Cooter, decided that they weren't going anywhere in life and thought they should go to college to get ahead. Bubba went first to see the professor, and the professor advised him to take math, history, and logic.

"What's logic?" asked Bubba. The professor answered, "Let me give you an example. Do you own a weed-eater?"

"I sure do," answered the redneck.

"Then I can assume, using logic, that you have a yard," replied the professor.

"That's real good," the redneck responded in awe. The professor continued, "Logic will also tell me that since you have a yard, you also have a house." Impressed, the redneck shouted, "AMAZIN'!"

"And since you own a house and a house is tough to take care of by yourself, logic dictates that you have a wife."

"Betty Mae! This is incredible!"

"Finally, since you have a wife, logically I can assume that you are heterosexual," said the professor.

"You're absolutely right! Why that's the most fascinatin' thing I ever heard of. I can't wait to take this here logic class."

Bubba, proud of the new world opening up to him, walked back into the hallway where Cooter was still waiting.

"So what classes are ya takin?" he asked.

"Math, history, and logic," replied Bubba.

"What in tarnation is logic?"

"Let me give you an example. Do ya own a weed-eater?"
"No."

"You're queer, ain't ya?"

Mirror, Mirror ...

After living in a remote wilderness all his life, an old codger decided it was time to visit the big city. In one of the stores he picked up a mirror and looked in it. Not knowing what it was, he remarked, "How about that! Here's a picture of my daddy."

He bought the "picture", but on the way home he remembered his wife, Lizzy, didn't like his father. So he hung it in the barn, and every morning before leaving for the fields, he would go there and look at it.

Lizzy began to get suspicious of these many trips to the barn. One day after her husband left, she searched the barn and found the mirror. As she looked into the glass, she fumed,

"So that's the ugly bitch he's runnin' after."

Redneck Engineering Exam

1. Calculate the smallest limb diameter on a persimmon tree that will support a ten-pound possum.

2. Which of the following cars will rust out the quickest when placed on blocks in your front yard?
a) a '66 Ford Fairlane
b) a '69 Chevrolet Chevelle
c) a '64 Pontiac GTO

3. If your uncle builds a still that operates at a capacity of 20 gallons of shine per hour, how many car radiators are necessary to condense the product?

4. A pulpwood cutter has a chainsaw that operates at 2700 rpm. The density of the pine trees in a plot to be harvested is 470 per acre. The plot is 2.3 acres in size. The average tree diameter is 14 inches. How many Budweiser Tall-Boys will it take to cut the trees?

5. If every old refrigerator in the state vented a charge of R-12 simultaneously, what would be the decrease in the ozone layer?

6. A front porch is constructed of 2-inch by 8-inch pine on 24-inch centres with a field rock foundation. The span is 8 feet and the porch length is 16 feet. The porch floor is 1-inch rough-sawn pine. When the porch collapses, how many hound dogs will be killed?

7. A man owns an Arkansas house and 3.7 acres of land in a hollow with an average slope of 15%. The man has five children. Can each of the children place a mobile home on the man's land?

8. A 2-ton pulpwood truck is overloaded and proceeding down a steep grade on a secondary road at 45 mph. The brakes fail. Given the average traffic loading of secondary roads, how many people will swerve to avoid the truck before it crashes at the bottom of the mountain? For extra credit, how many of the vehicles that swerved will have mufflers and uncracked windshields?

9. A coal mine operates a NFPA Class 1, Division 2 Hazardous Area. The mine employs 120 miners per shift. A gas warning is issued at the beginning of third shift. How many cartons of unfiltered Camels will be smoked during the shift?

📥 💾 Fishing Trip

Two redneck guys were going on a fishing trip. They rented all the equipment: the reels, the rods, the wading suits, the rowboat, the car, and even a cabin in the woods. They spent a fortune.

The first day fishing they didn't catch anything. The same thing happened on the second day, and on the third day. It went on like this until finally, on the last day of their vacation, one of the men caught a fish.

Driving home they felt really depressed. One guy turned to the other and says, "Do you realize that this one lousy fish we caught cost us 1500 dollars?" To which the other guy replied,

"Wow! It's a good thing we didn't catch any more!"

📥 💾 Redneck Computer Test

How can you tell if a redneck has been working on a computer?

10. The monitor is up on blocks.

9. Outgoing faxes have tobacco stains on them.

8. The six front keys have rotted out.

7. The extra RAM slots have Dodge truck parts installed in them.

6. The numeric keypad only goes up to six.

5. The password is "Bubba".

4. The CPU has a gun-rack.

3. There is a Skoal can in the CD-ROM drive.

2. The keyboard is camouflaged.

And, The Number One Way To Tell If A Redneck Has Been Working On A Computer …

1. The mouse is referred to as a "critter".

Good Ol' Southern Wisdom

If you're Southern, you'll know …

** The difference between a hissie fit and a conniption.

** Pretty much how many fish make up a mess.

** What general direction cattywumpus is.

** That "gimme sugar" don't mean pass the sugar.

** When "by and by" is.

** How to handle your "pot likker".

** The best gesture of solace for a neighbour who's got trouble is a plate of cold potato salad.

** The difference between "purt' near" and "a right far piece".

** The differences between a redneck, a good ol' boy, and trailer trash.

** Never to go snipe hunting twice.

** Never to assume that the other car with the flashing turn signal is actually going to make a turn.

** You should never loan your tools, pick-up, or gun to nobody! But nobody!

📥🖥 Favourite Redneck Movies

Alabama Jones and the Last Beer Run

S*O*U*R*M*A*S*H

Thelma-Louise

Back to the Future IV: I'm My Own Daddy!

9½ Teeth

Three to Tango – But Two Have to Hold the Cow Steady So You Don't Get Knocked Off The Footstool

And the Band Played "Freebird"

Three Brides for Seven Brothers

Dog, Ma

Honey, I Blew My Cousin!

Three Men and Ned Beatty

Austin Texas: The Uncle Who Shagged Me

Being John Deere

How Stella Got Her Tooth Back

The Green Smile

West Virginia

Q: What does it mean when a girl in West Virginia has cum running out of both sides of her mouth?
A: The trailer is level.

Ending It All

An Irishman, a Mexican and a redneck were doing construction work on a tall building. At lunchtime, the Irishman opened his lunch box and said, "Corned beef and cabbage! If I get corned beef and cabbage one more time for lunch, I'm going to jump off this building."

The Mexican opened his lunch box and exclaimed, "Burritos again! If I get burritos one more time, I'm going to jump off, too!"

The redneck opened his lunch and said, "Bologna again! If I get a bologna sandwich one more time, I'm jumping, too!"

Next day the Irishman opens his lunch box, sees corned beef and cabbage and jumps to his death. The Mexican opens his lunch, sees a burrito and jumps too. The Redneck opens his lunch, sees the bologna and jumps to his death as well.

At the funeral, the Irishman's wife is weeping. She says, "If I'd known how really tired he was of corned beef and cabbage, I never would have given it to him again!"

The Mexican's wife also weeps and says, "I could have given him tacos or enchiladas! I didn't realize he hated burritos so much." Everyone turns and stares at the redneck's wife.

"Hey, don't look at me," she says.

"He always made his own lunch."

Send Her Back

A redneck couple were in bed on their wedding night, and were about to consummate their marriage. The wife stopped the husband, saying, "Be gentle. I'm still a virgin." The man was astounded. He had never been with a virgin before. He decided to call his father for advice.

"Dad," said the newly married young man. "My new wife is a virgin! What do I do?"

"Better come on home, son," replied his father.

"If she ain't good enough for her own family, she sure ain't good enough for ours."

Driving Like Momma

One day, a hitch-hiker gets a ride from Billy Bob. They come to an intersection with a stoplight. The light showed red. Billy Bob went right through the red light. The passenger looked at Billy Bob and screamed, "What the heck are you doing? You're going to get us killed!" Billy Bob responded, "Don't worry, my momma always drives like this."

Later on, the two guys came to another stoplight and that too was red. Billy Bob sped right through the light. Again the passenger looked at the driver and said, "I thought I told you, you're gonna get us killed! Would you please stop this nonsense!" Billy Bob looked at the passenger and responded, "All right! I get it, but I told you my momma drives like this all the time!"

Soon, the two guys ran into another light. This time it was green. Billy Bob slammed on his brakes and the truck skidded to a stop.

"What the hell are you doing?" The passenger screamed. "This is the third time you almost got us killed. Why did you stop at a green light?"

"Well," said Billy Bob, "my momma might be coming the other way!"

Taking Precautions

Billy Bob and Luther were talking one afternoon when Billy Bob tells Luther, "Ya know, I reckon I'm 'bout ready for a vacation. Only this year I'm gonna do it a little different. The last few years, I took your advice about where to go. Three years ago you said to go to Hawaii. I went to Hawaii and Earline got pregnant. Then two years ago, you told me to go to the Bahamas, and Earline got pregnant again. Last year you suggested Tahiti and darned if Earline didn't get pregnant again."

"So, what you gonna do this year that's different?" asked Luther.

"This year I'm taking Earline with me."

Hick Medical Terms Translated

ARTERY	The study of paintings
BENIGN	What you be after you be eight
BACTERIA	Back door to cafeteria
BARIUM	What doctors do when patients die
CAESARIAN SECTION	A neighbourhood in Rome
CATSCAN	Searching for Kitty
CAUTERIZE	Made eye contact with her
COLIC	A sheep dog
COMA	A punctuation mark
D&C	Where Washington is

DILATE	To live long
ENEMA	Not a friend
FESTER	Quicker than someone else
FIBULA	A small lie
GENITAL	Non-Jewish person
HANGNAIL	What you hang your coat on
IMPOTENT	Distinguished, well known
LABOUR PAIN	Getting hurt at work
MEDICAL STAFF	A Doctor's cane
MORBID	A higher offer than I bid
NITRATES	Cheaper than day rates
NODE	I knew it
OUTPATIENT	A person who has fainted
PAP SMEAR	A fatherhood test
PELVIS	Second cousin to Elvis
POST-OPERATIVE	A letter carrier
RECOVERY ROOM	Place to do upholstery
RECTUM	Darn near killed him
SECRETION	Hiding something
SEIZURE	Roman emperor
TABLET	A small table

TERMINAL ILLNESS	Getting sick at the airport
TUMOUR	More than one
URINE	Opposite of "You're out"
VARICOSE	Nearby

The Cadillac Tourist

A man and his wife were touring in the Deep South. Looking at his fuel gauge, the man decided to stop at the next gas station and fill up. About 15 minutes later, he spotted a Mobil station and pulled over to the high-octane pump.

"What can I do for ya'll?" asked the attendant.

"Fill 'er up with high test," replied the driver. While the attendant filled up the tank, he looked the car up and down.

"What kinda car is this?" he asked. "I never seen one like it before."

"Well," responded the driver, his chest swelling up with pride, "this, my boy, is a 1999 Cadillac DeVille."

"What all's it got in it?" asked the attendant.

"Well," said the driver, "it has everything. It's loaded with power steering, power seats, power sun roof, power mirrors, AM/FM radio with a ten-deck CD player in the trunk with 100 watts per channel, eight-speaker stereo, rack and pinion steering, disk brakes all around, leather interior, digital instrument package, and best of all, a 8.8 litre V12 engine."

"Wow," said the attendant, "that's really something!"

"How much do I owe you for the gasoline?" asked the driver.

"That'll be $30.17," says the attendant. The driver pulls out his money clip and peels off a $20 and a $10. He goes into his other pocket and pulls out a handful of change. Mixed up with the change are a few golf tees.

"What are those little wooden things?" asked the attendant.

"That's what I put my balls on when I drive," said the driver.

"Wow," said the attendant,

"those Cadillac people think of everything!"

In Louisiana ...

Bordeaux and Thibodeaux found themselves out of a job when the underwear factory in Port Bare shut down. But their boss said they could go to the LSU office, you know, the Louisiana State Unemployment office. So as Thibodeaux waited, Bordeaux sat down at the desk and was interviewed by the lady there.

"And what was your former occupation?" she asked.

"Me, I was a crotch stitcher. I specialized in ladies underpants," Bordeaux proudly replied. So the lady looked it up in her big book and said, "OK, you're eligible for $50 a week."

"Hot damn, you mean I don't gotta do nothin' and I can get $50 a week. Man, that even beats crawfishin'!" Bordeaux shouted.

Then Thibodeaux sat down and the lady asked him the same question. Thibodeaux looked her straight in the eye and said, "I was a diesel fitter." She looked up in her big book again and said, "Very good then, you're eligible for $200 a week in unemployment benefits."

"WAIT A HOT DAMN MINUTE!" Bordeaux shouted. "How come he gets $200 a week, and me, I only get $50. I told you I used to be a crotch stitcher; you know you gotta be real good to do that kind of work so the seams are all nice and straight and smooth so nothing scratches you down there. And Thibodeaux here, he's only a diesel fitter. And he's gonna make four times more than I'm making?"

"Oh," the lady replied, "but he's a skilled labourer with an education. Diesel fitters are in high demand especially by oilfields and heavy equipment users. There's not many diesel specialists around."

"Whoa, whoa, whoa, lady," Bordeaux continued, "you got it all wrong. Yeah, Thibo's a diesel fitter, all right. But what that means is that after I do all the fine work on the lady drawers, he picks them up, looks 'em over and stretches them this way and that, and then says …

"'Yep, dese'll fit her!'"

In an Arkansas Bar

A man walked into a bar in Arkansas and ordered a white wine. Everybody sitting around the bar looked up, surprised, and the bartender looked around and said, "You ain't from around here, are ya … Where ya from, boy?"

"I'm from Iowa," said the man. The bartender asks, "What th' hell you do in Iowa?"

"I'm a taxidermist," replied the man.

"A taxidermist … now just what in th' hell is a taxidermist?"

"I mount and stuff animals," said the man. The bartender grins in relief and shouts out to the whole bar,

"It's OK boys, he's one of us!"

Kids' Stuff

Passing for Dumb

There was a little fellow named Junior who hung out at the local grocery store. The manager didn't know what Junior's problem was, but the other boys liked to tease him. The boys said he was two bricks short of a load, or two pickles shy of a barrel. To prove it, sometimes the boys would offer Junior his choice between a nickel and a dime. He always took the nickel, they said, because it was bigger.

One day after Junior grabbed the nickel, the store manager got him off to one side and said, "Junior, those boys are making fun of you. They think you don't know the dime is worth more than the nickel. Are you grabbing the nickel because it's bigger, or what?"

"No sir," said Junior.

"But if I took the dime, they'd quit doing it!"

Potential and Reality

A kid came home from school with a writing assignment and asked his father for help.

"Dad, can you tell me the difference between potential and reality?"

His father looked up, thoughtfully, and said, "I'll demonstrate it for you. Go ask your mother if she would sleep with Robert Redford for a million dollars. Then go ask your sister if she would sleep with Brad Pitt for a million dollars. Then come back and tell me what you've learned."

The kid was puzzled, but decided to see if he can figure out what his father meant. He asked his mother, "Mom, if someone gave you a million dollars, would you sleep with Robert Redford?" His mother looked around slyly, and then with a little smile on her face said, "Don't tell your father, but yes, I would."

Then he went to his sister's room and asked, "Sis, if someone gave you a million dollars, would you sleep with Brad Pitt?" His sister looked up and said, "Omigod! Definitely!"

The kid goes back to his father and said, "Dad, I think I've figured it out. Potentially, we are sitting on two million bucks,

"but in reality, we are living with a couple of tramps."

Lessons from Mother

My Mother taught me TO APPRECIATE A JOB WELL DONE – "If you are going to kill each other, do it outside because I just finished cleaning."

My Mother taught me RELIGION – "You'd better pray that will come out of the carpet."

My Mother taught me about TIME TRAVEL – "If you don't straighten up, I'm going to knock you into the middle of next week."

My Mother taught me LOGIC – "Because I said so, that's why."

My Mother taught me LOGIC #2 – "If you fall out of that swing and break your neck, you are not going to the store with me."

My Mother taught me FORESIGHT – "Make sure you wear clean underwear, in case you are in an accident."

My Mother taught me IRONY – "Keep crying and I'll give you something to cry about."

My Mother taught me about OSMOSIS – "Shut your mouth and eat your supper."

My Mother taught me about CONTORTIONISM – "Will you look at the dirt on the back of your neck."

My Mother taught me about STAMINA – "You will sit there till all that spinach is finished."

My Mother taught me about WEATHER – "It looks as if a tornado swept through your room."

My Mother taught me how to solve PHYSICS PROBLEMS – "If I yelled because I saw a meteor coming toward you, would you listen then?"

My Mother taught me about HYPOCRISY – "If I've told you once, I've told you a million times – don't exaggerate."

My Mother taught me THE CIRCLE OF LIFE – "I brought you into this world, and I can take you out."

My Mother taught me about ENVY – "There are millions of less fortunate children in this world who don't have wonderful parents like you do."

My Mother taught me about ANTICIPATION – "Just wait until we get home."

My Mother taught me MEDICAL SCIENCE – "If you don't stop crossing your eyes, they are going to freeze that way."

My Mother taught me to THINK AHEAD – "If you don't pass your spelling test, you will never get a good job."

My Mother taught me ESP – "Put your sweater on; don't you think I know when you are cold?"

My Mother taught me HUMOUR – "When that lawnmower cuts off your toes, don't come running to me."

My Mother taught me about GENETICS – "You are just like your Father."

My Mother taught me about my ROOTS – "Do you think you were born in a barn."

My Mother taught me about WISDOM OF AGE – "When you get to be my age, you will understand."

And my all time favourite that my Mother taught me was JUSTICE – "One day you will have kids … and I hope they all turn out just like you."

Definitions

A school teacher said to her class one day, "Who can use the word 'definitely' in a sentence?" The first little boy said, "The sky is definitely blue."

"Sorry, Amy, but the sky can be grey, or orange …" corrected the teacher. The second little boy said, "Trees are definitely green."

"Sorry, but in the autumn, the trees are brown …"

Little Johnny at the back of the class stood up and asked, "Does a fart have lumps?" The teacher looked horrified.

"Johnny! Of course not!"

"OK … then I DEFINITELY shit my pants …"

Learning Maths

A ten-year-old Jewish boy was failing maths. His parents tried everything from tutors to hypnosis; but to no avail. Finally, at the suggestion of a family friend, they decided to enroll their son in a private Catholic school.

After the first day, the boy's parents were surprised when he walked in after school with a stern, focused and very determined expression on his face. He went straight past them, right to his room and quietly closed the door.

For nearly two hours he toiled away in his room – with maths books strewn about his desk and the surrounding floor. He emerged long enough to eat, and after quickly cleaning his plate, went straight back to his room, closed the door and worked feverishly at his studies until bedtime.

This pattern of behaviour continued until it was time for the first term report. The boy walked in with it unopened, laid it on the dinner table and went straight to his room. Cautiously, his mother opened it and, to her amazement, she saw a large red 'A' under the subject of Maths. Overjoyed, she and her husband rushed into their son's room, thrilled at his remarkable progress.

"Was it the nuns that did it?" the father asked.

The boy shook his head and said, "No."

"Was it the one-to-one tutoring? The peer mentoring?"

"No."

"The textbooks? The teachers? The curriculum?"

"No," said the son.

"But on that first day, when I walked in the front door and saw that guy nailed to the plus sign, I KNEW they meant business!"

Where No Man Has Gone Before

Two young brothers, aged five and six, are listening through the keyhole as their older sister is getting it on with her new boyfriend. They hear her say, "Oh, Jim, you're going where no man has gone before!"

The six-year-old says to his brother, "He must be fucking her up the ass!"

Two Teenagers

Two teenagers were found naked and smoking a joint in the middle of the town's park. They were both arrested for indecent exposure and possession of marijuana and taken to the town jail. The arresting officer was unable to reach either parent, so he advised them they were entitled to one phone call.

A while later, a man entered the station. As he was approaching the desk, the Sergeant said to him, "I assume you're the kids' lawyer."

"Heck, no," the man replied.

"I'm here to deliver their pizza."

Sex Education

Three boys got their grades from their female sex education teacher. One of them got a D+, the second one got a D- and the third got an E.

"We should get her for this," said the first boy.

"Yeah, let's grab her ..." said the second.

"Yeah," interrupted the third,

"and then let's kick her in the nuts."

What Dad Did

A teacher asked her pupils to discuss what their dads did for a living.

Little Mary says: "My Dad is a lawyer. He puts the bad guys in jail."

Little Jack says: "My Dad is a doctor. He makes all the sick people better."

All the kids in the class had their turn except little Johnny.

Teacher says: "Little Johnny, what does your Dad do?"

Little Johnny says: "My Dad is dead."

Teacher says: "I'm sorry to hear that, but what did he do before he died?"

"He turned blue and shit on the carpet."

Childhood Is So Precious

A father asked his son, little Mikey, if he knew about the birds and the bees.

"I don't want to know!" little Mikey said, exploding and bursting into tears. Confused, his father asked little Mikey what was wrong.

"Dad," Mikey sobbed, "for me there was no Santa Claus at age six, no Easter Bunny at seven, and no Tooth Fairy at eight.

"And if you're telling me now that grown-ups don't really fuck, I've got nothing left to believe in!"

Letter Home

Dear Dad,

$chool i$ really great. I am making lot$ of friend$ and $tudying very hard. With all my $tuff, I $imply can't think of anything I need, $o if you would like, you can ju$t $end me a card, a$ I would love to hear from you.

Love, Your $on.

Dear Son,

I kNOw that astroNOmy, ecoNOmics, and oceaNOgraphy are eNOugh to keep even an honOur student busy. Do NOt forget that the pursuit of kNOwledge is a NOble task, and you can never study eNOugh.

Love, Dad

His Dad Has Two Dicks

Little Johnny was in the boys' room at school taking a pee. Another boy entered the boys' room and also started to take a pee. The other boy said, "Hey Johnny, your dick is bigger than mine," to which little Johnny replied, "That's nothing, my father has two dicks!"

"That's not possible!" the other boy said. But little Johnny said it was and that he had seen them. The other boy said "Oh yeah, what do they look like, then?"

"One is small and wrinkly and he uses it for peeing," said little Johnny,

"The other is long and stiff and he uses it for brushing mum's teeth."

Big Boy

A group of third, fourth and fifth graders accompanied by two female teachers went on a field trip to the local racetrack to learn about thoroughbred horses and the supporting industry. During the tour some of the children wanted to go to the toilet so it was decided that the girls would go with one teacher and the boys would go with the other.

As the teacher assigned to the boys waited outside the men's toilet, one of the boys came out and told her he couldn't reach the urinal. Having no choice, she went inside and began hoisting the little boys up by their armpits, one by one. As she lifted one, she couldn't help but notice that he was unusually well endowed for an elementary school child.

"I guess you must be in the fifth," she said.

"No ma'am," he replied,

"I'm in the seventh, riding Silver Arrow. Thanks for the lift anyhow."

The Farmer's Son

A farmer advertised that his prize bull was available for stud service. The next day another farmer and his wife arrived in their truck with two cows, a white cow and a brown cow. They put the cows in the corral with the bull, and both couples went in the house to have coffee while the deed was done. The farmer left his little four-year-old son outside to watch, telling him, "Son, you stay here and watch, and come in and tell us if anything happens."

In a short while the boy rushed into the house and excitedly proclaims, "Daddy, daddy, guess what happened, guess what happened?"

"What happened son?" asked the farmer, to which the boy replied, "The bull just fucked the brown cow!" Everyone was shocked, but the boy's father remained calm.

"That's fine, son," he said, "but you should really say the bull 'surprised' the brown cow. Now go out and watch again, and let us know if anything else happens."

After a short while, the boy came running into the house again, saying, "Daddy, daddy, guess what happened, guess what happened!" The farmer asked, "What happened, son, did the bull surprise the white cow?"

"He surprised both of them," said the boy.

"Don't be silly, son," said the father, "a bull can't surprise two cows at once."

"Yes he can," said the boy.

"He just fucked the horse!"

Mommy, How Old Are You?

Eight-year-old little Mary and her mother were walking through the mall together one day when Mary asked, "Mommy, how old are you?"

"Darling, you should never ask a woman what her age is," her mother replied.

"Why not?" demanded the child.

"Well, that is something you will understand one day when you're grown up."

"Mommy," asked Mary again, "how much do you weigh?"

"Never mind," answered her mother.

"Why can't you tell me?"

"Because grown-ups never talk about how much they weigh. This is something you will learn and understand someday."

"Mommy," insisted the child, "can you tell me why you and Daddy got divorced?"

"Darling," responded the mother in exasperation, "that's something still very painful for Mommy, and I really just can't talk about it now."

A few days later, little Mary recounted this conversation to a friend at school. The friend explained how to overcome these problems.

"All you have to do is get your mother's driver's licence. It has all the information about any grown-up you want on it. You just read it like a report card and it'll give you anything you need."

So little Mary did as her friend recommended. That night she snuck into her mother's room while her mom was cooking dinner. She rummaged through her purse and found the driver's licence. After examining it carefully she went to her mother and said, "I know how old you are! You are 35!" Her mother was very surprised.

"And, I know how much you weigh. You weigh 136 pounds, right?" Her mother was shocked.

"And, I know why you and Daddy got a divorce."

The mother, dumbfounded, asked, "Why?"

"It's because you got an F in sex."

Dark in Here

A bored wife takes a lover during the day while her husband is at work. Her nine-year-old son comes home unexpectedly, so she puts him in the closet and shuts the door. Her husband also comes home, so she quickly puts her lover in the closet with her little boy.

The boy says, "Dark in here."

The man says, "Yes it is."

Boy: "I have a baseball."

Man: "That's nice."

Boy: "Want to buy it?"

Man: "No thanks."

Boy: "My Dad's outside."

Man: "OK, how much?"

Boy: "$25."

In the next few weeks, it happens again that the boy and the lover are in the closet together.

Boy: "Dark in here."

Man: "Yes, it is."

Boy: "I have a baseball glove."

The lover, remembering the last time, asks the boy how much.

Boy: "$75."

Man: "Fine."

A few days later, the father says to the boy "Grab your bat and glove, let's go outside and toss a few balls."

Boy: "I can't, I sold them."

Father: "How much did you sell them for?"

Boy: "$100."

Father: "That's terrible to overcharge your friends like that. That is way more than those two things cost. I'm going to take you to church and make you confess to the priest what you did."

They go to the church and the father makes his little boy sit in the confessional where the priest is and closes the door.

The boy says, "Dark in here."

The priest says, "Don't start that shit with me again."

Do You Know Who I Am?

It was the final examination for an introductory English course at the local university. Like many such freshman courses, it was designed to weed out new students, there being over 700 students in the class.

The examination was two hours long, and exam booklets were provided. The professor was very strict and told the class that any exam that was not on his desk in exactly two hours would not be accepted and the student would fail. Half an hour into the exam, a student came rushing in and asked the professor for an exam booklet.

"You're not going to have time to finish this," the professor stated sarcastically as he handed the student a booklet.

"Yes I will," replied the student. He then took a seat and began writing.

After two hours, the professor called for the exams, and the students filed up and handed them in. All except the late student, who continued writing.

Half an hour later, the last student came up to the professor, who was sitting at his desk preparing for his next class. He attempted to put his exam on the stack of exam booklets already there.

"No you don't, I'm not going to accept that. It's late."

The student looked incredulous and angry, "Do you know WHO I am?"

"No, as a matter of fact I don't," replied the professor with an air of sarcasm in his voice.

"DO YOU KNOW WHO I AM?" the student asked again.

"No, and I don't care," replied the professor with an air of superiority.

"Good," replied the student, who quickly lifted the stack of completed exams, stuffed his in the middle, and walked out of the room.

Saving It for Marriage

One day, a mother walked by her young son's room and saw little Johnny masturbating. Later, she had a talk with him and told him that good little boys save it until they are married.

A few weeks later, the mom had another talk with little Johnny.

"How are you doing with that problem we talked about, dear?" she asked. Little Johnny cheerfully replied,

"Great! So far I've saved nearly a quart!"

The Amazing Body Part

The sixth-grade science teacher, Mrs Parks, asked her class, "Which human body part increases to ten times its size when stimulated?"

No one answered until little Mary stood up, angry, and said, "You should not be asking sixth graders a question like that! I'm going to tell my parents, and they will go and tell the principal, who will then fire you!" With a sneer on her face, she sat back down.

Mrs Parks ignored her and asked the question again, "Which body part increases to ten times its size when stimulated?" Little Mary's mouth fell open; then she said to those around her, "Boy, is she gonna get in big trouble!" The teacher continued to ignore her and said to the class, "Anybody?"

Finally, Billy stood up, looked around nervously, and said, "The body part that increases to ten times its size when stimulated is the pupil of the eye."

"Very good, Billy," said Mrs Parks, then turned to Mary and continued, "As for you, young lady, I have three things to say:

"1) you have a dirty mind,
 2) you didn't read your homework, and
 3) one day you are going to be very, very disappointed."

New Nursery Rhymes

Mary had a little lamb,
Her father shot it dead.
Now it goes to school with her,
Between two chunks of bread.

Little Miss Muffet sat on a tuffet,
Her clothes all tattered and torn.
It wasn't the spider that crept beside her,
But Little Boy Blue and his horn.

Simple Simon met a Pieman, going to the fair.
Said Simple Simon to the Pieman,
What have you got there?
Said the Pieman unto Simon,
"Pies, you dickhead."

Humpty Dumpty sat on a wall,
Humpty Dumpty had a great fall.

All the king's horses and all the king's men,
Said, "F*ck him, he's only an egg."

Mary had a little lamb,
It ran into a pylon.
10,000 volts went up its ass,
And turned its wool to nylon

Georgie Porgy pudding and pie,
Kissed the girls and made them cry.
When the boys came out to play,
He kissed them too, 'cause he was gay.

Jack and Jill
Went up the hill
To have a little fun.
Jill, that dill,
Forgot her pill
And now they have a son.

Old Mother Hubbard
Went to the cupboard
To fetch her poor dog a bone.
When she bent over
Rover took over,
And gave her a bone of his own.

Little Boy Blew.
Hey, he needed the Money.

Mostly for the Brits

Barmy British Place Names: Part I

Evenjobb,
Fatfield,
Fitful Head,
Flash,
Floors,
Fockerby,
Foul Mile,
Frenchbeer,
Frisby on the Wreaks,
Frog End,
Germansweek,
Giggleswick,
Glasshouses,
Gotham,
Great Snoring,
Grimpo,
Guiting Power,
Gussage St Michael,
Gweek,
Halfway,
Hanging Langford,
Heavitree,
Homer,
Hose,
Houghton Conquest,
Hogland Nether,
Huish Episcopi,
Husbands Bosworth,
Henry,
Indian Queens,
Inkpen,
Jump,
Kettlesing Bottom,
Kirkby Overblow,
Lickey End,
Limpley Stoke,
Little Snoring,
Loose,
Love Clough,
Lower Dicker,
Lower Swell,
Lumbutts,
Merrymeet,
Middle Wallop,
Molehill Green,
Mork,
Mousehole,
Much Marcle,
Mucking.

How to Upset a Scouser

At the end of a tiny, deserted bar is a huge Scouse bloke – 6'5" and 18 stone. He's having a few beers when a short, well-dressed and obviously gay man walks in and sits beside him.

After three or four beers the gay fella finally plucks up the courage to say something to the big Liverpudlian. Leaning over towards the Scouser he whispers, "Do you want to get a blow job?"

At this the massive Merseysider leaps up with fire in his eyes and smacks the man in the face, knocking him off the stool. He proceeds to beat him all the way out of the bar before leaving him bruised and battered in the car park and returning to his seat.

Amazed, the barman quickly brings over another beer.

"I've never seen you react like that," he says, "just what did he say to you?"

"I'm not sure," the big Scouser replies.

"Something about getting a job."

Pop Idol

Pop Idol Will Young – number one for the second week – when interviewed said he'd rather be filling the number two slot.

Einstein, Picasso and Beckham

Einstein died and went to heaven. At the Pearly Gates, St Peter told him, "You look like Einstein, but you have NO idea the lengths that some people will go to sneak into Heaven. Can you prove who you really are?"

Einstein pondered for a few seconds and asked, "Could I have a blackboard and some chalk?" St Peter snapped his fingers and a blackboard and chalk instantly appeared. Einstein proceeded to describe with arcane mathematics and symbols his theory of relativity. St Peter was suitably impressed.

"You really ARE Einstein!" he said. "Welcome to heaven!"

The next to arrive was Picasso. Once again, St Peter asked for credentials. Picasso asked, "Mind if I use that blackboard and chalk?"

"Go ahead," said St Peter. Picasso erased Einstein's equations and sketched a truly stunning mural with just a few strokes of chalk. St Peter applauded.

"Surely you are the great artist you claim to be!" he said. "Come on in!"

Then Saint Peter looked up and saw David Beckham. St Peter scratched his head and said, "Einstein and Picasso both managed to prove their identity. How can you prove yours?"

Beckham looked bewildered and said, "Who are Einstein and Picasso?"

"Come on in, David."

Barmy British Place Names: Part II

Nasareth,	Piddlehinton,
Nasty,	Pill,
Nedging Tye,	Plumtree,
Neen Savage,	Pokesdown,
Nempnett Thrubwell,	Portwrinkle,
Nether Wallop,	Potters Crouch,
Nobottle,	Pratt's Bottom,
North Piddle,	Prickwillow,
Old Wives Lees,	Ripe,

Ripple,
Robin Hood,
St Bees,
St Erth,
St Fagans,
St Tudy,
St Veep,
Scrooby,
Seething,
Sheepy Magna,
Shop,
Sloley,

Sots Hole,
Spital,
Spital in the Street,
Steep,
Steeple Bumpstead,
Sticker,
Stiffkey,
Stratton Strawless,
Stroat,
Strubby,
Styrrup.

The Wonderful Waddell

For those of you who have been glued to Sky Sports watching the PDC World Championship Darts unfold, this is for you. Allow me to introduce to you Sid Waddell, the silver-tongued monolith from Geordieland.

CLASSICAL SID

* "That's the greatest comeback since Lazarus."

* "When Alexander of Macedonia was 33, he cried salt tears because there were no more worlds to conquer. Bristow's only 27."

* "It's the nearest thing to public execution this side of Saudi Arabia."

* "His physiognomy is that of a weeping Madonna."

* "Eat your heart out Harold Pinter, we've got drama with a capital 'D' in Essex."

* "If we'd had Phil Taylor at Hastings against the Normans, they'd have gone home."

SURREAL SID

* "He's as cool as a prize marrow!"

* "Under that heart of stone beat muscles of pure flint."

* "You couldn't get more excitement here if Elvis Presley walked in eating a chip sandwich!"

* "He's playing out of his pie crust."

* "He looks about as happy as a penguin in a microwave."

* "Here's Baxter doing a cock-a-leekie soup job on Ovens!"

STRANGE SID

* "The pendulum swinging back and forth like a metronome."

* "His face is sagging with tension."

* "The fans now, with their eyes pierced on the dart board."

* "He's been burning the midnight oil at both ends."

* "Bristow reasons … Bristow quickens … Aaah, Bristow."

* "They won't just have to play outta their skin to beat Phil Taylor. They'll have to play outta their essence!"

ARE YOU SURE SID?

* "Darts players are probably a lot fitter than most footballers in overall body strength."

The Disabled Scouser

A bartender was washing the glasses when an elderly Irishman came in. With great difficulty, the Irishman hoisted his bad leg over the barstool, pulled himself up painfully, and asked for a sip of Irish whiskey. The Irishman then looked towards the end of the bar and said, "Is that Jesus down there?" The bartender nodded, so the Irishman told him to give Jesus an Irish whiskey, too.

The next patron to come in was an ailing Italian with a hunched back, who moved very slowly. He shuffled up to the barstool and asked for a glass of Chianti. He also looked down the bar and asked if it was Jesus sitting at the end of the bar. The bartender nodded, so the Italian said to give him a glass of Chianti, too.

The third patron to enter the bar was a Scouser, who swaggered into the bar and yelled, "Barkeep, gis us a lager dere la! Hey, is dat dat God's boy down dere?" The barkeeper nodded, so the Scouser told him to give Jesus a lager, too.

As Jesus got up to leave, he walked over to the Irishman and touched him and said, "For your kindness, you are healed!" The Irishman felt the strength come back to his leg, so he got up and danced a jig out of the door.

Jesus went up and touched the Italian and said, "For your kindness, you are healed!" The Italian then felt his back straighten, so he raised his hands above his head and did a flip out of the door.

Jesus then walked towards the Scouser, but the Scouser jumped back exclaiming,

"Don't you fucking touch me! I'm on Disability!"

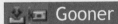 Gooner

Two boys were playing football in a north-west London park when one of them was attacked by a Rottweiler. Thinking quickly, his friend ripped a plank of wood from a fence, forced it into the dog's collar and twisted it around, breaking the dog's neck.

A newspaper reporter who was out taking a stroll saw the whole thing. He rushed over, introduced himself and took out his pad and pencil to start his story for the next edition.

He wrote, "QPR fan saves friend from vicious animal."

"But I'm not a QPR fan," said the lad.

The reporter began again, "Spurs fan saves friend from horrific attack."

"I'm not a Spurs fan either," the boy interrupted.

The reporter asked, "Who do you support then?"

"Arsenal," replied the boy. So the reporter takes his pencil and starts again,

"Gooner bastard kills family pet."

Essex Girl

An Essex girl was involved in a nasty car crash and was trapped bleeding in the wreckage. The paramedics soon arrived on site.

"It's OK," said the ambulanceman, "I'm a paramedic and I'm going to ask you some questions."

"OK," said the girl.

"What's your name?"

"Sharon."

"OK, Sharon, is this your car?"

"Yes."
"Where are you bleeding from?"

"Romford, mate."

Car Trouble

John Prescott: "My wife was driving me around last night, when the car broke down."
Tony Blair: "Puncture?"
John Prescott: "Yes, but she deserved it."

Barmy Place Names: Part III

Thong,
Three Cocks,
Three Holes,
Three Legged Cross,
Thwing,
Tiltups End,
Titterstone Clee Hill,
Tong,
Toot Baldon,
Trerulefoot,
Trumpet,
Turton Bottoms,
Twelveheads,
Ugley,
Undy,
Unthank,

Upper Dicker,
Upperthong,
Vange,
Vobster,
Warninglid,
Washaway,
Waterlooville,
Wendy,
West Curry,
Westley Waterless,
Westward Ho!,
Wetwang,
Whaplode,
Widecombe in the Moor,
Wide Open,
Willey,

Wincle,
Windrush,
Wittering,
Wombleton,

Woofferton,
Wormgay,
Wyre Piddle.

Tactics

The chancellor of Oxford University was delighted with his guest speaker for the day.

"I'm proud to announce David Beckham will today be giving a talk on the importance of tactics to the game of football, so without further ado, over to you David ..."

"Well," Becks started, "I always rely on tactics ...

"after all, they contain only two calories and keep your breath fresh all day."

Office Life

These are all allegedly true.

1. As of tomorrow, employees will only be able to access the building using individual security cards. Pictures will be taken next Wednesday and employees will receive their cards in two weeks. (Microsoft Corp.)

2. What I need is a list of specific unknown problems we will encounter. (Lykes Lines Shipping)

3. E-mail is not to be used to pass on information or data. It should be used only for company business. (Accounting manager, ElectricBoat Company)

4. This project is so important, we can't let things that are more important interfere with it. (Advertising/Marketing manager, United Parcel Service)

5. Doing it right is no excuse for not meeting the schedule. No one will believe you solved this problem in one day! We've been working on it for months. Now, go act busy for a few weeks and I'll let you know when it's time to tell them. (R&D supervisor, Minnesota Mining and Manufacturing, 3M Corp.)

9. We know that communication is a problem, but the company is not going to discuss it with the employees. (Switching supervisor, AT&T Long Lines Division)

10. This is to inform you that a memo will be issued today regarding the subject mentioned above. (Legal Affairs Division, Microsoft Corp.)

⬇ 🖳 Bullshit

Ever wonder about those people who say they are giving more than 100%? We have all been to those meetings where someone wants over 100%. How about achieving 103%? Here's a little math that might prove helpful. What makes life 100%?

If:
A B C D E F G H I J K L M N O P Q R S T U V W X Y Z is represented as:
1 2 3 4 5 6 7 8 9 10 11 12 13 14 15 16 17 18 19 20 21 22 23 24 25 26

Then,
H A R D W O R K
8 1 18 4 23 15 18 11 = 98%

K N O W L E D G E
11 14 15 23 12 5 4 7 5 = 96%

But,
A T T I T U D E
1 20 20 9 20 21 4 5 = 100%

And,
B U L L S H I T
2 21 12 12 19 8 9 20 = 103%

So, it stands to reason that hard work and knowledge will get you close, attitude will get you there, but bullshit will put you over the top.

Casual Day

>Memo 1:
Effective immediately, the company is adopting Friday as "Casual Day" so that employees may express their diversity.

>Memo 2:
Spandex and leather micro-miniskirts are not appropriate attire for Casual Day. Neither are string ties, rodeo belt buckles or moccasins.

>Memo 3:
Casual Day refers to dress only, not attitude. When planning Friday's wardrobe, remember image is a key to our success.

>Memo 4:
A seminar on how to dress for Casual Day will be held at 4.00 p.m. Friday in the cafeteria. Fashion show to follow. Attendance is mandatory.

>Memo 5:
As an outgrowth of Friday's seminar, a 14-member Casual Day Task Force has been appointed to prepare guidelines for proper dress.

>Memo 6:
The Casual Day Task Force has completed a 30-page manual. A copy of "Relaxing Dress Without Relaxing Company Standards" has been mailed to each employee. Please review the chapter "You Are What You Wear" and consult the "home casual" versus "business casual" checklist before leaving for work each Friday. If you have doubts about the appropriateness of an item of clothing, contact your CDTF representative before 7.00 a.m. on Friday.

>Memo 7:
Because of lack of participation, Casual Day has been discontinued, effective immediately.

While the Cat's Away

Top eight office activities when your boss is on the first day of his holiday:

8) "Best imitation of the boss" contest – victor wins everything in the supply room.

7) Lock-jimmying contest, immediately followed by a charity raffle of executive office furniture.

6) The battle begins for the coveted Solitaire/Minesweeper/Tetris Triple Crown.

5) Visit local nude beach for daily "staff" meeting.

4) Staple that dweeb from accounting to the wall.

3) Take pictures of his favourite coffee cup in the toilet – save for resignation day.

2) Purchasing vs. Receiving: Let's Get Ready to Rummmmblllle!

1) Convince the boss's daughter to be your intern.

Special High-Intensity Training

In order to ensure the highest levels of quality work and productivity from employees it will be our policy to keep all employees well trained through our programme of Special High-Intensity Training (S.H.I.T.).

We are trying to give our employees more S.H.I.T. than anyone else. If you feel that you do not receive your share of S.H.I.T. on the job, please see your manager. You will be immediately placed at the top of the

S.H.I.T. list, and they are especially skilled at seeing that you get all the S.H.I.T. you can handle. Employees who don't take their S.H.I.T. will be placed in Departmental Employee Evaluation Programmes (D.E.E.P. S.H.I.T.). Those who fail to take D.E.E.P. S.H.I.T. seriously will have to go to Employee Attitude Training (E.A.T. S.H.I.T.).

Since our managers took S.H.I.T. before they were promoted, they don't have to take S.H.I.T. anymore, and are full of S.H.I.T. already. If you are full of S.H.I.T. you my be interested in job training others. We can add your name to our Basic Understanding Lecture List (B.U.L.L. S.H.I.T.)

If you have further questions, please direct them to our Head of Training, Special High-Intensity Training (H.O.T. S.H.I.T.). Thank you.

Boss in General, Special High-Intensity Training (B.I.G. S.H.I.T.)

Puns, Double Meanings and Wordplay

A European Parliament spokesman has confirmed that in order to comply with the conditions for joining the single currency, the phrase "spending a penny" is not to be used after 31 December 2001.

From this date the correct terminology will be "euronating".

Each year the *Washington Post's* Style Invitational asks readers to take any word from the dictionary, alter it by adding, subtracting, or changing one letter and supply a new definition. Here are the 2001 winners:

Intaxication: Euphoria at getting a tax refund, which lasts until you realize it was your money to start with.

Reintarnation: Coming back to life as a hillbilly.

Foreploy: Any misrepresentation about yourself for the purpose of getting laid.

Giraffiti: Vandalism spray-painted very, very high.

Sarchasm: The gulf between the author of sarcastic wit and the person who doesn't get it.

Inoculatte: To take coffee intravenously when you are running late.

Hipatitis: Terminal coolness.

Osteopornosis: A degenerate disease. (This one got extra credit.)

Karmageddon: It's like, when everybody is sending off all these really bad vibes, right? And then, like, the Earth explodes and it's, like, a serious bummer.

Glibido: All talk and no action.

Dopeler Effect: The tendency of stupid ideas to seem smarter when they come at you rapidly.

Ignoranus: A person who's both stupid and an asshole.

Holes

A man, while playing on the front nine of a complicated golf course, became confused as to where he was on the course. Looking around, he saw a lady playing ahead of him. He walked up to her, explained his confusion and asked her if she knew what hole he was playing. She replied, "I'm on the seventh hole, and you are a hole behind me, so you must be on the sixth hole."

He thanked her and went back to his golf. On the back nine the same thing happened; and he approached her again with the same request. She said, "I'm on the 14th hole, you are a hole behind me, so you must be on the 13th hole."

Once again he thanked her and returned to his play. He finished his round and went to the clubhouse where he saw the same lady sitting at the end of the bar. He asked the bartender if he knew the lady. The bartender said that she was a sales lady and played the course often.

So the man approached her and said, "Let me buy you a drink in appreciation for your help. I understand that you are in the sales profession. I'm in sales, too. What do you sell?"

She replied, "If I tell you, you'll laugh."

"No, I won't."

"Well, if you must know," she answered, "I work for Tampax." With that, he laughed so hard he almost lost his breath. She said, "See, I knew you would laugh."

"That's not what I'm laughing at," he replied. "I'm a salesman for Preparation H,

"so I'm still a hole behind you."

William Tell

The world's greatest charade player bragged that he could guess any charade, so a TV producer decided to use the charade player in a TV special. He issued a challenge offering the charade player a million dollars to guess a very hard charade on television. The charade player agreed.

The big night arrived, all the world was watching. The charade player was sitting on stage in front of a curtain. Music blared and the curtain opened to reveal seven nude young women. The second and fourth ladies are holding their breasts, while the other five have their backs to him and are baring their behinds. The charade player barely glanced over them.

"The 'William Tell Overture' by Rossini," he said. The flabbergasted presenter exclaimed in awe, "You've done it! That's the right answer. You are indeed the greatest charade player!" and handed him a cheque for a million bucks.

As he was walking out, a reporter stopped the charade player and asked him how he did it.

"It's really simple," said the charade player. "One look at the positions of the seven women, and I realized it was the 'William Tell Overture' …

"Rump, titty, rump, titty, rump rump rump."

Dutch Girl

I met a Dutch girl with inflatable shoes last week, phoned her up to arrange a date but unfortunately she'd popped her clogs.

Vampire Slaying

Count Dracula was on the town on the pull. He spent the night drinking Bloody Marys in various clubs and biting on unsuspecting women's necks.

He was heading for home, wandering along the back streets sometime before sunrise, when suddenly he was hit on the back of the head. He looked round and saw nothing. He looked down and saw a small sausage roll.

"Mmmm," he thought, "what's going on here?"

He shrugged it off, and continued walking, and then wallop, right on the bonce! He looked around, but could see nothing. Then his eyes fell to the ground where lay a little prawn vol-au-vent. He peered into the darkness suspiciously, but decided to carry on regardless.

A few yards further on … bang! Smacked on the back of the head again. He whirled round – nothing! Again he looked down and there was a small triangular sandwich lying on the ground. How odd!

A few yards further along the street … crash! Smacked on the back of the head again. He turned round as quick as he could, but could see nothing. By now he was getting really angry. Again he looked down and there was a cocktail sausage lying on the ground. He stood and peered into the darkness but nothing was there.

He had walked a few yards further on, when he felt a tap on the shoulder. With a swirl of his cape and a cloud of mist, he turned as fast as he could. Suddenly he felt a sharp pain in his heart. He fell to the ground clutching his chest, which was punctured by a small cocktail stick laden with a chunk of cheese and a pickle.

As he lay on the ground dying, he looked up and saw a young female. With his dying breath, he gasped, "Who are you?", to which she replied,

"Buffet, the Vampire Slayer!"

A Dog with Three Legs

A dog with three legs walked into a western bar and said to the bartender...

"I'm looking for the man who shot my paw."

Medicated Pun No.1

A man went to his GP with a peanut stuck in his left ear.

"What can I do to get it out?" he asked pathetically.

"Pour warm chocolate in the right ear and tilt your head," replied the doctor.

"How the bloody hell will that help?"

"Easy," replied the doctor.

"When the chocolate cools it should come out a Treat."

Medicated Pun No. 2

A surgeon was performing an operation. He was about to finish when, surprisingly, the patient awoke, sat up and demanded to know what was going on.

"I'm about to close," said the surgeon.

The patient grabbed the surgeon's hand saying, "I'm not going to let you do that. I'll close my own incision." The surgeon handed him the thread saying,

"Suture self."

Glass Eye

A man who lived in a block of apartments thought it was raining and put his head out the window to check. As he did so a glass eye fell into his hand. He looked up to see where it came from in time to see a young woman looking down.

"Is this yours?" he asked. She said, "Yes, could you bring it up?" and the man agreed. On arrival she was profuse in her thanks and offered the man a drink. As she was very attractive he agreed. Shortly afterwards she said, "I'm about to have dinner. There's plenty. Would you like to join me?" He readily accepted her offer and both enjoyed a lovely meal.

As the evening was drawing to a close the lady said, "I've had a marvellous evening. Would you like to stay the night?" The man hesitated then said, "Do you act like this with every man you meet?"

"No," she replied, "only those who catch my eye."

Eight Inches

An allegedly true story from Michigan:

The day after it was supposed to have snowed and didn't, a female TV news anchor turned to the weatherman and asked,

"So Tim, where's that eight inches you promised me last night?"

Infertility

The couple left the gynaecologist's office with the wife in tears. They had just been told that she could never become pregnant. They would never have the family they both desired so fervently. Suddenly, a masked man appeared before them.

"I think I can help you," he said, handing them a card.

"Why are you masked?" the husband asked.

"Because the government has declared our activities illegal. Go to the address on this card. The doctor will take a scraping from your mouth and culture it. In less than a year, we will have your baby for you." Turning to her husband, the wife exclaimed, "This is the answer to our prayers!" Then she turned back to thank the stranger but he was gone.

"Who was that masked man?" she asked her husband. He replied,

"Why, that was … the Clone Arranger."

Today's Stock Market Report

Helium was up.
Paper was stationary.
Fluorescent tubing was dimmed in light trading.
Knives were up sharply.
Cows steered into a bull market.
Pencils lost a few points.
Hiking equipment was trailing.
Elevators rose, while escalators continued their slow decline.
Weights were up in heavy trading.
Light switches were off.
Mining equipment hit rock bottom.

Diapers remained unchanged.
Shipping lines stayed at an even keel.
The market for raisins dried up.
Coca Cola fizzled.
Caterpillar stock inched up a bit.
Sun peaked at midday.
Balloon prices were inflated.
Scott Tissue touched a new bottom.
And batteries exploded in an attempt to recharge the market.

Family Affairs

Many, many years ago,
When I was twenty-three,
I got married to a widow,
Pretty as could be.

This widow had a grown-up daughter
With flowing hair of red.
My father fell in love with her,
And soon the two were wed.

This made my dad my son-in-law
And changed my very life.
Now my daughter was my mother,
For she was my father's wife.

To complicate the matters worse,
Although it brought me joy,
I soon became the father
Of a bouncing baby boy.

My little baby then became
A brother-in-law to dad.
And so became my uncle,
Though it made me very sad.

For if he was my uncle,
Then that also made him brother
To the widow's grown-up-daughter
Who, of course, was my step-mother.

Father's wife then had a son,
Who kept them on the run.
And he became my grandson,
For he was my daughter's son.

My wife is now my mother's mother
And it makes me blue.
Because, although she is my wife,
She is my grandma too.

If my wife is my grandmother,
Then I am her grandchild.
And every time I think of it,
It simply drives me wild.

For now I have become
The strangest case you ever saw.
As the husband of my grandmother,
I am my own grandpa!

At the Doctor's

A man walked into a doctor's office. He had a cucumber up his nose, a carrot in his left ear and a banana in his right ear.

"So Doc, what do you think is the matter with me?" he asked. The doctor replied,

"You're not eating properly."

The Almost Intelligent Horse

A bunch of Indians captured a cowboy and brought him back to their camp to meet the chief. The chief said to the cowboy, "You going to die. But we sorry for you, so give you one wish a day for three days. On sundown of third day, you die. What is first wish?" The cowboy thought for a moment and then responded, "I want to see my horse." The Indians fetched his horse. The cowboy grabbed the horse's ear and whispered something, then slapped the horse on the ass. The horse took off.

Two hours later, the horse comes back with a naked blonde. She jumped off the horse and went into the teepee with the cowboy. The Indians looked at each other, figuring, "Typical white man – can only think of one thing."

The second day, the chief asked, "What your wish today?" The cowboy said, "I want to see my horse again." The Indians brought him his horse. The cowboy leant over to the horse and whispered something in the horse's ear, then slapped it on the ass.

Two hours later, the horse came back with a naked redhead. She got off and went into the teepee with the cowboy. The Indians shook their heads, figuring, "Typical white man – going to die tomorrow and can only think of one thing."

The last day came, and the chief said, "This your last wish, white man. What you want?" The cowboy said, "I want to see my horse again." So the Indians brought him his horse. The cowboy grabbed the horse by both ears, twisted them hard and yelled,

"Read my lips! POSSE, damnit! P-O-S-S-E!"

Read Marx?

There were two old men, one a retired professor of psychology and the other a retired professor of history. Their wives had talked them into a two-week stay at a hotel in the Catskills. They were sitting around on the porch of the hotel watching the sun set. The history professor said to the psychology professor, "Have you read Marx?" To which the professor of psychology replied,

"Yes, I think it's the wicker chairs!"

Valley Girl Pun

Q: What do you call a Valley Girl with one leg shorter than the other?
A: Like, not even!

How to Stop Choking

Two men from Texas were sitting at a bar, when a young lady nearby began to choke on a hamburger. She gasped and gagged, and one Texan turned to the other and said, "That little gal is havin' a bad time. I'm agonna go over there and help."

He ran over to the young lady, held both sides of her head in his big Texan hands, and asked, "Kin ya swaller?" Gasping, she shook her head no. He asked, "Kin ya breathe?" Still gasping, she again shook her head no. With that, he yanked up her skirt, pulled down her panties and licked her on the butt. The young woman was so shocked that she coughed up the piece of hamburger and began to breathe on her own. The Texan sat back down with his friend and said,

"Ya know, it's sure amazin' how that hind-lick manoeuvre always works."

In Heaven

Queen Elizabeth and Dolly Parton died on the same day, and they both went before St Peter to find out if they would be admitted to heaven. Unfortunately, there was only one space left that day, so St Peter had to decide which of them would get in. St Peter asked Dolly if there was some particular reason why she should go to heaven, so she took off her top.

"Look at these," she said, displaying her breasts. "They're the most perfect ones God ever created, and I'm sure it will please him to be able to see them every day for eternity." St Peter thanked Dolly, and asked Queen Liz the same question.

Elizabeth dropped her skirt and panties, took a bottle of Perrier out of her purse, shook it up, and proceeded to douche with it. St Peter conceded, "OK, your Majesty, you may go in."

Dolly was outraged and screamed, "What was that all about? I show you two of God's own creations, she performs a disgusting hygiene act, and gets in and I don't?!!!"

"Sorry, Dolly," said St Peter, "but a royal flush beats a pair any day."

📥🖥 In a Bar

>Four fonts walked into a bar. The barman said, "Oi – get out! We don't want your type in here."

>Two peanuts walk into a bar. One was a salted.

>A pair of jump-leads walk into a bar. The barman says, "I'll serve you, but don't start anything."

>A priest, a rabbi and a vicar walk into a bar. The barman says, "Is this some kind of joke?"

>A woman walks into a bar and asks the barman for a double entendre. So he gives her one.

>A dyslexic man walks into a bra …

📥🖥 Justin the Prawn

Far away, in the tropical waters of the Caribbean, two prawns were swimming around in the sea – one called Justin and the other Christian. The prawns were constantly being harassed and threatened by sharks who patrolled the area.

Finally, during a tropical storm, Justin said to Christian, "I'm bored and frustrated at being a prawn, I wish I was a shark, then I wouldn't have any worries about being eaten."

As Justin had his mind firmly on becoming a predator, a flash of lightning hit the water and, lo and behold, Justin turned into a shark. Shocked and horrified, Christian immediately swam away, afraid of being eaten by his old mate.

Time went by (as it invariably does) and Justin found himself becoming bored and lonely as a shark. All his old mates simply swam away whenever he came close. Justin finally realized that his new menacing appearance was the cause of his sad plight.

During the next tropical storm, Justin figured that the same lightning force could change him back into a prawn. Lightning never strikes twice except in stories like these, but while he was thinking of being a prawn, a flash of lightning struck the water next to Justin and, lo and behold, he turned back into prawn.

With tears of joy in his tiny little eyes, Justin swam back to his friends and bought them all a cocktail. (The punch line does not involve a prawn cocktail … it's much worse.) Looking around the gathering at the reef, he searched for his old pal.

"Where's Christian?" he asked.

"He's at home, distraught that his best friend changed sides to the enemy and became a shark," came the reply.

Eager to put things right again and end the mutual pain and torture, he set off to Christian's house. As he opened the coral gate, the memories came flooding back. He banged on the door and shouted, "It's me, Justin, your old friend, come out and see me again."

Christian replied, "No way, man, you'll eat me. You're a shark, the enemy, and I'll not be tricked."

Justin cried back, "No I'm not. That was the old me. I've changed …

"I'm a prawn again, Christian."

The Speaking Clock

Following a night out, a man brought a few friends back to show off his new flat. After the grand tour, the visitors were rather perplexed by the large gong taking pride of place in the lounge.

"What's that big brass gong for?" one of the guests asked.

"Why, that's my speaking clock," the man replied.

"How does it work?"

"I'll show you," the man said, giving the gong an ear-shattering blow with an unpadded hammer. Suddenly, a voice from the other side of the wall screamed,

"For fuck's sake, you bastard, it's twenty to two in the fucking morning!!"

The Pepsi Salesman

A Pepsi salesman went missing out in the jungles far, far away and was gone for a long time. The office back home started to get worried about him, so they sent out a big search party to look for him. The search party trekked around for a couple of days, and eventually found a trail of Pepsi cans. They asked one of the natives in the next village if he had seen the guy who had all of these cans.

"Oh, yes, we ate him," the native said.

"What do you mean, you ate him? You ate all of him?"

"Yes, we ate him all up."

"Like everything? You ate all of him? You ate his arms and legs?"

"Yes."

"You ate his head, and his stomach?"

"Yes."

"What about his … thing, did you eat that too?"

"Nope, we didn't eat his thing …

"Things go better with Coke."

Religion

One fine day in Ireland, a guy was out golfing and got up to the 16th hole. He teed up and cranked one. Unfortunately, it went into the woods on the side of the fairway. He went looking for his ball and came across a little guy with a huge bump on his head and a golf ball lying right beside him.

"Goodness," said the golfer, as he proceeded to revive the poor little guy.

Upon awakening, the little guy said, "Well, you caught me fair and square. I am a leprechaun. I will grant you three wishes."

"I can't take anything from you," said the man. "I'm just glad I didn't hurt you too badly," and walked away. Watching the golfer depart, the leprechaun said, "Well, he was a nice enough guy, and he did catch me, so I have to do something for him. I'll give him the three things that I would want. I'll give him unlimited money, a great golf game, and a great sex life."

Well, a year went past and the same golfer was out golfing on the same course at the 16th hole. He teed off and hit the ball into the same woods and went off looking for his ball. When he found the ball he saw the same little guy and asked how he was doing.

"I'm fine," said the leprechaun, "and might I ask how's your golf game?"

"It's great!" the golfer replied. "I hit under par every time."

"I did that for you," said the leprechaun. "And might I ask how your money is holding out?"

"Well, now that you mention it, every time I put my hand in my pocket, I pull out a 100-dollar bill" he replied. The leprechaun smiled and said, "I did that for you. And might I ask how is your sex life?"

Now the golfer looked at him a little shyly and said, "Well, maybe once or twice a week."

"Once or twice a week?" stammered the leprechaun, floored. The golfer looked at him sheepishly and said,

"Well, that's not too bad for a Catholic priest in a small parish."

At the Pearly Gates

A guy arrived at the pearly gates, waiting to be admitted. St Peter read through the Big Book to see if the guy's name was written in it.

After several minutes, St Peter closed the book, furrowed his brow, and said, "I'm sorry, I don't see your name written in the Book."

"How current is your copy?" the guy asked.

"I get a download every ten minutes," St Peter replied. "Why do you ask?"

"I'm embarrassed to admit it," said the guy, "but I was always the stubborn type. It wasn't until my death was imminent that I cried out to God, so my name probably hasn't arrived in your copy yet."

"I'm glad to hear that," St Peter said, "but while we're waiting for the update to come through, can tell me about a really good deed that you did in your life?"

The guy thought for a moment and said, "Hmm, well there was this one time when I was driving down a road and I saw a giant group of biker gang members harassing this poor girl. I slowed down, and sure enough, there they were, about 20 of them torturing this poor woman. Infuriated, I got out of my car, grabbed a tyre iron out of my trunk, and walked up to the leader of the gang. He was a huge guy: 6' 4", 260 pounds, with a studded leather jacket and a chain running from his nose to his ears. As I walked up to the leader, the bikers formed a circle around me and told me to get lost or I'd be next.

"So I ripped the leader's chain out of his face and smashed him over the head with the tyre iron. Then I turned around and yelled to the rest of them, 'Leave this poor innocent girl alone! You're all a bunch of SICK, deranged animals! Go home before I really teach you a lesson in PAIN!'" St. Peter, duly impressed, says, "Wow! When did this happen?"

"About three minutes ago."

Golfing Nuns

A nun sat with her Mother Superior chatting.

"I used some horrible language this week and feel absolutely terrible about it."

"When did you use this awful language?" asked the elder.

"Well, I was golfing and hit an incredible drive that looked like it was going to go over 280 yards, but it struck a phone line that was hanging over the fairway and fell straight down to the ground after going only about 10 yards."

"Is that when you swore?"

"No, Mother," said the nun. "After that, a squirrel ran out of the bushes and grabbed my ball in its mouth and began to run away."

"Is THAT when you swore?" asks the Mother Superior again.

"Well, no," says the nun. "You see, as the squirrel was running, an eagle came down out of the sky, grabbed the squirrel in his talons and began to fly away!"

"Is THAT when you swore?" asks the amazed elder nun.

"No, not yet. As the eagle carried the squirrel away in its claws, it flew near the green and the squirrel dropped my ball."

"Did you swear THEN?" asked Mother Superior, becoming impatient.

"No, because the ball fell on a big rock, bounced over the sand trap, rolled onto the green, and stopped about six inches from the hole." The two nuns were silent for a moment. Then Mother Superior sighed and said,

"You missed the fucking putt, didn't you?"

That Was Then, This Is Now

Jesus and Moses were hanging out one afternoon by a lake, reminiscing about the good ol' days. Moses walked over to the water's edge, gestured with his arms and shouted, "Part!" As the water rolled back on itself, creating a path across the lake, Moses turned to Jesus and said, "Hey, I still got it!" He walked back towards Jesus, with the waters settling back into place behind him.

Not to be outdone, Jesus proceeded to the water's edge then stepped out across the water, but almost immediately began to sink. Perplexed, he returned to dry ground. Moses suggested he try it again; after all, why should the son of God lose his ability to walk on water? Jesus tried several more times, each time ending in wet, angry failure. Finally he returned to Moses and flopped down on the ground next to him.

After several moments of silently watching Jesus fuming and muttering to himself, Moses worked up the courage to ask, "Wait a second …

"did you ALWAYS have those holes in your feet?"

Delusions of Grandeur

Moses and Jesus were on a short par four with a large water hazard right in front of the green.

"You ought to lay up here," said Moses to Jesus.

"No way. I'm gonna drive the green just like Tiger Woods."

Jesus teed up and swung with his driver. The ball fell into the water hazard. Moses ran down, parted the water and retrieved Jesus's ball.

"Take a mulligan and lay up this time," Moses said.

"Nope," said Jesus. "Gonna drive the green just like Tiger." Another drive landed in the water. Moses retrieved it just as before.

"I'm not gonna get your ball again. Lay up!" said Moses.

"Nope. Gonna drive the green. Just like Tiger Woods," replied Jesus. Sure enough, his drive landed in the water. Moses refused to get his ball for the third time, so Jesus ran down, walked out on the water, reached down and retrieved his ball.

By this time the next foursome had arrived at the tee and they saw Jesus walking on the water.

"Wow!" said one of the golfers. "Does that guy think he's Jesus Christ?"

"Nope," replied Moses. "He thinks he's Tiger fuckin' Woods!"

The Girls' Prayer

Our men's cash
Which art on plastic
Hallowed be thy name
Thy Cartier watch
Thy Prada bag
In Harrods as it is in Selfridges
Give us each day our Platinum Visa
And forgive us our overdraft
As we forgive those who stop our MasterCard
And lead us not into Next
And deliver us from Benetton

For mine is the Cartier, the Dior and the Armani
For Chanel No 5 and Eternity
Amex.

The Boys' Prayer

Our beer
Which art in bottles
Hallowed be thy sport
Thy will be drunk
I will be drunk
At home as it is in the pub
Give us each day our daily beverage
And forgive us our spillage
As we forgive those who spillest against us
And lead us not into poofy wine tasting
And deliver us from tequila
For mine is the bitter, the chicks and the footy
Forever and ever
Barmen.

The Power of Prayer

A journalist assigned to the Jerusalem bureau took an apartment over-looking the historic Wailing Wall. Every day when she looked out, she saw an old bearded Jewish man praying vigorously. Certain he would be a good interview subject, the journalist went down to the Wall and introduced herself to the old man.

She asks, "You come every day to the Wall, sir. How long have you been doing that and what are you praying for?"

"I have come here to pray every day for 25 years," the old man replied. "In the morning I pray for world peace and for the brotherhood of man. I go home, have a cup of tea, and I come back and pray for the eradication of illness and disease from the earth. And very, very important: I pray for peace and understanding between the Israelis and Palestinians."

The journalist was very impressed. "How does it make you feel to come here every day for 25 years and pray for these wonderful things?" she asked. The old man replied calmly,

"Like I'm talking to a wall."

The Number of the Beast

666 Number of the Beast
DCLXVI Roman Numeral of the Beast
666.0000 Number of the High-Precision Beast
0.666 Number of the Millibeast
/666 Beast Common Denominator
(-666) ^ (1/2) Imaginary Number of the Beast
1010011010 Binary of the Beast
0666 Dialling Code of the Beast
00666 Zip Code of the Beast
£665.95 Retail Price of the Beast
£782.49 Price of the Beast plus VAT
Phillips 666 Petrol of the Beast
M666 Way of the Beast
666F Oven Temperature for Roast Beast
666k Retirement Plan of the Beast
666 mg Recommended Minimum Daily Requirement of Beast
6.66% Five-Year CD Interest Rate at Royal Beast of Hell National Bank
(£666 minimum deposit)

Lotus 6-6-6 Spreadsheet of the Beast
Word 6.66 Word Processor of the Beast
i66686 CPU of the Beast
666i BMW of the Beast
DSM-666 (revised) Diagnostic and Statistical Manual of the Beast
668 Next-Door Neighbour of the Beast
333 The Semi-Christ

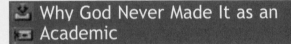

Why God Never Made It as an Academic

1. He had only one major publication.

2. It was in Hebrew.

3. It had no references.

4. It wasn't published in a referee journal.

5. Some even doubt he wrote it himself.

6. It may be true that he created the world, but what has he done since then?

7. His cooperative efforts have been quite limited.

8. The scientific community has a hard time replicating his results.

9. He never applied to the Ethics Board for permission to use human subjects.

10. When one experiment went awry he tried to cover it up by drowning his subjects.

11. When subjects didn't behave as predicted he deleted them from the sample.

12. He rarely came to class, just told students to read the Book.

13. Some say he had his son teach the class.

14. He expelled his first two students for learning.

15. Although there are only ten requirements, most students failed his test.

16. His office hours were infrequent and usually held on a mountain top.

Results Count ...

A minister died and went to heaven. Before him in the queue to see St Peter was a loudmouth man with a loud shirt, chain pants, and a loud hat. St Peter asked the guy what he had done for a living.

The man said, "I was a taxi cab driver in Noo Yawk city." St Peter handed him a silk robe, and a golden staff.

Next up was the minister. St Peter asked him what he had done for a living. He stood up very straight, and spoke in a loud, clear voice, "I am John C. Maxwell, bishop of St Mary's Church." St Peter handed him a cotton robe, and a regular staff.

"What?" said the bishop. "You let that taxi cab driver have a silk robe and golden staff but not me?"

St Peter replied, "Up here we work by results ...

"While you preached, people slept, while he drove, people prayed."

Sex, Lays and Duct Tape

All in the Name of Art

Jerry was hired to play his trumpet on the score of a movie, and he was excited. He was especially thrilled because he got to perform two long solos.

After the sessions, which went wonderfully, Jerry couldn't wait to see the finished product. He asked the producer where and when he could catch the film. A little embarrassed, the producer explained that the music was for a porno flick that would be out in a month, and he told Jerry where he could go to see it.

A month later, Jerry, with his collar up and wearing a false beard and glasses, went to the theatre where the picture was playing. He walked in and sat way in the back, next to an elderly couple who also seemed to be disguised and hiding.

The movie started, and it was the filthiest, most perverse porno flick ever … straight fucking, facials, S&M, anal, golden showers, fisting, sandwiches, two-in-a-hole, deep throat, the lot … and then, halfway through, a dog got in on the action.

Before anyone could blink an eye, the dog had sex with all the women, in every orifice, and most of the men. Embarrassed, Jerry turned to the old couple and whispered, "I'm only here for the music." The woman turned to Jerry and whispered back,

"That's okay, we're just here to see our dog."

Big Dick

A man was sitting at home with his wife. He said to her, "You know, I was thinking of going down to the bar tonight and entering that big dick contest."

"Oh honey," she exclaimed, "I don't want you taking that out in public!"

"But sweet thing," he said, "the prize is $100."

"I don't care," she said. "I don't want you showing that thing to everybody."

So he let the subject drop until the following night when his wife walked in on him in the bedroom, counting out a hundred dollars.

"Did you go down and enter that big dick contest last night after I told you not to?" she asked.

"Please forgive me, sweetheart." he said.

"You mean you took that thing out for everybody to see?" she asked, tears welling up in her eyes. The man looks at her fondly and said,

"Only enough to win."

Makes You Sick

A man went to a travel agent and booked a two-week cruise for himself and his girlfriend. A couple of days before the cruise, the travel agent called and said the cruise has been cancelled, but he could get them on a three-day cruise instead. The man accepted and in preparation for his holiday went to the chemist to buy three Dramamine and three condoms.

Next day, the agent called back and said that some space had been freed up and he could now book a five-day cruise. The man was pleased and accepted the change. Later that day he returned to the pharmacy and bought two more Dramamine and two more condoms.

The following day, the travel agent called again and said owing to last-minute cancellations he could now book an eight-day cruise. Again the man agreed and went back to the drugstore and asked for three more Dramamine and three more condoms. Overcome by curiosity and compassion the chemist finally felt compelled to ask,

"Look, if it makes you sick, how come you keep doing it?"

Postman Pat

It was Postman Pat's last day on the job after 35 years of carrying the post through all kinds of weather to the same houses in Greendale.

When he arrived at the first house on his route, he was greeted by the whole family there, who all hugged and congratulated him and sent him on his way with a gift cheque for £500.

At the second house they presented him with ten fine Cuban cigars in an 18-carat-gold box.

The folks at the third house handed him a case of 30-year-old single malt whisky.

At the fourth house he was met at the door by a blonde lady in her lingerie. She took him by the arm and led him up the stairs to the bedroom where she blew his mind with the most passionate love he had ever experienced.

When he had had enough they went downstairs, where she made him a giant breakfast: eggs, tomatoes, bacon, sausage, black pudding, mushrooms, toast and freshly squeezed orange juice. When he was truly satisfied, she poured him a cup of steaming coffee.

As she was pouring, he noticed a £5 note sticking out from under the cup's bottom edge.

"All this was just too wonderful for words," he said, "but what's the fiver for?"

"Well," said the blonde, "last night, I told my husband that today would be your last day, and that we should do something special for you. I asked him what to give you.

"He said, 'F**k him. Give him a fiver.' ... The breakfast was my idea."

Goodyear

Q: What's the difference between an airship and 365 blow jobs?
A: One's a Goodyear the other's an excellent year.

Newlyweds

Three couples got married on the same day and had their wedding night in the same hotel. All three couples went up to bed early (for whatever reason).

At 11.00 p.m., the barman was about to shut up the hotel bar when one of the grooms walked in and said, "A large whisky please."

"What's up – you look like you've had quite a shock?"

"Well, I come from a strict background and I had never seen my wife's breasts until this evening – they are huge! When I pointed this out to my wife she went mad and kicked me out the room!"

"That's tough pal. The whisky is on the house!"

A few minutes later, the second groom walked in and said, "A large whisky please."

"What's up – you look like you've had quite a shock too?"

"Well, I come from a strict background and I had never seen my wife's bottom until this evening – it's enormous! When I pointed this out to my wife she went mad and kicked me out the room!"

"That's tough too, pal. The whisky is on the house!"

A few minutes later the third groom walked in, looking really shocked.

The barman said, "Don't tell me – you've put your foot in it too?"

"No, but I could have done!"

Viagra for Sunburn

A doctor was making his rounds in the hospital when he came upon a guy with the worst case of sunburn he had ever seen. The poor guy was burnt raw from head to toe and was in agony. He turned to the doctor and said, "Is there anything you can give me to ease this terrible pain?"

"Yes, I'll prescribe you some Viagra," said the doctor.

"Viagra?" said the poor guy. "How will that help my sunburn?"

"It won't help your sunburn much," replied the doctor,

"but at least it'll keep the sheets off it!"

Bad News, Good News

Sherry the secretary walked into her boss's office and said, "I'm afraid I've got some bad news for you."

"Sherry honey, why do you always have to give me bad news?" he complained. "Tell me some good news for once."

"Alright, here's some good news," said the secretary.

"You're not sterile."

Chinese Torture

A young man was wandering lost in a forest when he came upon a small house. He knocked on the door and was greeted by an old Chinese man with a long grey beard.

"I'm lost," said the man. "Can you put me up for the night?"

"Certainly," the Chinese man said. "But on one condition. If you so much as lay a finger on my daughter I will inflict upon you the three worst Chinese tortures known to man." The man agreed, thinking that the daughter must be pretty old as well, and entered the house.

Over dinner the daughter came down the stairs. She was young, beautiful and had a fantastic body. She was obviously attracted to the young man as well, as she couldn't keep her eyes off of him during the meal. Remembering the old man's warning he ignored her and went up to bed alone.

During the night he could bear it no longer and snuck into her room for a night of passion. Near dawn, he quietly crept back to his room so the old man wouldn't hear, exhausted but happy.

He woke to feel a pressure on his chest. Opening his eyes he saw a large rock on his chest with a note on it that read: "Chinese Torture 1: Large rock on chest."

"Well, that's easy," he thought. "If that's the best the old man can do then I don't have much to worry about." He picked the boulder up, walked over to the window and threw it out. As he did so, he noticed another note on it that read: "Chinese Torture 2: Rock tied to left testicle."

In a panic he glanced down and saw that the rope was already getting close to taut. Figuring that a few broken bones were better than castration, he jumped out of the window after the boulder. As he plummeted toward the ground he saw a large sign on the ground that read:

"Chinese Torture 3: Right testicle tied to bed post."

 Fine Art

As Titian was mixing Rose Madder
His model reclined on a ladder.
Her position to Titian suggested coition
So her leapt up the ladder and had 'er.

Persons of Restricted Growth

Two dwarves decided to treat themselves to a vacation in the big city. At the hotel bar, they were dazzled by two hookers, and wound up taking them to their separate rooms. The first dwarf remained frustrated, however, as he was unable to achieve an erection. His depression was enhanced by the fact that, from the next room, he heard cries of, "ONE, TWO, THREE … HUH!" all night long.

In the morning, the second dwarf asked the first, "How did it go?"

"It was so embarrassing," whispered the first, "I simply couldn't get an erection."

"You think that's embarrassing?" the second dwarf said, shaking his head,

"I couldn't even get on the bed!"

Sexercise

It has been known for many years that sex is good exercise, but until recently nobody had made a scientific study of the caloric expenditure of different sexual activities. Now after original and proprietary research we are proud to present the results.

REMOVING HER CLOTHES:

With her consent	12 calories
Without her consent	187 calories

UNDOING HER BRA:

With both hands	8 calories
With one hand	12 calories
With your teeth	85 calories

PUTTING ON A CONDOM:

With an erection	6 calories
Without an erection	315 calories

PRELIMINARIES:

Trying to find the clitoris	8 calories
Trying to find the G-spot	92 calories

POSITIONS:

Missionary	12 calories
69 lying down	78 calories
69 standing up	112 calories
Wheelbarrow	216 calories
Doggy style	326 calories
Italian chandelier	912 calories

ORGASM:

Real	112 calories
False	315 calories

POST ORGASM:

Lying in bed hugging	18 calories
Getting up immediately	36 calories
Explaining why you got out of bed immediately	816 calories

GETTING A SECOND ERECTION: If you are

20–29 years old	36 calories
30–39 years	80 calories
40–49 years	124 calories
50–59 years	972 calories
60–69 years	2916 calories
70 and over	Results still pending

GETTING DRESSED AFTERWARDS:

Calmly	32 calories
In a hurry	98 calories
With her father knocking at the door	1218 calories
With your wife knocking at the door	3521 calories

Sick Guy

A guy started a new job on a Thursday. On Monday he called in and said, "I can't come in today. I'm sick." He worked the rest of the week, but the following Monday he called in again and said, "I can't come in today. I'm sick."

The boss asked the foreman about him, and the foreman said, "He's great. He does the work of two men. We need him."

So the boss called the guy into his office, and said, "You seem to have a problem getting to work on Mondays. You're a good worker and I'd hate to fire you. What's the problem? Anything we can help you with? Drugs? Alcohol?"

"No, I don't drink or do drugs," said the guy. "But my brother-in-law drinks every weekend, and then beats up my sister. So every Monday morning, I go over to make sure she's all right. She puts her head on my shoulder and cries, one thing leads to another, and the next thing you know, I'm screwing her."

"You screw your sister?!" asked the boss disgusted. The guy replied,

"Hey, I told you I was sick."

Always Let Your Conscience Be Your Guide

Dave had felt guilty all day long, no matter how much he tried to forget about it, he couldn't. The guilt and sense of betrayal were overwhelming. But every once in a while he'd hear that soothing voice trying to reassure him,

"Dave, don't worry about it. You weren't the first doctor to sleep with one of your patients and you won't be the last. And you're single. Let it go!"

But invariably the other voice would bring him back to reality,

"Dave, you're a vet."

Charging for It

A boy and his date were parked on a back road some distance from town, doing what boys and girls do on back roads some distance from town, when the girl stopped the boy.

"I really should have mentioned this earlier, but I'm actually a hooker and I charge $20 for sex." The boy reluctantly paid her, and they did their thing.

After a cigarette, the boy just sat in the driver's seat looking out the window. "Why aren't we going anywhere?" asked the girl.

"Well, I should have mentioned this before, but I'm actually a taxi driver,

"and the fare back to town is $25."

Worn-Out Squaw

Every time an Indian walked into the chief's teepee he found the chief masturbating. The tribe finally realized this was a serious problem, so they fixed him up with a nice woman, and she started living with him in his teepee.

One day, one of the Indians walked into to the chief's teepee and there was the chief masturbating again. He says, "Chief, what are you doing? We fix you up with a beautiful woman." The chief replied,

"Her arm get tired."

The 25 Lessons of Porn

1. Women wear high heels to bed.

2. Women have naturally trimmed pubic hair.

3. Women always look pleasantly surprised when they open a man's trousers and find a cock there.

4. If a woman is discovered masturbating by a strange man, she will not scream with embarrassment, but rather insist he have sex with her.

5. Watching a man masturbate always gives a woman an orgasm.

6. When going down on a woman, ten seconds is more than satisfactory.

7. Women moan uncontrollably when giving a blow job.

8. Men always pull out before they ejaculate.

9. Women smile appreciatively when men splat sperm in their face/tits/hair/vicinity.

10. Young, attractive women always enjoy having sex with ugly, middle-aged men.

11. Men always groan "OH YEAH" when they come.

12. Assholes are clean, and capable of orgasm.

13. When taking a woman from behind, a man can really excite her by slapping her butt.

14. A common and enjoyable sexual practice for a man is to take his half-erect penis and slap it repeatedly on a woman's butt/tits/face/feet.

15. Women always say "Fuck me" when they are being fucked.

16. Double penetration makes a woman smile.

17. If there are two men they will "high five" each other (and the girl won't be disgusted).

18. If you come across a guy and his girlfriend having sex in the bushes, the boyfriend won't knock the shit out of you if you shove your cock in his girlfriend's mouth.

19. When your girlfriend bursts in on you while you are are fucking her best friend, she'll only be momentarily pissed off before fucking both of you.

20. Mixed-sex swimming always leads to sex.

21. Nurses suck patients' cocks.

22. A blow job will always get a woman off a speeding ticket.

23. All male teachers get to fuck their most attractive female pupils.

24. All window cleaners get to screw their attractive female clients.

25. All Swedish people exist in a permanent state of sexual arousal.

🔽 💾 You Finish?

A virile young Italian soldier was relaxing at his favourite bar in Rome, when he managed to attract a spectacular young blonde. Things progressed to the point where he invited her back to his apartment and, after some small talk, they had sex.

After a pleasant interlude, he asked with a smile, "So ... you finish?" She paused for a second, frowned, and replied, "No."

Surprised, the young man reached for her; and the fucking resumed. This time, she thrashed about wildly, and there were screams of passion. The sex ended, and again, the young man smiled, and asked, "You finish?" And again, after a short pause, she returned his smile, cuddled closer to him, and softly said, "No."

Stunned, but damned if this woman was going to outlast him, the young man reached for the woman. Using the last of his strength, he barely managed it; but they climaxed simultaneously, screaming, bucking, clawing and ripping bed sheets.

The exhausted man fell onto his back, gasping. Barely able to turn his head, he looked into her eyes, smiled proudly, and asked, "You finish?"

"No!" she smiled back,

"I Sveedish!"

🔽 💾 "Clinton's Excuse", by Dr Seuss

I did not do it in a car
I did not do it in a bar
I did not do it in the dark
I did not do it in the park
I did not do it on a date

I did not ever fornicate
I did not do it at a dance
I did not do it in her pants
I did not get beyond first base
I did not do it in her face
I never did it in a bed
If you think that, you've been misled
I did not do it with a groan
I did not do it on the phone
I did not cause her dress to stain
I never boinked Saddam Hussein
I did not do it with a whip
I never fondled Linda Tripp
I never acted really silly
With volunteers like Kathleen Willey
There was one time, with Margaret Thatcher
I chased her 'round, but could not catch her
No kinky stuff, not on your life
I wouldn't, not even with my wife
And Gennifer Flowers' tale of woes
Was paid for by my right-wing foes
And Paula Jones, and those state troopers
Are just a bunch of party poopers
I did not ask my friends to lie
I did not hang them out to dry
I did not do it last November
But if I did, I don't remember
I did not do it in the hall
I could have, but I don't recall
I never did it in my study
I never did it with my dog, Buddy
I never did it to Sox, the cat

I might have once with Arafat
I never did it in a hurry
I never groped Ms Betty Currie
There was no sex at Arlington
There was no sex on Air Force One
I might have copped a little feel
And then endeavoured to conceal
But never did these things so lewd
At least, not ever in the nude
These things to which I have confessed
They do not count, if we stayed dressed
It never happened with cigar
I never dated Mrs Starr
I did not know this little sin
Would be retold on CNN
I broke some rules my Mama taught me
I tried to hide, but now you've caught me
But I implore, I do beseech
Do not condemn, do not impeach
I might have got a little tail
But never, never did I inhale.

The Carefully Nurtured Virgin

A man longed to wed a maiden with her virtue intact. He searched high and low for one but eventually resigned himself to the fact that every female over the age of ten in his town had been at it.

Finally he decided to take matters in hand and adopted a baby girl from the orphanage. He raised her until she was walking and talking and then sent her away to a monastery for safe keeping until marrying age. After many years she finally reached maturity and he retrieved her from the monastery and married her.

After the wedding they made their way back to his house and into the bedroom where they both prepared themselves for the consummation. They lay down together in his bed and he reached over for a jar of petroleum jelly.

"Why the jelly?" she asked him.

"So I do not hurt your most delicate parts during the act of love-making," he replied.

"But why don't you just spit on your cock like the monks did?"

Monica's Love Handles

The *Globe* reported today that Monica Lewinsky recently went to a plastic surgeon. Stung by all the jokes about being overweight, she was thinking about having her love handles removed. However, she decided not to go through with it after the doctor told her that removing both ears would cause complete and total deafness.

Good Heavens, Another Monica Dress Joke

Monica Lewinsky went in to a dry cleaners where a hard-of-hearing clerk had his back to her.

"I need to have this dress cleaned."

"Come again?" he said.

"No, mustard!"

Animals' Orgasms

A farmer and his wife were lying in bed one evening; she was knitting, he was reading the latest issue of *Animal Husbandry*. Eventually he looked up from the page and said to her, "Did you know that humans are the only species in which the female achieves orgasm?" She looked at him wistfully, smiled, and replied, "Oh yeah? Why don't you prove it." He frowned for a moment, then said, "Okay." He got up and walked out, leaving his wife with a confused look on her face.

About a half an hour later, he returned all tired and sweaty and proclaimed,

"Well, I'm sure the cow and sheep didn't, but the way that pig's always squealing, how can you tell?"

Somewhere Down There

A lady heard that the local drugstore was now featuring a mind-reading druggist. She couldn't believe it, so she went down to the store, and there was a sign, right in the window, "Mind-reading druggist."

She walked in, and the druggist said to her, "You're here for suppositories."

"Nope, I'm here for tampons," she replied.

"Hey, didn't miss it by much did I?"

Monkey Business

A police officer came upon a terrible wreck where the driver and passenger had been killed. As he looked upon the wreckage a little monkey came out of the brush and hopped around the crashed car. The officer looked down at the monkey and said, "I wish you could talk." The monkey looked up at the officer and shook his head up and down.

"You can understand what I'm saying?" asked the officer. Again, the monkey shook his head up and down.

"Well, did you see this?"

"Yes," motioned the monkey.

"What happened?" The monkey pretended to have a can in his hand and turned it up by his mouth.

"They were drinking?" asked the officer.

"Yes!" the monkey motioned.

"What else?" The monkey pinched his fingers together and held them to his mouth.

"They were smoking marijuana?"

"Yes," the monkey confirmed.

"What else?" The monkey motioned "Screwing."

"They were screwing, too?" asked the astounded officer.

"Yes."

"Now wait, you're saying your owners were drinking, smoking and screwing before they wrecked."

"Yes."

"What were you doing during all this?"

"Driving," motioned the monkey.

Hank's Beard

Best friends, Vinnie and Hank, were in their local bar one night, having a few drinks. All of a sudden Vinnie leaned over and started stroking Hank's beard.

"Your face feels just like my wife's pussy," exclaimed Vinnie. Hank gave it a stroke himself and said,

"Ya, you're right!"

The Toughest Whore

One day, after striking gold in Alaska, a lonesome miner came down from the mountains and walked into a saloon in the nearest town.

"I'm lookin' for the meanest, roughest and toughest whore in the Yukon!" he said to the bartender.

"We got her!" replied the barkeep. "She's upstairs in the second room on the right." The miner handed the bartender a gold nugget to pay for the whore and two beers. He grabbed the bottles, stomped up the stairs, kicked open the second door on the right and yelled, "I'm lookin' for the meanest, roughest and toughest whore in the Yukon!" The woman inside the room looked at the miner and said, "You found her!" Then she stripped naked, bent over and grabbed her ankles.

"How do you know I want to do it in that position?" asked the miner.

"I don't," replied the whore.

"I just thought you might like to open those beers first."

At the Doctor's

A guy went to see a doctor and after a series of tests the doctor came in and said, "I've got some good news and some bad news."

"What's the bad news?" asked the patient.

"The bad news is that, unfortunately, you've only got three months to live." The patient was shocked.

"Oh my god! Well what's the good news then, doctor?" The doctor pointed over to the secretary at the front desk.

"You see that blonde with the big breasts, tight ass and legs that go all the way up to heaven?"

"Yes," said the patient.

"I'm shagging her!"

Just Say No

Two young guys were picked up by the cops for smoking dope and appeared in court on Friday in front of the judge. The judge said, "You seem like nice young men, and I'd like to give you a second chance rather than jail time. I want you to go out this weekend and try to show others the evils of drug use and get them to give up drugs forever. I'll see you back in court on Monday."

The following Monday the two guys were in court, and the judge said to the first one, "How did you do over the weekend?"

"Well, your Honour, I persuaded 17 people to give up drugs for ever."

"Seventeen people? That's wonderful! What did you tell them?"

"I used a diagram, your Honour. I drew two circles like this: O o ... and told them the big circle is your brain before drugs and the small circle is your brain after drugs."

"That's admirable!" said the judge.

To the second boy the judge said, "And you, how did you do?"

"Well, your Honour, I persuaded 156 people to give up drugs forever."

"That's amazing! How did you manage to do that?"

"Well, I used a similar approach. I drew two circles: o O ... and pointed to the small circle and said,

"'this is your arsehole before prison ...'"

This Is Your Captain ...

A jumbo jet was just coming into an airport in Toronto on its final approach. The pilot came on over the intercom.

"This is Captain Johnson. We're on our final descent into Toronto. I want to thank you for flying with us today, and I hope you enjoy your stay in Toronto." Unfortunately he forgot to switch off the intercom, so the whole plane was treated to the subsequent conversation from the flight deck. The co-pilot said to the pilot, "Well skipper, watcha gonna do in Toronto?" Now all ears in the plane were listening in to this conversation.

"Well," said the skipper, "first I'm gonna check into the hotel and take a crap. Then I'm gonna take that new stewardess out for supper, you know, the one with the huge tits. I'm gonna wine and dine her, take her back to my room, and shag her all night." Everyone in the plane turned to look at the new stewardess. She was so embarrassed that she ran from the back of the plane to try and get to the cockpit to turn the intercom off. Halfway down the aisle, she tripped over an old lady's bag and down she went. The old lady leaned over and said,

"No need to run, dear, he's gotta take a shit first!"

Waiting for a Haircut

A guy stuck his head in the barber shop and asked, "How long before I can get a haircut?" The barber looked around the shop and said, "About two hours." The guy left.

A few days later, the same guy stuck his head in the door and asked, "How long before I can get a haircut?" The barber looked around the shop full of customers and said, "About two hours." Again the guy left.

A week later, the same guy stuck his head in the shop and asked, "How long before I can get a haircut?" The barber looked around the shop and said, "About an hour and a half." The guy left.

The barber looked over at a friend in the shop and said, "Hey Bill, follow that guy and see where he goes." In a little while, Bill came back into the shop laughing hysterically. The barber asked, "Bill, where did he go when he left here?" Bill looked up and said,

"To your house."

Men Like Drinks

Three women were sitting around one night talking about their boyfriends when they decided they would give their men nicknames based on kinds of drink. The first woman said, "I'm gonna call Tom 'Mountain Dew' because he is as strong as a mountain and always wants to do it!" The second woman said, "I'm gonna call Bruce '7-Up' because he has seven inches and it is always up!" The third woman said, "I'm gonna call my man 'Jack Daniels'." The other two women responded, "'Jack Daniels'? But that's a hard liquor." The third woman replied,

"THAT'S MY LEROY!"

Like a Virgin

A young couple on their first date became quickly involved with one another and finished making love in no time. The man, quite proud of himself, said, "If I had known that you were a virgin I would have taken more time." To which she replied,

"If I had known you were going to take more time I would have taken off my knickers."

🖼 A Riddle

Here is a riddle for the intellectually minded.

At the exact same time, there are two young men on opposite sides of the Earth: one is walking a tightrope between two skyscrapers, the other is getting a blow job from an 85-year-old woman. They are each thinking exactly same thing. What are they both thinking?

>
>
>
>
>
>
>
>
>
>

Don't look down.

🖼 Sex 'n' Booze

Seven bartenders were asked if they could identify personality on what drinks were chosen. Though interviewed separately, they concurred on almost all counts. The results:

IF WOMEN DRINK …

Drink: Beer
Personality: Casual, low maintenance, down-to-earth
Approach: Challenge her to a game of pool

Drink: Cocktails with umbrella
Personality: Flaky and a pain in the arse
Approach: Avoid her, unless you want to be her cabin boy

Drink: Cocktails, no umbrellas
Personality: Mature, has picky taste, knows what she wants
Approach: If she wants you, she'll send YOU a drink

Drink: Wine (bottled not four-litre cask)
Personality: Conservative and classy, sophisticated
Approach: Try and weave Paris and clothing into the conversation

Drink: Bacardi Breezer
Personality: Easy, thinks she is trendy and sophisticated, actually has absolutely no clue
Approach: Make her feel smarter than she is and you're in

Drink: Baileys
Personality: Annoying voice, bit of a tart
Approach: Stand close and mention the alley next to the pub

Drink: Shorts (Vodka, Aftershock etc.)
Personality: Hanging with male pals or looking to get drunk ... and naked
Approach: Easiest hit in the pub, nothing to do but wait

IF MEN DRINK (as always, very simple and clear cut) ...

Cider: He's probably under-age and wants to get laid.

Cheap Domestic Beer: He's poor/a student and wants to get laid.

Premium Local Beer: He likes good beer and wants to get laid.

Bitter: He's old, he likes good beer and wants to get laid.

Imported Beer: He likes expensive beer and wants to get laid.

Guinness: The man is determined and will get laid one way or another.

Wine: He's hoping that the wine thing will give him a sophisticated image and help him get laid.

Vodka or Brandy: Extremely horny hound, would shag a warm scarf, desperate to get laid.

Port: Thinks he's sophisticated, secretly likes men and wants to get laid.

Whisky: He doesn't give two shits about anything and will hit anyone who gets in the way of his getting laid.

Jack Daniels: Not as masculine as the whisky drinker, knows all about feminine activities (knitting, crochet etc.) to weasel himself into getting laid.

Tequila: Piss off you wankers, I'm gonna go shag anything with a pulse.

Bacardi Breezer: He's gay (blatantly).

The Punishment

A little boy came down to breakfast one morning. His mother asked if he had done his chores.

"Not yet," said the little boy. His mother told him he couldn't have any breakfast until he had done his chores.

Well, he was a little pissed off, so he went to feed the chickens, and kicked a chicken. He went to feed the cows, and he kicked a cow. He went to feed the pigs, and he kicked a pig. He went back in for breakfast and his mother gave him a bowl of dry cereal.

"How come I don't get any eggs and bacon? Why don't I have any milk on my cereal?" he asked.

"Well," his mother said, "I saw you kick a chicken, so you don't get any eggs for a week. I saw you kick the pig, so you don't get any bacon, for a week either. I also saw you kick the cow, so for a week you aren't getting any milk."

Just then, his father came down for breakfast, kicking the cat as he walked into the kitchen. The little boy looked up at his mother with a smile, and said,

"Are you going to tell him, or should I?"

In an Airplane Lavatory

Two voices – one male, one female – on a plane:

"I think everyone's asleep, let's go."

Sound of steps.

"This one's empty ... no one's looking ... you go in first."

"It's a bit cramped – let me sit down."

"Have you got the condom? Quick – put it on."

Sniff-sniff.

"God, that smells good."

"Jesus, this is great ..." (long sigh).

Static on the loudspeaker then a new voice.

"This is the captain speaking to those two people in the rear toilet. We know what you're doing and it is expressly forbidden by airline regulations ...

"Now put those cigarettes out and take the condom off the smoke detector!"

🔽 📼 Come Again?

ORGASM TYPES:

Sex for hours and hours on end	=	Soregasms
Sex with a nymphomaniac	=	Gimme Moregasms
Sex watching a dirty video	=	Hardcoregasms
Sex with three of your friends	=	Fourgasms
Sex that isn't very satisfying	=	There's the doorgasms
Sex with a competitive partner	=	Scoregasms
Sex while hopelessly drunk	=	Liquorgasms
Sex at the supermarket	=	Storegasms
Sex with a prostitute	=	Whoregasms
Sex on the beach	=	Shoregasms
Sex while hiking	=	Outdoorgasms
Sex in a boat	=	Oargasms
Sex while sightseeing	=	Tourgasms
Sex with a meat eater	=	Carnivoregasms
Sex when you're past it	=	Nomoregasms
Sex with a menstruating woman	=	Goregasms
Sex with a lion	=	Roargasms
Sex with the God of Thunder	=	Thorgasms
Sex with the needy	=	Poorgasms
Sex with someone you hate	=	Abhorgasms
Sex on a rainy day	=	Indoorgasms
Sex with the mentally retarded	=	IQ of Thirty-fourgasms
Sex with a chef	=	Soup de Jourgasms
Sex with an agnostic	=	Unsuregasms
Sex with someone who's asleep	=	Snoregasms
Sex with a judge	=	Lawgasms
Sex with a housewife	=	Choregasms
Sex with the military	=	Wargasms

Sex that's really not all that interesting =   Boregasms

Premature ejaculations   =   Beforegasms

And of course …

Anal sex   =   Backdoorgasms

The Cutting Edge of Technology

⬇ ✉ AOL Before Christmas

'Twas a month before Christmas,
From my wife came the wail,
"Take out the garbage
And go get the mail."

So I trudged to my mailbox
And what did I see?
Why, a miniature disc
And computer CD!

'Twas a limited offer
From America Online,
I knew in a twinkling
That this deal was fine!

"Unlimited" access
for one little fee,
And if I didn't like it
I could cancel it free.

So I plugged the thing in
And it just wouldn't load,
The message said "Error!"
And something in code.

And this was when I
Started getting real nervous

So I waited four hours
For "Customer Service".

This techno-geek helped me
To load and install it,
Then demanded the VISA
I keep in my wallet.

So I gave him my number
And what did I spy?
"Terms and Conditions" screens
Whistling by.

Then I got me a password
Now I'd surf the Net!
But I never hit waves,
Man, I never got wet.

I soon got so mad
I was shaking and dizzy
For my modem kept trying
But the lines were all busy!

And all through the month
I kept trying this thing
But all I would hear
Was the "busy" sound ring.

So I called 1-800
And the AOL number
And waited on hold
'Til I lapsed into slumber.

So I tried then to cancel
But where's the address?

Somewhere in Virginia?
It's anyone's guess.

And several days later
I heard on the news
That eight million people
Were trying to use

This AOL network
At the very same time.
And that's when this CEO,
Weasel-necked slime,

Announced the solution
To how to log on,
Don't hog the phone lines
And call in at dawn!

As you can imagine
This didn't sit well
With lots of mad users
Who started to yell.

And soon the AGs
Joined them in the attack,
"Give them their money
(Or at least part of it) back!"

And this weasel-man leader
Tried to calm down the throng:
"Hey, I wanted those refunds
For you all along!"

So in grandiose fashion
And a big press release

Members were told
How to get back their piece.

"Just call up this number
And ask for your money,"
But then something happened
That's practically funny.

When you call up the number
(Don't get in a tizzy)
You can't get your refund
Cause the damn number's busy!!!

Batteries Not Included

Jake was struggling through a bus station with two huge and obviously heavy suitcases when a stranger walked up to him and asked, "Have you got the time?" Jake sighed, put down the suitcases and glanced at his wrist.

"It's a quarter to six," he said.

"Hey, that's a pretty fancy watch!" exclaimed the stranger. Jake brightened a little.

"Yeah, it's not bad. It's an invention of mine I've been working on. Check this out." And he showed him a time zone display not just for every time zone in the world, but for the 86 largest metropolises.

He hit a few buttons and from somewhere on the watch a voice said, "The time is eleven 'til six" in a very West Texas accent. A few more buttons and the same voice said something in Japanese. Jake continued, "I've put in regional accents for each city. Listen." The watch said, "It's about ten to six-ish, near enough."

"That's London," said Jake. The display was unbelievably high quality and the voice was simply astounding. The stranger was struck dumb with admiration.

"That's not all," said Jake. He pushed a few more buttons and a tiny but very high-resolution map of New York City appeared on the display. "The flashing dot shows our location by satellite positioning," explained Jake. "Zoom out," Jake said, and the display changed to show all of eastern New York State.

"I want to buy this watch!" said the stranger.

"Oh, no, it's not ready for sale yet; I'm still working out the bugs," said the inventor. "But look at this," and he proceeded to demonstrate that the watch was also a very creditable little FM radio receiver with a digital tuner, a sonar device that could measure distances up to 125 metres, a pager with thermal paper printout and, most impressive of all, the capacity for voice recordings of up to 300 standard-size books.

"Though I only have 32 of my favourites in there so far," said Jake.

"I've got to have this watch!" said the stranger.

"No, you don't understand; it's not ready …"

"I'll give you $1000 for it!"

"Oh, no, I've already spent more than …"

"I'll give you $5000 for it!

"But it's just not …"

"I'll give you $15,000 for it!" And the stranger pulled out a chequebook.

Jake stopped to think. He had only put about $8500 into materials and development, and with $15,000 he could make another one and have it ready for merchandising in only six months. The stranger frantically finished writing the cheque and waved it in front of him.

"Here it is, ready to hand to you right here and now: $15,000. Take it or leave it." Jake abruptly made his decision.

"OK," he said, and peeled off the watch. They made the exchange and the stranger started happily away.

"Hey, wait a minute!" Jake called after the stranger, who turned around warily. Jake pointed to the two suitcases he'd been trying to wrestle through the bus station.

"Don't forget your batteries."

One-upmanship

Three men were sitting naked in the sauna. Suddenly there was a beeping sound. The first man pressed his forearm and the beeping stopped. The others looked at him curiously.

"That's my pager," he said. "I have a microchip under the skin of my arm."

A few minutes later a phone rang. The second man lifted his palm to his ear. When he had finished he explained, "That's my mobile phone. I have a microchip in my hand."

The third man, feeling decidedly low-tech, stepped out of the sauna. In a few minutes he returned with a piece of toilet paper hanging from his arse. The others raised their eyebrows.

"I'm getting a fax," he explained.

Happily Addicted to the Web

To be sung to the tune of "Winter Wonderland"

Doorbell rings, I'm not list'nin',
From my mouth, drool is glist'nin',
I'm happy, although
My boss let me go
Happily addicted to the Web.

All night long, I sit clicking,
Unaware time is ticking,
There's beard on my cheek,
Same clothes for a week,
Happily addicted to the Web.

Friends come by; they shake me,
Saying, "Yo, man!
Don't you know that life keeps moving on?"
With a listless shrug, I mutter, "No, man;
I just discovered letterman-dot-com!"

I don't phone, don't send faxes,
Don't go out, don't pay taxes,
Who cares if someday
They drag me away?
I'm happily addicted to the Web!

Twelve-Step Recovery Programme for Internet-aholics

1) I will have a cup of coffee in the morning and read my newspaper like I used to, before the Internet.

2) I will eat breakfast with a knife and fork and not with one hand typing.

3) I will get dressed before noon.

4) I will make an attempt to clean the house, wash clothes, and plan dinner before even thinking of the Internet.

5) I will sit down and write a letter to those unfortunate few friends and family that are Internet-deprived.

6) I will call someone on the phone whom I cannot contact via the Internet.

7) I will read a book ... if I still remember how.

8) I will listen to those around me and their needs and stop telling them to turn the TV down so I can hear the music on the Internet.

9) I will not be tempted during TV commercials to check for e-mail.

10) I will try and get out of the house at least once a week, whether it is necessary or not.

11) I will remember that my bank is not forgiving if I forget to balance my chequebook because I was too busy on the Internet.

12) Last, but not least, I will remember that I must go to bed sometime ... and the Internet will always be there tomorrow!

Nerd Season

A truck driver hauling a load of computers interstate stopped for a beer. As he approached the bar he saw a big sign on the door saying, "NERDS NOT ALLOWED – ENTER AT OWN RISK!" He went in and sat down. The bartender came over to him and sniffed.

"You smell kind of nerdy," said the bartender suspiciously. "What do you do for a living?"

"I drive a truck," replied the truck driver. "That smell is just from the computers I'm hauling." The bartender said OK, truck drivers were not nerds, and served him a beer.

As the truck driver was sipping his beer, a skinny guy walked in with tape around his glasses, a pocket protector with twelve kinds of pen and pencil, and a belt at least a foot too long. The bartender, without saying a word, pulled out a shotgun and blew the guy away.

"What did you do that for?" asked the truck driver.

"Not to worry," replied the bartender, "the nerds are overpopulating Silicon Valley, and are in season now. You don't even need a licence."

So the truck driver finished his beer, got back in his truck, and headed back onto the motorway. Suddenly a car skidded in front of him and he veered to avoid an accident, causing the load to shift. The back door broke open and computers spilled out all over the road. He jumped out and saw a crowd already forming, grabbing up the computers. They were all engineers, accountants and programmers wearing the nerdiest clothes he had ever seen. He couldn't let them steal his whole load. So remembering what happened in the bar, he pulled out his gun and started blasting away, felling several of them instantly. A highway patrol officer came zooming up and jumped out of the car screaming at him to stop.

The truck driver said, "What's wrong? I thought nerds were in season."

"Well, sure," said the patrolman,

"but you can't bait 'em."

The Olden Days

POEM FOR COMPUTER USERS OVER 40

A computer was something on TV
From a science-fiction show of note,
A window was something you hated to clean
And ram was the father of a goat.*

Meg was the name of my girlfriend
And gig was a job for the nights.
Now they all mean different things
And that really mega bytes.

An application was for employment,
A program was a TV show,
A cursor used profanity,
A keyboard was a piano.

Memory was something that you lost with age,
A CD was a bank account
And if you had a three-inch floppy
You hoped nobody found out.

Compress was something you did to the dustbin
Not something you did to a file
And if you unzipped anything in public
You'd be in jail for a while.

Log on was adding wood to the fire,
Hard drive was a long trip on the road,
A mouse pad was where a mouse lived,
And a backup happened to your commode.

Cut you did with a pocket knife,
Paste you did with glue,
A web was a spider's home,
And a virus was the flu.

I guess I'll stick to my pad and paper
And the memory in my head;
I hear nobody's been killed in a computer crash
But when it happens you wish you were dead.

*oh, all right then, a SHEEP, but it doesn't rhyme.

How to Please Your IT Department

1. When you call us to have your computer moved, be sure to leave it buried under half a ton of postcards, baby pictures, stuffed animals, dried flowers, bowling trophies and children's art. We don't have a life, and we find it deeply moving to catch a fleeting glimpse of yours.

2. Don't write anything down. Ever. We can play back the error messages from here.

3. When an IT person says he's coming right over, go for coffee. That way you won't be there when we need your password. It's nothing for us to remember 700 screensaver passwords.

4. When you call the helpdesk, state what you want, not what's keeping you from getting it. We don't need to know that you can't get into your mail because your computer won't power on at all.

5. When IT support sends you an e-mail flagged high importance, delete it at once. We're just testing.

6. When an IT person is eating lunch at his desk, walk right in and spill your guts right out. We exist only to serve.

7. Send urgent e-mail all in upper case. The mail server picks it up and flags it as a rush delivery.

8. When the photocopier doesn't work, call computer support. There's electronics in it.

9. When something's wrong with your home PC, dump it on an IT person's chair with no name, no phone number and no description of the problem. We love a puzzle.

10. When an IT person tells you that computer screens don't have cartridges in them, argue. We love a good argument.

11. When an IT person tells you that he'll be there shortly, reply in a scathing tone of voice: "And just how many weeks do you mean by shortly?" That motivates us.

12. When the printer won't print, resend the job at least 20 times. Print jobs frequently get sucked into black holes.

13. When the printer still won't print after 20 tries, send the job to all 68 printers in the company. One of them is bound to work.

14. Don't learn the proper term for anything technical. We know exactly what you mean by "My thingy blew up."

15. Don't use on-line help. On-line help is for wimps.

The Assisted Computing Facility

THE TOUGHEST DECISION: SHOULD MY LOVED ONE BE PLACED IN AN ASSISTED COMPUTING FACILITY?

For family members, it is often the most difficult and painful decision they will face: to accept that a loved one – a parent, a spouse, perhaps a sibling – is technologically impaired and should no longer be allowed to live independently, or come near a computer or electronic device without direct supervision. The time has come to place that loved one into the care of an Assisted Computing Facility.

But you have questions. So many questions. We at Silicon Pines want to help.

* WHAT EXACTLY IS AN "ASSISTED COMPUTING FACILITY"?
Sometimes referred to as "Homes for the Technologically Infirm", "Technical Invalid Care Centres" or "Homes for the Technically Challenged", Assisted Computing Facilities (ACFs) are modelled on assisted living facilities, and provide a safe, structured residential environment for those unable to handle even the most common, everyday multitasks. Most fully accredited ACFs, like Silicon Pines, are oases of hope and encouragement that allow residents to lead productive, technologically relevant lives without the fear and anxiety associated with actually having to understand or execute the technologies themselves.

* WHO SHOULD BE IN AN ACF?
Sadly, technology is advancing at such a dramatic rate that many millions, of all ages, will never truly be able to understand it, putting an undue burden on those friends and family members who must explain it to them. But unless the loved one is suffering from a truly debilitating affliction, such as Reinstallzheimers, the decision to commit is entirely personal.

You must ask yourself, "How frustrated am I that my parent/sibling/spouse is unable to open an e-mail attachment?", "How much of my time should be taken up explaining how RAM is different from hard-drive memory?", "How many times can I bear to hear my dad say, 'Hey, can I replace the motherboard with a fatherboard? Ha ha ha!'?" To make things easier, we have prepared a list of Warning Signs which we encourage you to return to often or, if you can't figure out how to bookmark, print out. Also, please take a moment to read "I'm Glad I'm in Here! – A Resident's Story".

* MUST IT BE FAMILY, OR CAN I PLACE ANYONE IN AN ACF?
Several corporations have sought permission to have certain employees, or at times entire sales departments, committed to ACFs. At present, however, individuals can be committed only by direct family, or self-internment.

The reason is simple: there are not nearly enough ACFs in the world to accommodate all the technologically challenged. For example, there are currently only 860,000 beds available in ACFs, but there are 29 million AOL users.

* HOW MUCH WILL IT COST?
ACF rents range from free up to $12,500 per month. The disparity is currently a point of contention in the ACF industry. Many residents are covered through government programs such as Compucaid or Compucare, but reimbursement rates are low and only cover a portion of the fees.

Exacerbating the situation are the HMOs (Helpdesk Maintenance Organizations), which often deny coverage, forcing residents to pay out of pocket or turn to expensive private techcare insurers such as BlueCache/BlueScreen.

Offsetting the costs are technology companies themselves, many of which subsidize ACFs. Firms such as Microsoft, Dell, Qualcomm, and America Online will pay up to 100 per cent of a resident's monthly bill, but there is a catch. ISPs, for instance, require residents to sign service contracts lasting a year or more. Microsoft, meanwhile, prohibits the installation of any competitive software, while Priceline requires that residents buy shares of its stock, which seems onerous but saves residents on lavatory tissue.

* HOW OLD MUST I BE TO HAVE SOMEONE COMMITTED?

Until very recently, you had to be 18 or older to legally commit a family member. However, the now famous British court case Frazier vs. Frazier and Frazier has cleared the way for minors to commit their parents. In that case, 15-year-old Bradley Frazier of Leicester had his 37-year-old parents committed to an ACF in Bournemouth after a judge ruled Ian and Janet Frazier were a "danger to themselves and the community". According to court records, Bradley told his parents about the ILoveYou virus and warned them not to click attachments, then the next day his parents received an ILoveYou email and clicked on the attachment because, they explained, "it came from someone we know".

* WHAT SHOULD I LOOK FOR IN AN ACF?

First, make sure it's a genuine Assisted Computing Facility, and not an Assisted Living Facility. To tell the difference, observe the residents. If they look rather old and tend to openly discuss bowel movements, this is probably "assisted living". On the other hand, if they vary in age and say things like "I'm supposed to figure that out? I'm not Bill goddamned Gates you know!", this is probably "assisted computing".

Also, at a well-run ACF, residents should lead full, independent lives, and should be allowed the use of many technology devices, including telephones, electric toothbrushes, and alarm clocks. However, only a facility's Licensed Techcare Professionals (LTPs) should perform computational or technological tasks such as installing programs or saving e-mail attachments. And LTPs should NEVER answer residents' questions because studies have shown that answering user questions inevitably makes things worse. Instead, residents should simply have things done for them, relieving them of the pressure to "learn" or "improve".

* CAN A RESIDENT EVER GET OUT?
No.

* OK, THIS SOUNDS PROMISING. HOW CAN I LEARN MORE?
For your enlightenment, we offer extensive information on Silicon Pines and the ACF lifestyle, which can be found by clicking one of the links in the navigation bars found at both the top and bottom of this page. But whatever you decide, keep in mind that due to demand, ACFs now have long waiting lists. WebTV subscribers alone will take years to absorb.

The Magic of Married Life

Services Rendered

A husband is at home watching the match when his wife interrupts, "Darling, could you fix the light in the hallway? It's been flickering for weeks now." He looks at her and says angrily, "Fix the light? Now does it look like I have 'Powergen' written on my forehead? I don't think so."

"Well, then, could you fix the fridge door? It won't close right." To which he replies, "Fix the fridge door? Does it look like I have 'Zanussi' written on my forehead? I don't think so."

"Fine," she says, "then could you at least fix the steps to the front door? They're about to break."

"I'm not a damn carpenter and I don't want to fix the steps," he says. "Does it look like I have 'B&Q' written on my forehead? I don't think so. I've had enough of you. I'm going to the pub!" So he goes to the pub and drinks for a couple of hours. He starts to feel guilty about how he treated his wife, and decides to go home and help out.

As he walks into the house, he notices the steps are already fixed. As he enters the house, he sees the hall light is working. As he goes to get a beer, he notices the fridge door is fixed. "Honey, how'd this all get fixed?"

She said, "Well, when you left, I sat outside and cried. Just then a nice young man asked me what was wrong, and I told him. He offered to do all the repairs, and all I had to do was either bake him a cake or give him a blow job."

The husband asked, "So, what kind of cake did you bake him?"

She replied, "Do you see Delia Smith written on my forehead? I don't think so."

The Thoughtful Christmas Present

A rich man and a poor man were drinking in a bar.

Rich man: "Ya know what I'm gonna get my wife for Christmas?"
Poor man: "What?"
Rich man: "A diamond bracelet, and a new Mercedes."
Poor man: "Why?"
Rich man: "So if she doesn't like the bracelet she can drive her new car to return it."
Poor man: "That makes sense, I think I'll get mine a hairbrush and a dildo."
Rich man: "Why?"
Poor man: "So if she doesn't like the hairbrush she can go fuck herself."

You Are What You Eat

A very traditional elderly woman was enjoying a good game of bridge with her girlfriends one evening.

"Oh, no!" she exclaimed suddenly. "I have to rush home and fix dinner for my husband! He's going to be really ticked if it's not ready on time!"

When she got home, she realized that she didn't have enough time to go to the supermarket, and all she had in the cupboard was a wilted lettuce leaf, an egg, and a can of cat food. In a panic, she opened the can of cat food, stirred in the egg, and garnished it with the lettuce leaf just as her husband pulled up. She greeted her husband and then watched in horror as he sat down to his dinner. To her surprise, the husband really enjoyed his dinner.

"Darling, this is the best dinner you have made for me in 40 years of marriage. You can make this for me any old day."

Needless to say, every bridge night from then on, the woman made her husband the same dish. She told her bridge cronies about it and they were all horrified.

"You're going to kill him!" they exclaimed, and indeed two months later, her husband died.

The women were sitting around the table playing bridge when one of the cronies said, "You killed him! We told you that feeding him that cat food every week would do him in! How can you just sit there so calmly and play bridge knowing you murdered your husband?"

The wife stoically replied, "I didn't kill him.

"He fell off the mantel while he was cleaning himself."

Breaking the News

Harry answered the telephone one day to the Emergency Room doctor.

"Your wife was in a serious car accident," said the doctor, "and I have bad news and good news. The bad news is she has lost all use of both arms and both legs, and will need help eating and going to the bathroom for the rest of her life."

"My God. What's the good news?" asked Harry.

"I'm kidding. She's dead."

At the Zoo

It was a beautiful, warm spring morning and a man and his wife were spending the day at the zoo. She wore a cute, loose-fitting, pink spring dress, sleeveless with straps. He wore his normal jeans and a T-shirt. The zoo was not very busy that morning.

As they walked through the ape exhibit, they passed in front of a very large hairy gorilla. Noticing the girl, the gorilla went ape. (No pun intended.) He jumped up on the bars, and holding on with one hand (and two feet), he grunted and pounded his chest with his free hand, obviously excited by the pretty lady in the flimsy dress.

The husband, noticing the excitement, thought it was funny. He suggested that his wife tease the poor fellow some more. He suggested she pucker her lips, wiggle her bottom at him, and play along. She did so and the gorilla became more and more excited, making noises that would wake the dead.

Then the husband suggested that she let one of her straps fall to show a little more skin. This she did, whereupon the gorilla looked about ready to tear the bars down.

"Now try lifting your dress up your thighs and sort of fan it at him," the man said. This drove the gorilla absolutely crazy and he started doing backflips.

Then the husband grabbed his wife by the hair, ripped open the door to the cage, flung her in with the gorilla and slammed the cage door shut.

"Now, tell HIM you have a headache."

Paternity Pain Transfer

A married couple went to the hospital to have their baby delivered. Upon their arrival, the doctor said he had invented a new machine that would transfer a portion of the mother's labour pain to the father. He asked if they were willing to try it out. They were both very much in favour of it.

The doctor set the pain transfer to 10% for starters, explaining that even 10% was probably more pain than the father had ever experienced before. But as the labour progressed, the husband felt fine and asked the doctor to go ahead and bump it up a notch. The doctor then adjusted the machine to 20% pain transfer. The husband was still feeling fine. The doctor checked the husband's blood pressure and was amazed at how well he was doing. At this point they decided to try for 50%. The husband continued to feel quite well.

Since the pain transfer was obviously helping out the wife considerably, the husband encouraged the doctor to transfer ALL the pain to him. The wife delivered a healthy baby with virtually no pain. She and her husband were ecstatic.

When they got home, the milkman was dead upon the porch.

Romance Mathematics

Smart man + smart woman = romance
Smart man + dumb woman = affair
Dumb man + smart woman = marriage
Dumb man + dumb woman = pregnancy

Butler

A wealthy couple had plans to go to an evening ball. So they advised their butler that they were giving him the evening off to do as he pleased since they would be out until quite late. The couple went to the ball and dinner. After an hour and a half, the wife told her husband that she was horribly bored and that she would rather go home and finish some work for the next day. The husband responded that he had to stay for a few more hours to meet some very important people who were his new business partners.

So, the wife went home alone and found the butler spread out on the couch watching TV. She slowly moved towards him and sat down very seductively. She asked him to come closer. Then even closer. She moved forward and whispered in his ear, "Take off my dress … Now, take off my bra … Next, remove my shoes and stockings." She then looked deep into his eyes and in a sharp voice shouted,

"The next time I catch you wearing my clothes, you're fired!"

Off to the Pub

A man walked into the lounge and said to his wife, "The pub's open so get your coat on." Delighted she replied, "Great, I haven't been to the pub with you for a long time."

"No," he said, "I'm going on my own and I'm turning the heating off!"

Unsatisfied Wife

A young couple, Louise and Peter, had been married for about a year when the sex dropped off leaving the bride highly unsatisfied. Just about every night Peter came home, had a shower, got changed and went down to the pub. Louise was getting increasingly frustrated as the days went on, but each night she was disappointed as Peter came back from the pub completely hammered and unfit for sexual activity.

One particular night when Peter got in from work, Louise was seated provocatively on the sofa, wearing the skimpiest dress she had, suspenders, stockings and very sexy lace panties and bra. As was always the case, Peter came home, ran upstairs, got ready and went to the pub. Once again Louise was rejected, so she sat back with a bottle of wine to console herself.

Then at 11.00 p.m. (well before normal) she heard Peter coming up the driveway and opening the front door. Louise readopted her sexually provocative pose on the sofa and to her surprise, Peter's first words were "Right woman, get upstairs and into the bedroom."

"YES!" she said under her breath as she ran upstairs. "This is the night, I'm gonna finally get some!"

When Louise reached the bedroom, she removed her outer garments and sat on the edge of the bed in her black lace panties ready for Peter, as he stomped up the stairs. As Peter pushed the bedroom door open he said, "Right, now get your clothes off!" Louise didn't need telling twice – off it all came.

"Now get over in front of the mirror ..." said Peter.

"Kinky," she thought. "Great!"

"And do a handstand ..." said Peter.

"Oh god, I've been waiting for this for f**king ages," thought Louise.

Peter walked over to Louise parted her legs and placed his chin in her crotch,

"Perhaps the chaps were right ... a beard wouldn't suit me!"

On His Mobile

"Hello?"

"Honey, it's me. Are you at the club?"

"Yes."

"Great! I am at the mall two blocks from where you are. I just saw a beautiful mink coat. It's absolutely gorgeous!! Can I buy it?"

"What's the price?"

"Only $1500."

"Well, OK, go ahead and get it, if you like it that much."

"Ahhh, and I also stopped by the Mercedes dealership and saw the 2001 models. I saw one I really liked. I spoke to the salesman, and he gave me a really good price ... and since we need to exchange the BMW that we bought last year ..."

"What price did he quote you?"

"Only $60,000."

"OK, but for that price I want it with all the options."

"Great! But before we hang up, something else,"

"What?"

"It might look like a lot, but I was reconciling your bank account and ... I stopped by to see the real estate agent this morning and saw the house we looked at last year. It's on sale!! Remember? The one with a pool, English garden, acre of park area, beachfront property ..."

"How much are they asking?"

"Only $450,000 – a magnificent price ... and I see that we have that much in the bank to cover ..."

"Well, then go ahead and buy it, but just bid $420,000. OK?"

"OK, sweetie. Thanks! I'll see you later! I love you!!!"

"Bye ... I do too ..."

The man hung up, closed the phone's flap, held it up in the air and asked all those present,

"Does anyone know who this phone belongs to?"

Phone a Friend

One night after watching *Who Wants To Be A Millionaire*, a man and his wife went to bed and the man was getting very frisky. He asked his wife if she was in the mood.

His wife answered, "Not tonight dear, I have a headache."

"Is that your final answer?" asked the man.

"Yes," she said.

"OK then," he replied,

"in that case I'd like to phone a friend."

Catholic Marriage

Mrs O'Donovan was walking down O'Connell Street in Dublin, and coming in the opposite direction was Father Rafferty.

"Hello," said the Father, "and how is Mr O'Donovan? Didn't I marry you two years ago?"

She replied, "That you did Father."

The priest asked, "And are there any little ones yet?"

"No, not yet Father," said she.

"Well, now, I'm going to Rome next week, and I'll light a candle for you."

"Thank you, Father." And away she went.

A few years later they met again.

"Well, now, Mrs O'Donovan," said the Father, "how are you?"

"Oh, very well," said she.

"And tell me," he said, "have you any little ones yet?"

"Oh yes, Father. I've had three sets of twins, and four singles – ten in all."

"Now isn't that wonderful," he said. "And how is your lovely husband?"

"Oh," she said, "he's gone to Rome."

"What for, now?" asked the Father.

"To blow out the damn candle!"

The World Women's Conference

At the 1997 World Women's Conference the first speaker from England stood up.

"At last year's conference we spoke about being more assertive with our husbands. Well after the conference I went home and told my husband that I would no longer cook for him and that he would have to do it himself. After the first day I saw nothing. After the second day I saw nothing. But after the third day I saw that he had cooked a wonderful roast lamb." The crowd cheered.

The second speaker from America stood up, "After last year's conference I went home and told my husband that I would no longer do his laundry and that he would have to do it himself. After the first day I saw nothing. After the second day I saw nothing. But after the third day I saw that he had done not only his own washing but my washing as well." The crowd cheered.

The third speaker from Ireland stood up, "After last year's conference I went home and told my husband that I would no longer do his shopping and that he would have to do it himself. After the first day I saw nothing. After the second day I saw nothing.

"But after the third day I could see a little bit out of my left eye."

The Unkindest Cut

A guy walked into a bar with a sullen look on his face. His bartender friend asked him, "What's the matter buddy?"

"It's my wife," he replied, "she's cut my sex time down to once a month." The bartender quipped, "Aw, don't be so down,

"I know a couple of guys in town she's cut off altogether."

I'm the Boss!

The boss was complaining in our staff meeting the other day that he wasn't getting any respect. Later that morning he went to a local sign shop and bought a small sign that read, "I'm the Boss!" He then attached it to his office door.

Later that day when he returned from lunch, he found that someone had taped a note to the sign that said, "Your wife called, she wants her sign back!"

Learning from Bulls

A man took his wife to the stock show. They started heading down the alley that had the bulls. They came up to the first bull and his sign stated, "This bull mated 50 times last year." The wife turned to her husband and said, "He mated 50 times in a year, you could learn from him."

They proceed to the next bull and his sign stated, "This bull mated 65 times last year." The wife turned to her husband and said, "This one mated 65 times last year. That is over five times a month. You can learn from this one, also."

They proceeded to the last bull and his sign said, "This bull mated 365 times last year." The wife's mouth dropped open and she said, "WOW! He mated 365 times last year. That is ONCE A DAY!!! You could really learn from this one." The man turns to his wife and says,

"Go up and enquire if it was 365 times with the same cow."

Revenge

A man left for work one Friday afternoon. But, being payday, instead of going home, he stayed out the entire weekend partying with the boys and spending his entire paycheque. When he finally appeared at home, Sunday night, he was confronted by a very angry wife and was barraged for nearly two hours with a tirade befitting his actions.

Finally his wife stopped the nagging and simply said to him, "How would you like it if you didn't see me for two or three days?"

"That would be fine with me," replied the husband.

Monday went by and he didn't see his wife. Tuesday and Wednesday came and went with the same results. Come Thursday, the swelling went down just enough so that he could see her a little out of the corner of his left eye.

Mother-in-law on Safari

A big game hunter went on safari with his wife and his mother-in-law. One morning, the wife woke up to find her mother gone. Immediately, she woke up her husband and they both set off to find the old woman.

Suddenly, they broke into a clearing and there was the mother-in-law, standing face-to-face with a ferocious lion!

"Quick, darling," the wife shouted frantically, "Do something!"

"Oh, no," the husband said.

"That lion got himself into this mess. Let him get himself out!"

Freudian Slip

Bob arrived in his office one morning to find his colleague Simon roaring with laughter.

"What's the big joke?" Bob asked.

"Well," Simon replied, "I made a hilarious Freudian slip this morning."

"What's a Freudian slip?" asked Bob.

"It's when you mean to say one thing," said Simon, "but what comes out is what is really on your mind. So, this morning I was queuing at the train station to buy a return to Tooting, and I noticed that the girl behind the counter had enormous breasts. When I got to the front of the queue,

I asked for a return to Titting. The girl went bright red, I went bright red and the entire queue wet themselves laughing."

"Oh right," said Bob chuckling away.

The next morning, the situation was reversed and Bob arrived in the office first. He was chortling away to himself when Simon arrived.

"What's so funny?" asked Simon.

"Well," replied Bob, "I've made one of your Freudian slips."

"What happened?"

"I was sitting in the kitchen this morning, having breakfast. I looked over at my wife and instead of saying 'Pass the milk, dear',

"I said 'F*!@ off you fat bitch, you've ruined my life.'"

Trades and Professions

The Lawyer's Burst Pipe

A pipe burst in a lawyer's house, so he called a plumber. The plumber arrived, unpacked his tools, did mysterious plumber-type things for a while, and handed the lawyer a bill for £350 plus VAT.

"This is ridiculous!" exclaimed the lawyer, "I don't even make that much as a lawyer!"

"No," replied the plumber quietly,

"Neither did I when I was a lawyer."

Just Kidding

Reaching the end of a job interview, the Human Resources person asked a young engineer fresh out of college, "And what starting salary were you looking for?" The engineer replied, "In the neighborhood of 125,000 a year, depending on the benefits package."

"Well," said the interviewer, "what would you say to five weeks paid holiday, 14 paid public holidays, full medical and dental cover, company matching retirement fund to 50% of salary, and a company car leased every two years – say, a BMW?" The engineer sat up straight and said, "Wow! Are you kidding?"

"Yeah," replied the interviewer,

"but you started it."

The Free Haircut

A barber gave a haircut to a priest one day. The priest tried to pay for the haircut, but the barber refused, saying, "You do God's work." The next morning the barber found a dozen Bibles at the door to his shop.

A policeman came to the barber for a haircut, and again the barber refused to pay, saying, "You protect the public." The next morning the barber found a dozen doughnuts at the door to his shop.

A lawyer came to the barber for a haircut, and again the barber refused payment, saying, "You serve the justice system." The next morning the barber found a dozen lawyers waiting for a free haircut.

The Oldest Profession

A doctor, an engineer, a rabbi and a lawyer were debating who was the world's first professional.

The doctor said, "It must have been a doctor. Who else could have helped with the world's first surgery: taking a rib from Adam to create Eve, the first woman?"

"No," said the rabbi. "It must have been a rabbi, since the Lord needed someone to help preach his message to Adam and the world."

"Wait," said the engineer. "The world was created in six days from nothing. Do you know what an engineering feat it must have been to create the whole world into an organized, civilized place from utter chaos?"

"Yes, but who created the chaos?" asked the lawyer.

📥 🖻 In the Bank Queue

In a long line of people waiting for a bank teller, one guy suddenly started massaging the back of the person in front of him. Surprised, the man in front turned and snarled, "Just what the hell are you doing?"

"Well," said the guy, "you see, I'm a chiropractor and I could see that you were tense, so I had to massage your back. Sometimes I just can't help practising my art!"

"That's the stupidest thing I've ever heard!" the guy replied. "I'm a tax inspector.

"Do you see me screwing the guy in front of me?"

📥 🖻 Lawyer Season

State laws governing attorney hunting:

1. Any person with a valid state hunting license may harvest attorneys.
2. The taking of attorneys with traps or deadfalls is permitted; the use of currency as bait is prohibited.
3. The killing of attorneys with a vehicle is prohibited; if accidentally struck, remove roadkill to roadside, then proceed to nearest car wash.
4. It is unlawful to chase, herd, or harvest attorneys from a helicopter or other aircraft.
5. It shall be unlawful to shout, "whiplash", "ambulance" or, "free Perrier!" for the purposes of trapping attorneys.
6. It shall be unlawful to use cocaine, young boys, $100 bills, prostitutes, or vehicle accidents to attract attorneys.
7. It shall be unlawful to hunt attorneys within 200 yards of whorehouses, health spas, ambulances, or hospitals.

8. If an attorney is elected to government office, there will be a $500 bounty on the pelt.

9. Stuffed or mounted attorneys must have a state health department inspection for rabies, vermin and contagious diseases.

10. It shall be illegal for a hunter to disguise himself as a reporter, drug dealer, pimp, female law clerk, sheep, accident victim, bookie, or tax accountant for the purposes of hunting attorneys.

Attorney Bag Limits:

Yellow-bellied Sidewinder = 5
Hairless Civil Libertarian = 7
Skinny-assed Ambulance Chaser = 12
Horse or Cattle Rustler Defender = 20
Silver-tongued Murderer Defender = 50
Jack-legged Divorce Litigator = No limit
Honest Attorney = Extinct

Bumble Bee

One day a young man and woman were in their bedroom making love. All of a sudden a bumble bee entered the bedroom window. As the young lady parted her legs the bee entered her vagina. The woman started screaming, "Oh my god, help me, there's a bee in my vagina!" The husband immediately took her to the local doctor and explained the situation.

The doctor thought for a moment and said, "Hmm, tricky situation. But I have a solution to the problem if young sir would permit."

The husband, being very concerned, agreed that the doctor could use whatever method he liked to get the bee out of his wife's vagina. The doctor said "OK, what I'm gonna do is rub some honey over the top of my penis and insert it into your wife's vagina. When I feel the bee getting closer to the tip of my penis I shall withdraw it and the bee should hope-fully follow my penis out of your wife's vagina."

The husband nodded and gave his approval. The young lady said, "Yes, yes, whatever. Just get on with it."

So the doctor, after covering the tip of his penis with honey, inserted it into the young lady's vagina. After a few gentle strokes, the doctor said, "I don't think the bee has noticed the honey yet. Perhaps I should go a bit deeper." So the doctor went deeper and deeper.

After a while the doctor began shafting the young lady very hard indeed. The young lady began to quiver with excitement. She began to moan and groan aloud. The doctor, concentrating very hard, looked like he was enjoying himself. He put his hands on the young lady's breasts and started making loud noises. The husband at this point suddenly became very annoyed.

"Now wait a minute!" he shouted. "What the hell do you think you're doing?" The doctor, still concentrating, replied, "Change of plan …

"I'm gonna drown the bastard!"

The Three Kick Rule

A big city Californian lawyer went duck hunting in rural Arkansas. He shot and dropped a bird, but it fell into a farmer's field on the other side of a fence. As the lawyer climbed over the fence, an elderly farmer drove up on his tractor and asked him what he was doing. The litigator responded, "I shot a duck and it fell in this field, and now I'm going in to retrieve it." The old farmer replied, "This is my property, and you are not coming over here."

"I am one of the best trial attorneys in the US," the lawyer replied, "and, if you don't let me get that duck, I'll sue you and take everything you own." The old farmer smiled and said, "Apparently, you don't know how we do things in Arkansas. We settle small disagreements like this with the Arkansas Three Kick Rule."

"What's the Arkansas Three Kick Rule?" asked the lawyer. The Farmer replied, "Well, first I kick you three times and then you kick me three times, and so on, back and forth, until someone gives up." The attorney thought over the proposed contest and quickly decided that he could take the old codger. He agreed to abide by the local custom.

The old farmer slowly climbed down from the tractor and walked up to the city feller. His first kick planted the toe of his heavy work boot into the lawyer's groin and dropped him to his knees. His second kick nearly ripped the man's nose off his face. The barrister was flat on his belly when the farmer's third kick to a kidney nearly caused him to give up.

The lawyer summoned every bit of his will and managed to get to his feet and said, "Okay, you old coot, now it's my turn." The old farmer smiled and said,

"Naw, I give up. You can have the duck."

Emergency Landing

An airliner was having engine trouble, and the pilot instructed the cabin crew to have the passengers take their seats and get prepared for an emergency landing.

A few minutes later, the pilot asked the flight attendants if everyone was buckled in and ready.

"All set back here, Captain," came the reply,

"except for one lawyer who is still going around passing out business cards."

Three Engineers

Three engineers were in the bathroom standing at the urinals. The first finished and walked over to the sink to wash his hands. He then proceeded to dry his hands very carefully. He used paper towel after paper towel to insure that every single spot of water on his hands was dried. Turning to the other two engineers he explained, "At Opel, we are trained to be extremely thorough."

The second engineer finished his task at the urinal and he too proceeded to wash his hands. He used a single paper towel and made sure that he dried his hands using every available portion of the paper towel. He turned and said, "At Volkswagen not only are we trained to be extremely thorough but we are also trained to be extremely efficient."

The third engineer finished and walked straight to the door shouting over his shoulder,

"At Rolls-Royce we don't piss on our hands."

Lawyer in Heaven (Surely Not)

A lawyer died in a car accident on his 40th birthday and found himself greeted at the Pearly Gates by a brass band. St Peter ran over and shook his hand saying, "Congratulations!!!"

"Congratulations for what?" asked the lawyer.

"Congratulations for what?!?!?" said St Peter. "We're celebrating the fact that you lived to be 160 years old."

"But I didn't," said the lawyer. "I only lived to be 40."

"That's impossible," said St Peter.

"We've added up your time sheets."

Every Last Penny

In the market with his dad, a little boy was flipping a quarter into the air and then catching it with his teeth. Someone bumped the little boy at the wrong moment and the quarter came down and lodged in his throat. The boy started to choke and his father started to hollering for help. A middle-aged man heard the commotion, casually put his cart to the side, straightened his coat and tie, and made his way over to the boy and his father.

"Excuse me, sir," the man said to the boy's father. He then reached down to the still standing (but still choking) boy, carefully took hold of the kid, and squeezed gently but firmly. After a few seconds, the boy convulsed violently and coughed up the quarter, which the man caught in his free hand. He then released the boy and walked back over to his cart.

After making sure his son was OK, the father went over to the man and thanked him profusely for saving his son's life.

"I've never seen anyone do that," he said, "– that's amazing! Are you a surgeon?"

"Oh good heavens, no," replied the slightly embarrassed man.

"I work for the IRS."

Naming Children

Lawyer's daughter: Sue
Lawyer's son: Will
Thief's son: Rob
Fisherman's son: Rod
Fisherman's daughter: Annette

Backhoe operator's son: Doug
Homeopathic doctor's son: Herb
Justice of the Peace's daughter: Mary
Hot-dog vendor's son: Frank
Gambler's daughter: Bette
Gambler's son: Chip
Cattle thief's son: Russell
Painter's son: Art
Iron worker's son: Rusty
TV star's daughter: Emmy
Movie star's son: Oscar
Marksmanship instructor's daughter: Amy
Brick-layer's son: Mason
Knight's son: Lance
Swimmer's son: Wade
Lion tamer's son: Rory
Ex-lion tamer's son: Claude
Mountain climber's son: Cliff
Entomologist's son: Nat
Carpenter's son: Woody
Bird-watcher's daughter: Robin
Bird-watcher's son: Jay
Auto mechanic's son: Jack
Burger King manager's daughter: Patti
Heredity expert's son: Gene
Clothier's daughter: Jean
Fence-wire distributor's daughter: Barb
Oysterman's daughter: Shelley

The Volunteer Firemen

A fire started on some grassland near a farm in Indiana. The fire department from the nearby town was called to put the fire out. The fire proved to be more than the small-town fire department could handle, so someone suggested that a rural volunteer fire department be called. Though there was some doubt that they would be any use at all, the call was made.

The volunteer fire department arrived in a dilapidated old fire truck. They drove straight towards the fire and stopped in the middle of the flames. The volunteer firemen jumped off the truck and frantically started spraying water in all directions. Soon they had snuffed out the centre of the fire, breaking the blaze into two easily controllable parts. The farmer was so impressed with the volunteer fire department's work and so grateful that his farm had been spared, that he presented the volunteer fire department with a cheque for $1000.

A local news reporter asked the volunteer fire captain what the department planned to do with the funds.

"That should be obvious," he responded.

"The first thing we're gonna do is get the brakes fixed on that stupid fire truck."

The Smuggler

A fellow tried to cross the Mexican border on a bicycle with two big bags balanced on his shoulders. The border guard stopped him and asked, "What's in the bags?" The fellow said, "SAND!" The guard decided to examine them. He made the fellow get off the bike, place the bags on the ground, and open them up. The guard looked inside ... only to find sand.

The fellow packed up the sand again, placed the bags on his shoulders, and pedalled his bike across the border. Two weeks later, the same situation – he was back …

"What have you there?"

"Sand."

"We want to examine." Same results … the border guard opened up the bags and found nothing but sand. Once again the fellow went on his way. Every two weeks for six months the inspections continued.

Finally, one week the fellow didn't show up. However, the guard saw him downtown and said to the fellow, "Buddy, you had us crazy. We sort of knew you were smuggling something. I won't say anything … What were you smuggling?"

"Bicycles," the fellow replied.

Doctors and Lawyers

Two doctors boarded a flight out of Seattle. One sat in the window seat, the other sat in the middle seat. Just before takeoff, a lawyer got on and took the aisle seat next to the two doctors. The lawyer kicked off his shoes, wiggled his toes and was settling in when the doctor in the window seat said, "I think I'll get up and get a Coke."

"No problem," said the lawyer, "I'll get it for you."

While he was gone, one of the doctors picked up the lawyer's shoe and spat in it. When he returned with the Coke, the other doctor said, "That looks good, I think I'll have one too." Again, the lawyer obligingly went to fetch it and while he was gone, the other doctor picked up the other shoe and spat in it.

The lawyer returned and they all sat back and enjoyed the flight. As the plane was landing, the lawyer slipped his feet into his shoes and knew immediately what had happened. "How long must this go on?" he asked.

"This fighting between our professions? This hatred? This animosity?

"This spitting in shoes and pissing in Cokes?"

Blind Pilots

The passengers on a commercial airliner were seated, waiting for the cockpit crew to show up so they could get under way. The pilot and co-pilot finally appeared in the rear of the plane, and began walking up to the cockpit through the centre aisle. Both of them appeared to be blind. The pilot was using a white cane, bumping into passengers right and left as he stumbled down the aisle, and the co-pilot was using a guide dog. Both had their eyes covered with huge sunglasses.

At first the passengers did not react, thinking that it must be some sort of practical joke. However, after a few minutes the engines started spooling up and the airplane started moving down the runway. The passengers looked at each other with some uneasiness, whispering among themselves and looking desperately to the stewardesses for reassurance.

When the aeroplane started to accelerate rapidly the passengers began to panic. Some passengers were praying, and as the plane got closer and closer to the end of the runway, the voices were becoming more and more hysterical.

Finally, when the aeroplane had less than 20 feet of runway left, there was a sudden change in the pitch of the shouts as everyone screamed at once, and at the very last moment the plane lifted off and was airborne.

Up in the cockpit, the co-pilot breathed a sigh of relief and turned to the Captain,

"You know, one of these days the passengers aren't going to scream, and we're gonna get killed!"

🔁 📼 Plan Ahead

An elderly spinster called the lawyer's office and told the receptionist she wanted to see the lawyer about having a will prepared. The receptionist suggested they set up an appointment for a convenient time for the spinster to come into the office. The woman replied, "You must understand, I've lived alone all my life, I rarely see anyone, and I don't like to go out. Would it be possible for the lawyer to come to my house?"

The receptionist checked with the attorney, who agreed, and he went to the spinster's home for the meeting to discuss her estate and the will.

The lawyer's first question was, "Would you please tell me what you have in assets and how you'd like them to be distributed under your will?" She replied, "Besides the furniture and accessories you see here, I have £30,000 in my savings account at the bank."

"Tell me," the lawyer asked, "how would you like the £30,000 to be distributed?" The spinster said, "Well, as I've told you, I've lived a reclusive life, people have hardly ever noticed me, so I'd like them to notice when I pass on. I'd like to provide £25,000 for my funeral." The lawyer remarked, "Well, for £25,000 you will be able to have a funeral that will certainly be noticed and will leave a lasting impression on anyone who may not have taken much note of you!

"But tell me," he continued, "what would you like to do with the remaining £5000?" The spinster replied, "As you know, I've never married, I've lived alone almost my entire life, and in fact I've never slept with a man. Before I die, I'd like you to use the £5000 to arrange for a man to sleep with me."

"This is a very unusual request," the lawyer said, adding, "but I'll see what I can do to arrange it and get back to you."

That evening, the lawyer was at home telling his wife about the eccentric spinster and her weird request. After thinking about how much she could do around the house with £5000, and with a bit of coaxing, she got her husband to agree to provide the service himself. She said, "I'll drive you over tomorrow morning, and wait in the car until you're finished."

The next morning, she drove him to the spinster's house and waited while he went into the house. She waited for over an hour, but her husband didn't come out. So she blew the car horn.

Shortly, the upstairs bedroom window opened, the lawyer stuck his head out and yelled, "Pick me up tomorrow!

"She's going to let the council bury her!"

Looking Important

I was in the airport VIP lounge en route to Seattle a couple of weeks ago. While in there, I noticed Bill Gates sitting comfortably in the corner, enjoying a drink. I was meeting a very important client who was also flying to Seattle, but she was running a little bit late.

Well, being a straightforward kind of guy, I approached the Microsoft chairman, introduced myself, and said, "Mr Gates, I wonder if you would do me a favour."

"Yes?"

"I'm sitting right over there," pointing to my seat at the bar, "and I'm waiting on a very important client. Would you be so kind when she arrives as to come walk by and just say, 'Hi, Ray'?"

"Sure." I shook his hand and thanked him and went back to my seat.

About ten minutes later, my client showed up. We ordered a drink and started to talk business. A couple of minutes later, I felt a tap on my shoulder. It was Bill Gates.

"Hi, Ray," he said.

I replied, "Get lost, Gates, I'm in a meeting."

🖳 🖴 Executive Fantasy

A rich business executive saw an ad in the *Wall Street Journal* for the world's fastest and most expensive car, the Tri-Turbo Convertible Fantasy. It cost over $1 million, nevertheless the mogul decided that he must have it, and assigned half a dozen assistants to track the car down for him.

After months of searching, the car was found, bought, and delivered. Eager to play with his new toy, the executive took it for a spin. At the first stop light, an young man rode up next to the Fantasy on an old Vespa. Without an invitation, the young man stuck his head in the car and said, "Quite a ride you got here – how fast will she go?"

"About 270," answered the executive.

"No way," said the young man.

Just then, the light turned green and the executive decided to show the young man what the car was capable of. He floored it, and within seconds the car was doing 270.

But suddenly, he noticed in his rear-view mirror a dot that seemed to be getting closer and closer, so he came to a stop. Then, whooooooooooosh, something went flying by.

"What the heck was that?" said the executive. "What can go faster than my Fantasy?"

Suddenly, the same blur came racing back toward him, and whooooooosh, passed right by. This time the executive got a better look and could have sworn it looked like the young man on the Vespa.

"That just couldn't be," he said to himself.

Suddenly, he saw it again in his rear view mirror and WHAM!!!! it smashed into the back of the Fantasy. The executive jumped from his car, and sure enough, it was the young man on the Vespa that had crashed into him.

"Are you okay?" asked the executive. "Is there anything I can do for you?"

"Yes," replied the young man.

"Unhook my suspenders from your side-view mirror, please."

Doctor on Call

A well-respected surgeon was relaxing on his sofa one evening just after arriving home from work. As he was tuning into the evening news, the phone rang. The doctor calmly answered it and heard the familiar voice of a colleague on the other end of the line.

"We need a fourth for poker," said the friend.

"I'll be right over," whispered the doctor. As he was putting on his coat, his wife asked, "Is it serious?"

"Oh yes, quite serious," said the doctor gravely.

"In fact, three doctors are there already!"

The Road Cop

Two guys were driving through Alabama when they got pulled over by a state trooper. The trooper walked up and tapped on the window with his nightstick. The driver rolled down the window and the trooper smacked him on the head with the stick.

"Why'd you do that?" asked the driver.

"You're in Alabama, son," said the trooper. "When I pull you over you'll have your licence ready."

"I'm sorry, officer, I'm not from around here," said the driver. The trooper ran a check on the guy's licence, and he was clean. He gave the guy his licence back and walked around to the passenger side and tapped on the window. The passenger rolled his window down, and the trooper smacked him with the nightstick.

"What'd you do that for?" asked the passenger.

"Just making your wishes come true," said the trooper.

"Huh?"

"I know that two miles down the road you're gonna say,

"'I wish that jerk had tried that shit with me.'"

Things You Don't Want to Hear During Surgery

** BoBo! Come back with that! Bad dog!

** Wait a minute, if this is his spleen, then what's that?

** Hand me that … that uh … thingie.

** Well I guess that just about sews it up! Little joke there!

** Oh no, where's my Rolex?

** Oops! Hey, has anyone ever survived 500 ml of this stuff before?

** Who's been sipping from the anaesthetic bottle again?

** Your scalpel-hand is shaking, Johnson.

** There go the lights again.

** Quick! Call the plastic surgeon!

** Ya know, there's big money in kidneys.

** Everybody stand back! I lost my contact lens!

** Could you stop that thing from beating; it's throwing my concentration off.

** What's this doing here?

** I hate it when they're missing stuff in here.

** Sterile, schmerile. The floor's clean, right?

** What do you mean he wasn't in for a sex change?

** Now take a picture from this angle. This is truly a freak of nature.

** Nurse, did this patient sign the organ donation card?

** What do you mean, you want a divorce?

** Fire! Fire! Everyone get out!
** Hey!!!! Page 47 of this manual is missing!
** That's cool! Now can you make his leg twitch?

Army Tactics

During an army war game the Commanding Officer's jeep got stuck in the mud. The CO saw some men lounging around nearby and asked them to help him get unstuck.

"Sorry sir," said one of the loafers, "but we've been classified dead and the umpire said we couldn't contribute in any way."

The CO turned to his driver and said, "Go drag a couple of those dead bodies over here and throw them under the wheels to give us some traction."

New Squawks

Aircraft pilots submit maintenance complaints/problems, generally known as squawks, from time to time. After attending to the squawks, maintenance crews are required to log the details of the action taken to solve the problem the pilot logged. Here are some squawks, recently submitted by QANTAS pilots and the action taken thereafter.

P = The problem logged by the pilot.
S = The solution and action taken by the mechanics.

P – Something loose in cockpit.
S – Something tightened in cockpit.

P – Dead bugs on windshield.
S – Live bugs on backorder.

P – Autopilot in altitude-hold mode produces a 200 fpm descent.
S – Cannot reproduce problem on ground.

P – DME volume unbelievably loud.
S – Volume set to more believable level.

P – IFF inoperative.
S – IFF always inoperative in OFF mode.

P – Suspected crack in windscreen.
S – Suspect you're right.

P – Mouse in cockpit.
S – Cat installed.

World of Blondes

Getting Away with It

Three women worked in the same office with the same female boss. Every day, they noticed the boss left work early. One day, the girls decided that, when the boss left, they'd be right behind her. After all, she never called or came back, so how was she to know?

The brunette was thrilled to be home early. She did a little gardening and went to bed early. The redhead was elated to be able to get in a quick workout at her spa before meeting a dinner date. The blonde was happy to be home, but when she got to her bedroom she heard a muffled noise from inside. Slowly, quietly, she cracked open the door and was mortified to see her husband in bed with HER BOSS!! Ever so gently, she closed the door and crept out of her house.

The next day, at coffee break, the brunette and redhead mentioned leaving early again, and asked the blonde if she was with them.

"NO WAY," she exclaimed,

"I almost got caught yesterday!"

Two Blondes and a Banana

Two blondes were riding a train for the first time. They had brought along a bag of bananas for lunch. Just as one bit into her banana, the train entered a tunnel under a mountain. In the darkness was overheard, "Did you take a bite of your banana?"

"No."

"Well, don't.

"I did and I just went blind."

Anheuser-Busch

A drunken blonde went into a bar. The bartender asked her what she would like, and she replied, "Gimme a beer."

"Anheuser-Busch?" asked the barman.

"Fine thanks," she replied,

"and how's your cock?"

Exposed Tit

A blonde was walking down the street with her blouse open and her right breast hanging out. A policeman approached her and said, "Ma'am, are you aware that I could cite you for indecent exposure?"

"Why, officer?" she asked.

"Because your breast is hanging out."

She looked down and said, "OH MY GOD,

"I left the baby on the bus again!"

Passing for Brunette

A young brunette went into the doctor's office and reported that her body hurt wherever she touched it.

"Impossible," said the doctor. "Show me what you mean."

So, she took her finger, pressed it against her elbow and screamed in agony. Then she pressed her knee and screamed, pressed her ankle and screamed and so it went on, everywhere she touched made her scream.

Finally the doctor said, "You're not really a brunette, are you?"

"No, I'm actually a blonde," she replied.

"I thought so," said the doctor.

"Your finger is broken."

Blond Olympian

Q: Did you hear about the blond man who won the gold medal in the Olympics?
A: He had it bronzed.

Blondes and Mosquitoes

Q: What is the difference between a blonde and a mosquito?
A: The mosquito stops sucking after you smack it.

Blonde in a Casino

Two bored casino dealers were waiting at a craps table. A very attractive blonde woman arrived and bet 20,000 dollars on a single roll of the dice. She said, "I hope you don't mind, but I feel much luckier when I'm completely nude."

With that she stripped from her neck down, rolled the dice and yelled, "Mama needs new clothes!"

Then she hollered, "YES! YES! I WON! I WON!" She jumped up and down and hugged each of the dealers. With that she picked up all the money and her clothes and quickly departed.

The dealers just stared at each other dumbfounded. Finally, one of them asked, "What did she roll?"

The other answered, "I thought YOU were watching!"

Moral: not all blondes are dumb, but most men are perverts.

Well Hung

A white guy was walking along a beach when he came across a lamp partially buried in the sand. He picked up the lamp and gave it a rub. Two blonde genies appeared and they told him he had been granted three wishes.

The guy made his three wishes and the blonde genies disappeared. The next thing the guy knew, he was in a bedroom in a mansion surrounded by 50 beautiful women. He made love to all of them and began to explore the house. Suddenly he felt something soft under his feet; he looked down and the floor was covered in $100 bills.

Then, there was a knock at the door. He answered the door and standing there were two people dressed in Ku Klux Klan outfits. They dragged him outside to the nearest tree, threw a rope over a limb and hanged him by the neck until he was dead.

The Klansmen walked off. As they were walking away, they removed their hoods, and it was the two blonde genies. One blonde genie said to the other one, "Hey, I can understand the first wish, having all these beautiful women in a big mansion to make love to. I can also understand him wanting to be a millionaire …

"But to be hung like a black man is beyond me."

Blonde Revenge

WHAT'S BLACK AND BLUE AND BROWN AND LYING IN A DITCH?
>A brunette who's told too many blonde jokes.

WHAT DO YOU CALL GOING ON A BLIND DATE WITH A BRUNETTE?
>Brown-bagging it.

WHAT'S THE REAL REASON A BRUNETTE KEEPS HER FIGURE?
>No one else wants it.

WHY ARE SO MANY BLONDE JOKES ONE-LINERS?
>So brunettes can remember them.

WHAT DO YOU CALL A BRUNETTE IN A ROOM FULL OF BLONDES?
>Invisible.

WHAT'S A BRUNETTE'S MATING CALL?
>"Has the blonde left yet?"

WHY DIDN'T INDIANS SCALP BRUNETTES?
>The hair from a buffalo's butt was more manageable.

WHY IS BRUNETTE CONSIDERED AN EVIL COLOR?
>When was the last time you saw a blonde witch.

WHAT DO BRUNETTES MISS MOST ABOUT A GREAT PARTY?
>The invitation.

WHAT DO YOU CALL A GOOD-LOOKING MAN WITH A BRUNETTE?
>A hostage.

WHO MAKES BRAS FOR BRUNETTES?
>Fisher-Price.

WHY ARE BRUNETTES SO PROUD OF THEIR HAIR?
>It matches their moustache.

Blonde General Knowledge

A blonde was playing Trivial Pursuit one night. When it came to her turn, she rolled the dice, moved the counter and landed on "Science & Nature".

Her question was, "If you are in a vacuum and someone calls your name, can you hear it?" She thought for short while and asked,

"Is it on or off?"

God Grants the Blonde's Request

One night a blonde nun was praying in her room when God appeared before her.

"My daughter, you have pleased me greatly. Your heart is full of love for your fellow creatures and your actions and prayers are always for the benefit of others. I have come to you, not only to thank and commend you, but to grant you anything you wish," said God.

"Dear Heavenly Father," said the nun, "I am perfectly happy. I am a bride of Christ. I am doing what I love. I lack for nothing material since the Church supports me. I am content in all ways," said the nun.

"There must be something you would have of me," said God.

"Well, there is one thing," she said.

"Just name it," said God.

"It's those blonde jokes. They are so demeaning to blondes everywhere, not just to me. I would like blonde jokes to stop."

"Consider it done," said God. "Blonde jokes shall be stricken from the minds of humans everywhere. But surely there is something that I could do just for you."

"There is one thing. But it's really small, and not worth your time," said the nun.

"Name it. Please," said God.

"It's the M&Ms," said the blonde nun.

"They're so hard to peel."

Blonde Subcontractors

A woman decided to have the inside of her house painted, so she called a contractor in to help her. As they wandered around the house, she pointed out the colours she wanted.

"Now, in the living room," she said, "I'd like to have a neutral beige, very soft and warm." The contractor nodded, pulled out his pad of paper and wrote on it. Then he went to the window, leaned out and yelled, "Green side up!"

The woman was most perplexed but decided to ignore it. They wandered into the next room.

She said, "In the dining room I'd like a light white, not stark, but very bright and airy." The contractor nodded, pulled out his pad of paper and wrote on it. Then he went back to the window, leaned out, and yelled, "Green side up!"

The woman was even more perplexed but said nothing as they continued into the next room.

"In the bedroom," she said, "I'd like blue. Restful, peaceful, cool blue." The contractor nodded, pulled out his pad of paper and wrote on it. Then once more he went over to the window, leaned out and yelled, "Green side up!"

This was too much. The woman had to ask. So she said, "Every time I tell you a colour, you write it down, but then you yell out the window 'Green side up'. What on earth does that mean?"

The contractor shook his head and said, "No, no, it's nothing to do with you,

"I have four blondes laying turf across the road."

Xenophobes' Corner

🔽 🖥 Down Under

A Frenchman, an American and an Australian were in a bar.

The Frenchman said, "My name's Pierre, I come from Paris and I have a swimming pool so big that I need a motor boat to travel from one end to the other!"

The American said, "My name's Chuck, I come from Dallas and I have a ranch so big that it takes me two days to drive around it!"

The Australian said, "My name's Bruce, I come from Sydney and I've got an 18-inch penis!"

The Frenchman and the American looked at each other and the Frenchman said, "Okay, okay. I lied. My pool is really just Olympic size."

The American said, "Yeah, well, I lied too. I can drive round my ranch in a coupla hours."

The Australian said, "Okay. I admit it, I lied as well.

"My name's Cuthbert."

🔽 🖥 The Fly

An Englishman, an Irishman, and a Scot went out to a pub and ordered three pints. They each found a fly floating on the top of their mugs. The Englishman said, "Bartender, can I have a spoon?" and quietly removed the fly from his brew. The Irishman said, "Get out of there!" and flicked the fly away with a finger. The Scot picked up the fly with his fingers and said, "Alreet ya wee bastard.

"Spit it oot. Now!"

Irish Borderguards

Five Englishmen in an Audi Quattro arrived at an Irish border check-point. Paddy the officer stopped them and said, "It is illegal to put five people in a Quattro, Quattro means four."

"Quattro is just the name of the car," the Englishmen retorted disbelievingly. "Look at the papers: this car is designed to carry five persons."

"You cannot pull that one on me," replied Paddy. "Quattro means four. You have five people in your car and you are therefore breaking the law."

The Englishmen replied angrily, "You idiot! Call your supervisor over – I want to speak to someone with more intelligence!"

"Sorry," said Paddy, "Murphy is busy with two guys in a Fiat Uno."

Fair Dinkum

A tourist arrived in Australia, hired a car and set off for the outback. On his way he saw a bloke having sex with a sheep. Deeply horrified, he pulled up at the nearest pub and ordered a straight Scotch. Just as he was about to throw it back, he saw a bloke with one leg masturbating furiously at the bar.

"For fuck's sake!" the bloke cried, "what the hell's going on here? I've been here one hour and I've seen a bloke shagging a sheep, and now some bloke's wanking himself off in the bar!"

"Fair dinkum, mate," the bartender said to him.

"You can't expect a man with one leg to catch a sheep."

Eminem Tours Australia

Eminem has controversially been given permission to tour Australia. The tour is to go ahead in spite of the incredibly obscene language, total lack of respect towards women, irresponsible attitude to sex and violence, and, of course, the dungarees.

In a spirit of generosity and open-mindedness, Eminem said he'd like to make up his own mind about Australians.

Half a Head of Lettuce

A man walked into the produce section of his local supermarket and asked to buy half a head of lettuce. The boy working in that department told him that they only sold whole heads of lettuce. The man was insistent that the boy ask his manager about the matter. Walking into the back room, the boy said to his manager, "Some asshole wants to buy a half a head of lettuce." As he finished his sentence, he turned to find the man standing right behind him, so he added, "and this gentleman kindly offered to buy the other half."

The manager approved the deal and the man went on his way. Later the manager found the boy and said, "I was impressed with the way you got yourself out of that situation earlier. We like people who think on their feet here. Where are you from, son?"

"Canada, sir," the boy replied.

"Well, why did you leave Canada," the manager asked.

The boy said, "Sir, there's nothing but whores and hockey players up there."

"Really!" said the manager. "My wife is from Canada!"

The boy replied, "No shit?

"What team did she play for?"

Corporate Cows

A twist on that old politics/dairy farming paradigm

A TRADITIONAL CAPITALIST CORPORATION
You have two cows. You sell one and buy a bull. Your herd multiplies, and the economy grows. You sell them and retire on the income.

AN AMERICAN CORPORATION
You have two cows. You sell one, and force the other to produce the milk of four cows. You are surprised when the cow drops dead.

A FRENCH CORPORATION
You have two cows. You go on strike because you want three cows.

A JAPANESE CORPORATION
You have two cows. You redesign them so they are one-tenth the size of an ordinary cow and produce 20 times the milk. You then create clever cow cartoon images called Cowkimon and market them worldwide.

A GERMAN CORPORATION
You have two cows. You re-engineer them so they live for 100 years, eat once a month, and milk themselves.

A BRITISH CORPORATION
You have two cows. Both are mad.

AN ITALIAN CORPORATION
You have two cows, but you don't know where they are. You break for lunch.

A RUSSIAN CORPORATION
You have two cows. You count them and learn you have five cows. You count them again and learn you have 42 cows. You count them again and learn you have 12 cows. You stop counting cows and open another bottle of vodka.

A SWISS CORPORATION
You have 5000 cows, none of which belong to you. You charge others for storing them.

A HINDU CORPORATION
You have two cows. You worship them.

A CHINESE CORPORATION
You have two cows. You have 300 people milking them. You claim full employment, high bovine productivity, and arrest the newsman who reported the numbers.

AN ISRAELI CORPORATION
So, there are these two Jewish cows, right? They open a milk factory, an ice cream store, and then sell the movie rights. They send their calves to Harvard to become doctors. So, who needs people?

AN ARKANSAS CORPORATION
You have two cows. That one on the left is kinda cute ...

ENRON
You have two cows. You sell three of them to your publicly listed company, using letters of credit opened by your brother-in-law at the bank, then execute a debt/equity swap with an associated general offer so that you get all four cows back, with a tax exemption for five cows. The milk rights of the six cows are transferred via an intermediary to a Cayman Island company secretly owned by the majority shareholder who sells the rights to all seven cows back to your listed company. The annual report says the company owns eight cows, with an option on one more. Sell one cow to buy a new president of the United States, leaving you with nine cows. No balance sheet provided with the release. The public buys your bull.

French Quickie

Q: What do you call a Frenchman in sandals?
A: Philippe Philoppe

African Roulette

An African leader made an official trip to Russia. At the end of the trip, the Russian leader told the African that in Russia they have a custom performed at farewells called "Russian Roulette" to demonstrate one's courage.

The Russian whipped out a revolver, loaded one chamber, gave the cylinder a spin, put the gun to his head and pulled the trigger ... CLICK ... empty chamber. He handed the revolver to his African guest, and said, "Your turn." Not to be outdone, the African repeated the ritual ... CLICK ... empty.

The next year, the Russian visited the African country. At the end of the trip, the African told his Russian peer that he was very impressed with "Russian Roulette" and that he had spent the last year devising an African ritual to demonstrate one's courage. He then disappeared through a door only to reappear a few minutes later smiling and announcing, "Your turn."

The African escorted the Russian through the door. In the room were six of the most beautiful, naked women he had ever seen. The African explained that he had to choose one of the women to perform oral sex on him. Absolutely dumbfounded, the Russian asked, "What kind of test of courage is this?"

"One of them is a cannibal."

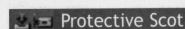 Protective Scot

One misty Scottish morning a man was driving through the hills to Inverness. Suddenly, he spotted a young woman standing by the road-side. She was absolutely beautiful, slim, shapely, fair complexion, golden hair … heart-stopping!

The driver stopped and stared, and his attention was only distracted from the lovely girl when a massive red-haired highlander stepped out of the darkness and opened the car door, dragging the terrified driver from his seat onto the road with a fist resembling a whole raw ham. The Highland monster was at least 6' 4" and built like a brick shithouse. He had a huge red beard and wore only a kilt and a tam-o'-shanter at a rakish angle.

"Right, lad," the massive Scotsman shouted, "Ah want ye tae mastur-bate!"

"But," stammered the driver.

"Dae it now … or I'll bluddy KILL yer!" So the driver turned his back on the girl, dropped his trousers and started to jack off. Thinking of the girl on the roadside, this didn't take him long.

"Right," snarled the highlander, "dae it again!"

"But …" said the driver.

"NOW, LAD!" So the driver did it again.

"Right laddie, dae it one more time," demanded the highlander. The driver tried, pulling at his limp dick in vain.

"Please, sir, I'm telling you, I can't do it anymore! You'll just have to kill me or let me go," he sobbed.

"Right then," said the highlander,

"now, wouldja mind givin' mae daughter a lift to Inverness?"

Chinese Dustman

A Chinese dustman noticed a bin was not placed out for collection and knocked on the door to find out why. A stunning woman opens the door covered in a great shimmering tan.

"Where you bin?" demanded the Chinese dustman.

"Oh I went to Barbados on a two-week five-star cruise," she replied, proud as punch.

The binman looked confused and said, "No, where you wheely bin?"

At this the girl frowned and snapped,

"On the bloody sunbed!" and slammed the door.

In an Irish Court

Mick was in court for a double murder and the judge said, "You are charged with beating your wife to death with a spanner." A voice at the back of the courtroom yelled out, "You bastard!"

The judge continued, "You are also charged with beating your daughter to death with a spanner." Again, the voice at the back of the courtroom yelled out, "You fucking bastard!!!"

The judge stopped, looked at the man in the back of the courtroom, and said, "Paddy, I can understand your anger and frustration at this crime, but I will not have any more of these outbursts from you or I shall charge you with contempt! Now what is the problem?"

Paddy stood up and responded, "For 15 years I lived next door to that bastard.

"And every time I asked to borrow a fucking spanner, he said he didn't have one!"

The Irish Genie

An Irishman found an old lamp and when he started to polish it, a genie appeared. After many thanks for his release, the genie granted Paddy three wishes.

"Well now," said Paddy, "I've always liked my Guinness in bottles so I want a bottle of the Guinness that will never be empty."

… Pooff!! …

It appeared and Paddy opened the bottle and took a drink.

"Jeez, that's wonderful. Did you say three wishes? Good man, yourself,

"I'll take two more of these."

Old Mr Campbell

An old-timer in Scotland, in a bar, said to a young man, "Lad, look out there to the field. Do ye see that wall? Look how well it's built. I built that wall stone by stone with my own two hands. I piled it for months. But do they call me Campbell-the-wall-builder? Nooooo!"

Then the old man gesturesd at the bar, "Look here at the bar. Do ye see how smooth and true it is? I planed that surface down by myself. I carved and jointed that wood with my own hard labour, for eight days. But do they call me Campbell-the-carpenter? Nooooo!"

Then the old man pointed out the window again, "Eh, laddy, look out to sea. Do ye see that pier that stretches out as far as the eye can see? I built that pier with the sweat off my back. I piled the blocks and nailed the deck board by board. But do they call me Campbell-the-pier-maker? Nooooo!"

Then the old man looked around nervously, trying to make sure no one was paying attention.

"But just for the sake of one lousy sheep …"

German Mute

A German couple had a baby and named him Klaus. As time went by Klaus grew up and yet never uttered a word. After years of trying to find out what was wrong with him, his parents just came to accept that he was mute.

On Klaus's 14th birthday he was given a slice of his favourite cake. Suddenly, Klaus turned to his mother and said, "Mother zis cake is dry." Overcome with emotion at his new verbal state his mother rushed to him.

"Klaus, you can speak," she cried. "Vy hef you never spoken before?"

"Vell," Klaus replied,

"up until now, everysing hes been kvite setisfectory."

Irish Gravestones

Three Irishmen, Paddy, Sean and Seamus, were stumbling home late one night and found themselves on the road which led past the old graveyard.

"Come have a look over here," said Paddy. "It's Michael O'Grady's grave. God bless his soul, he lived to the ripe old age of 87."

"That's nothing," said Sean, "here's one named Patrick O'Toole. It says here that he was 95 when he died."

Just then, Seamus yelled out, "But here's a fella that died when he was 145 years old!"

"What was his name?" asked Paddy. Seamus lit a match to see what else was written on the stone marker, and read out,

"Miles, from Dublin."

British Sex

In France when a lady is having a session she looks up and says:
"Je vous veux bébé!"

In Italy when a lady is having a session she looks up and says:
"Li desidero bambino!"

In Spain when a lady is having a session she looks up and says:
"Le deseco bebé!"

In Germany when a lady is having a session she looks up and says:
"Ich wünsche Sie Baby!"

In Britain when a lady is having a session she looks up and says:
"That ceiling needs doing, the paint's gone all flaky, I'll have to get a man in to sort it out!"

The Italian Rapist

A girl sat sobbing in the police station.
   "I was raped by an Italian." She wailed.
   "How do you know it was an Italian?" The detective asked.

"I had to help him," the girl replied.

How to Speak in New Zealand

(for bist efict, rid these out loud)

Amejen – visualise
Beard – a place to sleep

Beers – large savage animals found in US forests
Beggage Chucken – place to leave your suitcase at the earport
Bug hut – popular recording
Bun button – been bitten by insect
Duffy cult – not easy
Ear – mix of nitrogen and oxygen
Ear New Zulland – an extinct airline
Ear roebucks – exercise at the gym
Ever cardeau – avocado
Fear hear – blonde
Fitter cheney – type of pasta
Fush – marine creatures
Guess – vapour
Iggs Ecktly – Precisely
Inner me – enemy
Jumbo – pet name for someone called Jim
Jungle Bills – Christmas carol
Ken's – Cairns
Kiri Pecker – famous Australian businessman
Kittle crusps – potato chips
Leather – foam produced from soap
Lift – departed
McKennock – person who fixes cars
Mere – Mayor
Mess Kara – eye makeup
Milburn – capital of Victoria
Min – male of the species
Munner stroney – soup
Nin tin dough – computer game
One Doze – well-known computer program
Peck – to fill a suitcase
Pigs – for hanging out washing with

Pissed aside – chemical which kills insects
Pug – large animal with a curly tail
Pump – to act as agent for prostitute
Sucks – one less than sivven
Sucks Peck – Half a dozen beers
Veerjun – mythical New Zealand maiden

No Hidden Agenda Here, Then

The European Commission has just announced an agreement whereby English will be the official language of the EU rather than German, which was the other possibility. As part of the negotiations, Her Majesty's Government conceded that English spelling had some room for improvement and has accepted a five-year phase-in plan for what will be known as "EuroEnglish".

In the first year, "s" will replace the soft "c". Sertainly, this will make the sivil servants jump with joy. The hard "c" will be dropped in favour of the "k". This should klear up konfusion and keyboards kan have one less letter.

There will be growing publik enthusiasm in the sekond year, when the troublesome "ph" will be replased with the "f". This will make words like "fotograf" 20% shorter.

In the third year, publik akseptanse of the new spelling kan be expekted to reach the stage where more komplikated changes are possible. Governments will enkourage the removal of double letters, which have always ben a deterent to akurate speling. Also, al wil agre that the horible mess of the silent "e" should be removed.

By the fourth yar, peopl wil be reseptiv to steps such as replasing "th" with "z" and the "w" with "v".

During the fifz yar, ze unesesary "o" kan be dropd from vords kontaining "ou" and similar changes vud of kors be aplid to ozer kombinations of leters. After ze fifz yar, ve vil hav a realy sensibl vriten styl. Zer vil be no mor trubls or difikultis and evryvun vil find it easy tu understand each ozer.

ZE DREM VIL FINALI KUM TRU!

Yeeurch!

Last week I took some friends out to a restaurant, and noticed that the waiter who took our order carried a spoon in his shirt pocket. It seemed a little strange, but I ignored it. However, when the busboy brought out water and utensils, I noticed he also had a spoon in his shirt pocket. I then looked around the room and saw that all the waiters had a spoon in their pocket. When the waiter came back to check on our order I asked, "Why the spoon?"

"Well," he explained, "the restaurant's owners hired Andersen Consulting, experts in efficiency, in order to revamp all our processes. After several months of statistical analysis, they concluded that customers drop their spoons 73.84% more often than any other utensil. This represents a drop frequency of approximately three spoons per table per hour. If our personnel are prepared to deal with that contingency, we can reduce the number of trips back to the kitchen and save 1.5 man-hours per shift."

As we finished talking, a metallic sound was heard from behind me. Quickly, the waiter replaced the dropped spoon with the one in his pocket and said, "I'll get another spoon next time I go to the kitchen instead of making an extra trip to get it right now."

I was rather impressed. The waiter continued taking our order and while my guests ordered, I continued to look around. I then noticed that there was a very thin string hanging out of the waiter's fly. Looking around, I noticed that all the waiters had the same string hanging from their flies. My curiosity got the better of me and before he walked off, I asked the waiter, "Excuse me, but can you tell me why you have that string right there?"

"Oh, certainly!" he answered, lowering his voice. "Not everyone is as observant as you. That consulting firm I mentioned also found out that we can save time in the restroom."

"How so?"

"See," he continued, "by tying this string to the tip of my ... you know ... I can pull it out over the urinal without touching it and that way eliminate the need to wash my hands, shortening the time spent in the restroom by 76.39%."

"Okay, that makes sense, but if the string helps you get it out, how do you put it back in?"

"Well," he whispered, lowering his voice even further,

"I don't know about the others ... but I use the spoon."

In the Stalls

Ten sure-fire ways to entertain the person in the next toilet ...

1. Grunt and strain really loud for 30 seconds and then drop a melon into the toilet bowl from a height of six feet. Sigh relaxingly.
2. Fill up a large flask with Lucozade. Squirt it erratically under the stall walls of your neighbours while yelling, "Whoa! Easy big boy!"
3. Cheer and clap loudly every time somebody breaks the silence with a bodily function noise.
4. Using a small squeeze tube, spread peanut butter on a wad of toilet paper and drop the wad under the stall wall of your neighbour. Then say, "Whoops, could you kick that back over here please?"
5. Say, "C'mon Mr Happy!! Don't fall asleep on me!!"
6. Drop a D-cup bra on the floor under the stall where the person in the next stall can see it.
7. Say, "Damn, this water's cold!"

8. Say, "Hmm, I've never seen that colour before."
9. Say, "Interesting, more floaters than sinkers."
10. Drop a marble and say, "Oh noooo, my glass eye!!"

Tramps

A tramp walked into a bar and asked the barman for a cocktail stick. The barman handed one to him and the tramp promptly left. A few minutes later another tramp wandered in and also asked for a cocktail stick, and again the barman obliged. A little while later yet another tramp walked in and asked for a straw.

The barman said, "Why do you want a straw when the other tramps asked for cocktail sticks?"

The tramp replied, "Somebody's been sick outside,

"and all the good bits have gone."

Lucy's Op

After her fifth child, Lucy decided that she should have some cosmetic surgery "down below" to restore herself to her former youthful glory because her womanhood was dangling a bit too low and looked like a ripped-out fireplace. Time and childbirth had taken its toll and she reckoned that, with five children now being the limit, she'd tidy things with a nip here and a tuck there so it looked more like a piggy bank slot rather than a badly packed kebab.

Following the operation she awoke from her anaesthetic to find three roses at the end of the bed.

"Who are these from?" she asked the nurse. "They're very nice but I'm a bit confused as to why I've received them."

"Well," said the nurse, "the first is from the surgeon – the operation went so well and you were such a model patient that he wanted to say thanks."

"Ah, that's really nice," said Lucy.

"The second is from your husband – he's delighted the operation was such a success and he can't wait to get you home. Apparently it'll be the first time he's touched the sides for years and he's very excited!"

"Brilliant!" said Lucy. "And the third?"

"That's from Eric in the burns unit," said the nurse.

"He just wanted to say thanks for his new ears."

The Sexy Lady

A sexy lady in a bar walked up to the counter and motioned the bartender over. She started to run her fingers through his hair and asked to speak to the manager. The bartender says, "He isn't here but I can do anything the manger can do for you."

By this time the lady was running her fingers down his face and into his mouth and was letting him suck on her fingers.

She said, "You're sure he isn't here?"

The bartender said, "Yes, I'm very sure."

The lady said, "Well, I just wanted to tell him there's no toilet paper or soap in the women's restroom."

The Thlick Thalethman

The hare-lipped toothbrush salesman came in to his manager's office to give a report on his first week at work.

"Well, how'd you do?" asks the manager.

"Well thir, I thold two toothbrutheth," replied the salesman.

"Two!" shouted the manager. "You're never going to make a living that way."

"Well thir, I don't know what to do, people jutht won't buy my tooth-brutheth."

The manager thought for a mmoment and said, "Sounds to me like you need a gimmick."

The salesman asked, "Whath a geemick?"

The manager explained, "A gimmick is something you use to entice, excite and motivate your customer about your product or service. A jingle, a slogan, something to make your customer feel a need for your product or service."

The salesman said, "Hmm, I gueth I'll have to get me a geemick."

The salesman returns at the end of the next week to give his report.

The manager asked, "Well son, how'd you do this week?"

The salesman beamed, "Well thir, I thold 185,353 toothbrutheth."

The manager leapt up, "My gosh, what did you do?"

"I took your advith and got me a geemick," said the salesman.

The manager, excited now, said, "Well out with it son. What's your gimmick? We need to pass this on to the rest of the staff. We'll make millions!"

The salesman said, "Well thir, I found me a real bithy thtreet corner and I thet up a table and a chair. On the table I put out thum chipth and dip. People would come up to the corner waiting to croth the thtreet and I would thay, 'Hey, while you're waiting, how about thum chipth and dip?' They would thay, 'Thure!' Then they would take a chip, get 'em thum dip and thtart to eat it. Then they would thay, 'Hey thith dip tathteth like thit!' and thtart throwing up. I would say, 'It ith thit …

"'Want to buy a toothbruth?'"

Brown Balls

A father of 17 kids went to the doc's with a rash on his belly.

"All right," said the doc, "drop 'em and let's have a look."

Having been confronted with the evidence the doc exclaimed, "Yes, you've got a bad rash there, but my word, what brown balls you've got. They're truly remarkable!"

The patient was a bit embarrassed and said, "Look doc, what about the rash?"

"Oh that's easy," said the doc. "Here's some cream to rub on. By the way, those brown balls are amazing, may I ask …"

"No," said the patient, "you may not. Now, is that all doc?"

"Well," said the doctor, "You could stop the rash coming back with a bit better hygiene. Tell your wife you need clean underpants every day, and those really are the brownest balls I've ever seen!"

The guy went home and told his wife that the doctor said he needed clean underpants every day.

"What?" she yelled. "Clean underpants every day, and me with 17 kids to chase after! Seventeen kids to wash, feed, clothe, get to school, tidy after, and you want clean underpants every day? You must be bloody joking, I haven't even got time to wipe my arse!"

"Ah," he said,

"and that's another thing I wanted to talk to you about …"

Cleaning the Duck

A fancy lady on vacation took a stroll through the woods. Suddenly a little white duck, all covered with crap, crossed her path.

"Oh, dear," exclaimed the lady. "Come on, I'll clean you!" She took a Kleenex from her purse and made a good job of cleaning the duck.

She walked on a little farther and another duck, with crap all over it, crossed her way. Again she took a Kleenex and cleaned the little bird.

Then she encountered a third duck, with the same problem. And for the third time, she acted like Florence Nightingale.

She walked on still farther and she heard a voice from the bushes calling, "Hey, lady!"

"Yes?" she responded.

"Do you have a Kleenex?" asked the voice from the bushes.

"No, not anymore," she answered.

"Too bad, I'll have to use another duck."

Fishing

A man went out to fish on a frozen lake. He cut a hole in the ice, dropped his line in and sat for hours without so much as a nibble.

After a while, a boy came along and cut a hole nearby. He baited his line, dropped it in the hole, and within a few minutes caught a fish. He baited his line again, and within another few minutes he had another fish. The man was incensed, so he went over to the boy and asked him his secret.

"Roo raf roo reep ra rums rrarm."

"What was that?" the man asked. Again the boy replied, "Roo raf roo reep ra rums rrarm."

"Look, I can't understand a word you're saying."

The boy spat into his hand and said,

"You have to keep the worms warm!"

Wrigley's

An Australian man was having coffee and croissants with butter and jam in a cafe when an American tourist sat down next to him chewing gum. The Australian politely ignored the American, who nevertheless started up a conversation.

The American snapped his gum and said, "You Australian folk eat the whole bread?" The Australian frowned, annoyed with being bothered during his breakfast, and replied, "Of course."

The American blew a huge bubble. "We don't. In the States, we only eat what's inside. The crusts we collect in a container, recycle them, transform them into croissants and sell them to Australia."

The American had a smirk on his face. The Australian listened in silence. The American persisted, "D'ya eat jam with the bread?" Sighing, the Australian replied, "Of course."

Cracking his gum between his teeth, the American said, "We don't. In the States, we eat fresh fruit for breakfast, then we put all the peels, seeds, and leftovers in containers, recycle them, transform them into jam and sell it to Australia."

The Australian then asked, "Do you have sex in the States?" The American smiled and said, "Why of course we do." The Australian leaned closer to him and asked, "And what do you do with the condoms once you've used them?"

"We throw them away, of course." Now it was the Australian's turn to smile.

"We don't. In Australia, we put them in a container, recycle them, melt them down into chewing gum and sell them to the United States.

"Why do you think it's called Wrigley's?"

📥 🖼 The Toupee

When Mr O'Leary died, an elaborate wake was planned. In preparation, Mrs O'Leary called the undertaker aside for a private little talk.

"Please be sure to fix his toupee to his head very securely. No one but I knew he was bald," she confided, "and he'd never rest in peace if anyone found out at this point. Our friends from the old country are sure to hold his hands and touch his head before they're through paying their last respects."

"Rest assured, Mrs O'Leary," comforted the undertaker. "I'll fix it so that toupee will never come off."

Sure enough, the day of the wake the old timers were giving O'Leary's ancient corpse quite a going over, but the toupee stayed firmly in place. At the end of the day, a delighted Mrs O'Leary offered the undertaker an extra hundred dollars for handling the matter so professionally.

"Oh, I couldn't possibly accept your money," protested the undertaker…

"What's a few nails?"

📥 🖼 I Say, I Say …

Q: What's blue and doesn't fit?
A: A dead epileptic.

Underground

If you are a regular traveller on the London Underground, here are some facts which you are going to wish you hadn't read.

During Autumn of 2000, a team of scientists at the Department of Forensics at University College London removed a row of passenger seats from a Central Line tube carriage for analysis into cleanliness. Despite London Underground's claim that the interiors of their trains are cleaned on a regular basis, the scientists made some alarming discoveries. This is what was found on the surface of the seats:

> four types of hair sample (human, mouse, rat, dog)
> seven types of insect (mostly fleas, mostly alive)
> vomit originating from at least nine separate people
> human urine originating from at least four separate people
> human excrement
> rodent excrement
> human semen

When the seats were taken apart, they found:

> the remains of six mice
> the remains of two large rats
> one previously unheard-of fungus

It is estimated that by holding one of the armrests, you are transferring to your body the natural oils and sweat from as many as 400 different people.

It is estimated that it is generally healthier to smoke five cigarettes a day than to travel for one hour a day on the London Underground.

It is far more hygienic to wipe your hand on the inside of a recently flushed toilet bowl before eating, than to wipe your hand on a London Underground seat before eating.

It is estimated that, within London, more work sick-days are taken because of bugs picked up while travelling on the London Underground than for any other reason (including alcohol).

Sick Baby Joke (Do Not Read If Easily Offended by Sick Baby Jokes)

A worried woman went to the psychiatrist.

"Doctor," she said, "I can't sleep at night. When I'm in the next room, I have this dreadful fear that I won't hear the baby if he falls out of the crib at night. What should I do?"

"Easy," said the doctor.

"Just take the carpet up."

Even Sicker Baby Joke (Do Not Read If Easily Offended by Even Sicker Baby Jokes)

It was the first of April, and Joe was out of town on business. He returned home to find out that his wife was at the hospital in labour having their first child.

He rushed to the hospital, and hurried to his wife's side. She had already had the child. He went to the nursery to see the baby.

He spotted the name on a crib and motioned to the nurse. She pointed at the crib and Joe said, "Yes, he's my son."

The nurse picked up the baby and dropped it on the floor. Joe was aghast. The nurse said, "Don't worry." She picked up the baby and slapped it hard across the face several times. Joe turned white in horror as she threw the baby across the nursery. Joe was about to faint as she held the baby by its testicles and swung it around her head.

Joe screamed, "Stop! You're killing my baby!"

"April Fool," laughed the nurse.

"It was born dead."

Sick Paedophile Joke (Do Not Read If Easily Offended by Sick Paedophile Jokes)

Two paedophiles were walking down the street one day when they came across a pair of small lacey knickers on the ground. The first one picked them up, smelled them and said, "Aahhh … A seven-year-old girl."

The other paedophile grabbed them from him and also took a smell and said, "No, no … Definitely an eight-year-old girl!"

The two of them continued sniffing the knickers in turns and arguing. "An eight-year-old!", "No, a seven-year-old!", "Definitely an eight-year-old!" and so on.

The local priest was walking past as the two men argued and couldn't help but ask them what the commotion was all about. The first paedophile told the priest, and asked him if he could sort out the argument. The priest took the knickers, had a good long sniff, and after pondering for a few moments he looked at the two men and said,

"Definitely an eight-year-old girl … but not from my parish!"

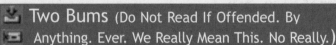

Two Bums (Do Not Read If Offended. By Anything. Ever. We Really Mean This. No Really.)

Two bums were walking along the railroad tracks one day and one bum said to the other, "I'm the luckiest guy in the world."

"Why is that?" asked the other bum.

"Well, I was walking down these tracks last week and I found a $20 bill. I went into town and bought me a case of Thunderbird wine and was drunk for three days."

The other bum said, "That was pretty good, but I think I'm the luckiest guy in the world. I was walking down these very tracks about two weeks ago, and just up ahead was a gorgeous naked woman tied to the tracks. I untied her and took her up there into the trees and I had sex with her for two days."

"Jesus," said the first bum. "You are the luckiest guy; did you get a blow job, too?"

"Well no," the other bum said,

"I never found her head."

Zone of Unclassifiability

A Better Idea

The most unfair thing about life is the way it ends. I mean, life is tough. It takes up a lot of your time. What do you get at the end of it? Death. What's that, a bonus?

I think the life cycle is all backwards. You should die first, get it out of the way. Then you live in an old people's home. You get kicked out when you're too young, You get a gold watch, you go to work. You work forty years until you're young enough to enjoy your retirement. You do drugs, alcohol, you party, you get ready for high school. You go to grade school, you become a kid, you play, you have no responsibilities, you become a little baby, you go back into the womb, you spend your last nine months floating …

… and you finish off as an orgasm.

Window Display

A tourist in a strange town noticed that her wristwatch was broken. She started looking for a repair shop. After a long and frustrating search she found herself in an area where many shop signs were in Hebrew. Finally, she noticed that one of the stores had all kinds of clocks and wristwatches displayed merrily in the window. She walked into the shop and put her wristwatch on the counter in front of the proprietor.

"Would you please fix my wristwatch?" she asked.

The proprietor replied, "Madam, I do not repair clocks or wristwatches. I perform circumcisions."

Puzzled, she asked, "Then why on earth do you have all these clocks and wristwatches in your window?"

"Well, what should I have in my window?"

The Cat Collector

A famous art collector was walking through the city when he noticed a mangy cat lapping milk from a saucer in the doorway of a store and he did a double take. Recognizing that the saucer was extremely old and very valuable, he walked casually into the store and offered to buy the cat for two dollars.

The store owner replied, "I'm sorry, but the cat isn't for sale."

The collector said, "Please, I need a hungry cat around the house to catch mice. I'll pay you 20 dollars for that cat."

And the owner said, "Sold," and handed over the cat.

The collector continued, "Hey, for the 20 bucks I wonder if you could throw in that old saucer. The cat's used to it and it'll save me from having to get a dish."

And the owner said, "Sorry buddy, but that's my lucky saucer.

"So far this week I've sold 68 cats."

The Parade Inspection

It was 0500 in the morning at the US Marine boot camp, well below freezing, and the soldiers were asleep in their barracks. The drill sergeant walked in and bellowed, "This is an inspection! I wanna see you all formed up outside butt naked NOW!"